Critical and Post-Critical Political Economy

Also by Gary Browning

PLATO AND HEGEL: Two Models of Philosophising about Politics

HEGEL AND THE HISTORY OF POLITICAL PHILOSOPHY

LYOTARD AND THE END OF GRAND NARRATIVES

RETHINKING R.G. COLLINGWOOD: Philosophy, Politics and the Unity of Theory and Practice

POLITICS: An Introduction

UNDERSTANDING CONTEMPORARY SOCIETY: Theories of the Present (*co-editor*)

THE POLITICAL ART OF BOB DYLAN (*co-editor*)

HEGEL'S PHENOMENOLOGY OF SPIRIT: A Reappraisal (*editor*)

Critical and Post-Critical Political Economy

Gary Browning
Professor of Politics, Oxford Brookes University, UK

and

Andrew Kilmister
Senior Lecturer in Economics, Oxford Brookes University, UK

First published 2006 by
PALGRAVE MACMILLAN
Houndmills, Basingstoke, Hampshire RG21 6XS and
175 Fifth Avenue, New York, N.Y. 10010
Companies and representatives throughout the world

PALGRAVE MACMILLAN is the global academic imprint of the Palgrave Macmillan division of St. Martin's Press, LLC and of Palgrave Macmillan Ltd. Macmillan® is a registered trademark in the United States, United Kingdom and other countries, Palgrave is a registered trademark in the European Union and other countries.

ISBN-13: 978-0-333-96355-5   hardback
ISBN-10: 0-333-96355-5   hardback

This book is printed on paper suitable for recycling and made from fully managed and sustained forest sources.

A catalogue record for this book is available from the British Library.

Library of Congress Cataloging-in-Publication Data

Browning, Gary K.
    Critical and post-critical political economy / Gary Browning and Andrew Kilmister.
        p. cm.
    Includes bibliographical references and index.
    ISBN 0-333-96355-5 (cloth)
        1. Economics—Political aspects. 2. Economics—Sociological aspects.
    I. Kilmister, Andrew, 1957–II. Title.

    HB74.P65B76 2006
    306.3—dc22   2006043208

10   9   8   7   6   5   4   3   2   1
15   14   13   12   11   10   09   08   07   06

Printed and bound in Great Britain by
Antony Rowe Ltd, Chippenham and Eastbourne

Contents

Acknowledgements

The authors would like to thank participants at the Critical Political Economy panel of the Political Studies Association Conference in Aberdeen in 2002, notably Terrell Carver and Harriet Bradley, for their comments on papers containing early drafts of the material included here. They are also grateful to Alison Howson of Palgrave Macmillan for being a wise and gifted editor.

Gary Browning would like to thank the following academics and friends for offering valuable insights; Diana Coole, Kimberly Hutchings, Jules Townshend, Nick Hewlett and Raia Prokhovnik. He is very grateful to his family and to students past and present who have to, or in, some degree considered, and debated some of the issues in this book.

Andrew Kilmister would like to thank his parents and his sisters, Sally Kilmister and Penny Longman, and their families for their constant encouragement over the years. He also received inspiration throughout from his Stoke Newington family: Maggie Usher, Bridget Fleetwood, Joseph Usher and Thomas Usher.

In addition he depended greatly on the support of many friends while working on this book, particularly Sedat Aybar, Marilyn Booth, Eileen Byrne, Prue Dawson, Gus Fagan, Jo Feehily, Judy Kendall, Jeremy Krikler, Matthew Lockwood, Jon Lunn, Francesca Nicolas, Berry O'Donovan, Tracy Parr, Judith Piggott, Stephen Salter, Siobhan Wall and Wan Ching Yee. The advice and example of Andrew Glyn and Jonathan Rée were very important in developing the ideas set out here, although it is unlikely that they would agree with all of them.

He would further like to thank Oxford Brookes University Business School for the award of an Internal Research Fellowship during the 2001–2 academic year.

GARY BROWNING
ANDREW KILMISTER

1
Introduction

This book contrasts a tradition of thought, which we designate as 'critical political economy', with a challenge to that tradition described as 'post-critical political economy'. In this introductory chapter we try to set out the nature of this contrast in general terms. However, in order to do this it is first necessary to outline what is meant here by 'political economy'.

1.1 Political economy

Political economy in this book refers to a theoretical approach which situates the economy within a broader context in order to create a more wide-ranging social theory. We therefore distinguish political economy both from economics as narrowly conceived (for example in much of the neo-classical economics conventionally taught in British universities) and from conceptions of social theory which focus on cultural or ideological issues to the exclusion of concern with economic questions. We also use the term in a different sense from that employed by those economists who have tried to analyse political issues from within the neo-classical tradition (Drazen 2000). Rather than embedding economic questions within a wider framework, such writers tend to work in the other direction, absorbing political and social questions within economics and so potentially limiting the scope within which they can be analysed (Fine 1999).

The term political economy came into widespread use in the eighteenth century and gave rise to the tradition described by Marx and others as 'classical political economy', beginning with the physiocrats and Smith and continuing with writers such as Ricardo and Malthus. While this approach certainly does represent political economy in our sense, we would not restrict the term to writers in the classical tradition. For example, more recent thinkers such as Joseph Schumpeter and Friedrich von Hayek are in our view fruitfully seen as political economists, whose methods of thought differ decisively from neo-classical economics, even if their immediate conclusions in the area of practical policy recommendations are similar.

Descriptions of political economy in terms of spatial metaphors such as 'situating' and 'embedding' obviously raise questions of determination. We do not see theories of political economy as necessarily implying that economic factors unilaterally determine or cause political and social effects or as assigning the economic a privileged role within society. However, we would argue that the concept of political economy necessitates seeing the economy as an important part of a social whole and requires tracing in detail the links between economic, political and social developments. The particular direction of causation involved will differ both according to the issues being analysed and the thinker involved. This question is taken up in more detail in what follows.

1.2 Critical political economy

In the light of this view of what constitutes political economy we can now set out what we mean by critical political economy. For us the key distinguishing feature of a critical approach to political economy is the recognition, when the economy is placed within a wider context, of the need for radical revision of conventional economic concepts in the light of their inadequacy in dealing with the questions generated by that context. Rather than a social theory which simply incorporates economic approaches in an unchanged form, or even is subordinated to such approaches in the sense that they become its organising principle, critical political economy demands the transformation of the economic. This transformation does not mean a straightforward rejection of economic ideas, however. These ideas can continue to provide essential insights for social theory, but in order to do so they must be decisively altered from the form in which they appear in conventional economic thought. The nature of this transformation or alteration will differ according to the standpoint taken by differing critical political economists.

In our view the above conception of critical political economy is common to both Hegel and Marx, and consequently these thinkers inaugurate this approach. As with classical political economy above, however, we would not restrict critical political economy to Hegelian or Marxist writers. A wide range of theoretical and practical standpoints can form the basis of a critical approach in this sense. However, it is our view that

Hegel and Marx are important both in providing a foundation for critical thought, including the thought of a number of writers who differ sharply from them on both particular and general questions, and in continuing to provide important insights and raise key questions. For these reasons we examine the thought of these two writers in detail in Chapters 2 and 3 of this book.

The way in which economic ideas are seen as inadequate when viewed in isolation differs in the work of these two writers and this has resulted in a large literature tracing points of affiliation and disagreement between them. We do not have space in this book to examine this issue in detail. Our view is that there are important common elements in the method adopted by Hegel and Marx, in particular their commitment to a dialectical social theory, which justify grouping them together under the heading of critical political economy. Indeed these common elements become more apparent in the light of the criticisms made of both thinkers by the writers whom we describe as post-critical theorists. However, they differ in significant respects with regard to methodology and there are even more far-reaching differences in the conclusions which they draw from the difficulties they perceive within political economy.

Both Hegel and Marx, as dialectical theorists, found their account of the inadequacy of economic thought on the concept of contradiction. The need for a critical approach is justified by the contradictions which are manifest within economic thought and practice. In his analysis of civil society, which he sees as the location of the economic within modernity, Hegel identifies a conceptual contradiction arising from the one-sided nature of this sphere, insofar as it is founded purely on individuality and particularity. This is in turn mirrored by a practical critique, which is focused on the dehumanising effects of the division of labour, the egoism generated by market activity and the creation of an alienated rabble whose extreme poverty is exacerbated by the simultaneous promotion of market wealth. The solution to both of these contradictions lies in the existence and role of the state, which can both reconcile particularity with universality conceptually and intervene practically to correct market failings.

Hegel acknowledges modern economic practices, and modernity's very amenability to idiosyncratic forms of particularity and susceptibility to the development of a robust self-interest, as allowing for an enhancement of human freedom. The difficulty arises when such practices, and the theory which underpins them, are given a self-sufficiency which they do not possess. It is at this point that, viewed in isolation from a broader context, both the theory and practice of political economy become contradictory. Hegel's view that political economy is inadequate is thus integrally linked with the need to set it within a wider framework. When this is done the insights of political economy can be preserved, but this requires both a conceptual movement from civil society to the state and a practical movement to limit the scope of the market.

Marx also regards political economy as a theoretical advance and stresses the liberating potential of the rise of market relations, compared with more traditional ways of co-ordinating society. However, the nature of his critique differs from that of Hegel in two respects. On a conceptual level he identifies contradictory elements in the thought of classical economists such as Smith and Ricardo much more directly than does Hegel. These contradictions arise not only from the attempt to view economic categories in isolation from the social and political, though this is an important target of criticism for Marx as for his predecessor. They are also present in the foundations of classical economic thought itself, and this is not accidental for Marx, since such contradictions are rooted in the contradictory nature of economic reality (it should, however, be noted that this is a controversial point in the interpretation of Marx; see the very different accounts contained in Colletti 1973 and Elster 1978). This leads on to the second key difference between Marx and Hegel. While for Hegel the state can reconcile the differing interests generated by civil society through regulation, Marx does not regard such reconciliation as possible under capitalism. For Marx the practical solution to the conflict between universality and particularity is not state oversight of the economic sphere but revolution.

Despite these differences we would argue that Hegel and Marx have enough in common to justify grouping them together as critical political economists. Each sees their account of economic life as inextricably linked to a broader analysis of social reality, which in turn provides the basis for fundamental modification of economic categories. In addition, their dialectical approach allows for the joint recognition of the genuinely liberating impact of the rise of market relationships and of their deep inadequacy as the sole or main guiding principle of social life. Recognising this similarity between the two thinkers does not require seeing Marx's dialectic as identical with that of Hegel and, as we argue later, dialectical theory is compatible with a wide range both of methodological standpoints and substantive claims.

1.3 Challenges to critical political economy

Critical political economy, as discussed above, rests on two main pillars; the drawing of links between the economic and other areas of social life and the recognition of the need for re-conceptualisation of the economic when such links are drawn. There are thus two principal challenges that can be made to this tradition of thought, which have been influential since its founding in the nineteenth century, but have gained particular force in recent years. The first is the claim that it is neither necessary nor possible to embed economic thought within a wider conceptual framework. The second is the position that this can be done but that it requires no modification of economic theory; rather our understanding of other aspects of society should be altered to fit better with that theory. We consider each view in turn.

The basis on which the first challenge has been raised in contemporary social thought is predominantly that of suspicion of overarching 'grand narratives' and emphasis on contingency and difference as key aspects of social reality. Closely linked with this has been an attack on economic determinism and a stress on the autonomy of political, cultural and ideological factors. The argument is that different aspects of society possess their own internal logic and organising principles and must be understood in their own terms. Consequently, the attempt to link analysis of such aspects to the consideration of economic questions is seen as violating this specificity and as inevitably leading to a reductionist account, in which the economic is granted an unwarranted privilege as the cause of both theoretical and practical change. Such a view has been especially important among many theorists and activists concerned with oppression on the basis of gender, race or sexuality and also among many writers concerned with ecological questions. However, such a challenge to critical political economy is by no means limited to those concerned with social movements. It has also provided much of the impetus for the so-called 'cultural turn' in a wide range of subject areas, notably history and anthropology, and for the growth of cultural studies itself.

The extent to which this challenge, and the associated criticisms made of Hegel and Marx, is justified will be discussed in detail in the course of this book. It is worth noting though at this point that such a standpoint runs the risk of critical thought abandoning the terrain of the economy altogether. The reason for this is partly practical, in that concentration on the detail of other spheres of activity simply leaves no space or time for interrogating economic realities. It is also theoretical, in that if each sphere can only be criticised according to its own internal principles then an important resource for critique of economic thought, the use of categories derived from outside economics, is lost. There has been an increasing recognition that, while the theory and practice of social movements and the cultural turn have led to important insights, the full force of such insights will be only be realised if they are connected once more with economic issues (Ray and Sayer 1999).

The second challenge to critical political economy arises from the view that economic thought can provide the basis for a more general theory of society without needing to be modified as Hegel and Marx believed. In many ways this represents a reassertion of political economy as defined earlier in this chapter and this can be seen in the renewed interest shown in the work of writers such as Smith. However, it can also lead to a more simplistic approach in which all facets of social life are simply reinterpreted as expressions of economic behaviour (Becker 1976; Levitt and Dubner 2005).

The most pervasive example of this kind of challenge to the critical tradition is the debate around 'globalisation'. Here widely disparate social issues – the role of states and the possibility of conflict between them, the scope of political activity, the nature of cultural change – are typically related to economic developments to provide an all-encompassing account of contemporary life. Yet this account leaves the adequacy of the economic concepts used to frame it entirely unquestioned, while on a practical level, economic imperatives are seen as requiring social and political adjustments in an unambiguous way.

Writers such as Ben Fine have argued that concepts such as globalisation and social capital represent an advance over postmodernist analyses which stress the irreducible differences between levels of social reality. This is because, while they have up until now been used to support the status quo, they do at least allow for a holistic approach to social thought, which could in the future be appropriated for more critical purposes (Fine 2001). In terms of the language of this book, by renewing political economy such concepts can lay the basis for critical political economy.

We would adopt a slightly different analysis. In our view the emergence of concepts like these is not the result of recognition of the limits of postmodernism and the cultural turn. Rather they arise from the way in which social theory based on difference allows the immutability of economic ideas to remain unchallenged. In this way, the coexistence of localized critiques of cultural and ideological phenomena lacking an economic dimension with sweeping economic accounts of global trends to which political and social reality is required to adapt, is not surprising. The neglect of the economy by radical thought allows free rein to conventional economics both theoretically and practically.

1.4 Post-critical political economy

The above argument has been made by a number of writers in recent years, including observers such as Terry Eagleton, who have in the past played an important role in emphasising cultural factors (Eagleton 2000 chapter 5, especially pp. 130–1). However, in this book we attempt to extend it in one important respect. We argue that the gap that has opened up in recent years between radical thought and consideration of the economy has allowed for the development of a particular approach to social theory which we describe as post-critical political economy. This approach connects the economic with other elements of society, but in a decisively different way from critical political economy. It thus challenges the tradition of Hegel and Marx, but not in the same way either as more localised, cultural accounts or the analyses of social movements, although it draws upon these at particular points.

The main body of the book consists of a discussion of six examples of post-critical political economy; the work of Michel Foucault, Jean-François Lyotard, Jean Baudrillard, André Gorz, Nancy Fraser and Toni Negri in collaboration with Michael Hardt. This list may appear surprising in a number of respects. It includes writers who have been seen as closely affiliated with Marxism, such as Gorz and Negri, along with others who have counterposed their work to that of Marx quite sharply, such as Foucault. Conversely, Lyotard and Baudrillard have moved during their careers from a 'dissident' Marxism to a hostile stance. In a similar way, Gorz and Negri have maintained a consistent political involvement throughout their careers, while Fraser has written much more from within the academy. Lyotard and Baudrillard were committed to political activity in their youth but moved away from this in later years, while Foucault changed in the opposite direction, becoming more involved in practical campaigns, albeit in areas such as prison struggles which are not conventionally seen as linked to economic concerns. Thus, the group of writers we discuss can be seen as quite heterogeneous in several dimensions.

The post-critical theorists have also been taken to differ significantly in the aspects of social theory and practice which form their main concerns. While a writer like Gorz has generally been seen as operating in the area of political economy broadly conceived, this has been much less the case for Baudrillard, Lyotard and Foucault. While there have been particular studies which have looked at their work in relation to political and economic ideas the dominant way in which they have been received in the English-speaking world has been through their effect on debates in philosophy and cultural studies. Hardt and Negri and Fraser differ again. Their work is generally located clearly in the area of social theory rather than cultural analysis; however, it is often considered more in terms of the implications which arise for political philosophy and practice as opposed to being placed within a tradition of political economy even though they consider economic trends and injustices. Consequently, while Gorz, Fraser and Negri are often seen as exemplars of the thinking arising from the 'new social movements' (ecology, feminism, anti-globalisation), their work is rarely analysed together with that of writers like Baudrillard, Lyotard and Foucault. This latter grouping tends to be seen within the philosophical and cultural context of poststructuralism and postmodernism.

This raises the question of the rationale for seeing these writers as sharing a common involvement in post-critical political economy. To a large extent this issue constitutes the main subject of much of the remainder of this book, and is considered in detail both in the chapters dealing with individual authors and in the conclusion. It is not possible to describe post-critical thought in detail in this introduction. However, as an initial justification of our choice of writers for consideration we would argue that despite the surface differences between them all six are marked to some degree by a particular kind of engagement with critical political economy in general and the work of Hegel and Marx in particular.

There are two levels to this engagement that we want to raise at this point. The first relates to the kinds of questions which their work tries to answer and which, in turn, are raised by that work. We argue in what follows that the issues with which they are concerned necessarily connect with, and imply a relationship to, the concerns of critical political economy. Examples here include Baudrillard's attempt to analyse exactly what is specific about contemporary social relations and their mediation through consumption, Hardt and Negri's investigation of the distinguishing feature of the current organisation of the international state system and Fraser's studies of the preconditions for justice and equality in the distribution of goods and resources as well as cultural identities. Whatever the precise characteristics of the answers given to such questions, we believe that the questions themselves both demand a general involvement with issues that are central to the work of Hegel and Marx. In addition, more specifically, we argue that this involvement leads these writers to define their positions in large measure through their differences with the tradition of critical political economy.

This leads to the second level of the engagement of these writers with that tradition, which we wish to emphasise. We argue that viewing their work through the prism of political economy can clarify and explicate many of their theoretical emphases in a fruitful and illuminating way. For example, many of Baudrillard's claims about the relationship between simulation and the real, which, judged as the starting point of a theoretical account, appear arbitrary and so unconvincing, can be understood much better when seen as the consequence of a lengthy argument rooted in the concerns of critical political economy. In a similar way, the rationale of key aspects of Foucault's approach to social theory becomes much clearer when set against his detailed analysis of the links between the classical economists and Marx. Further, Lyotard's scepticism of grand narratives and emphasis on difference derive much of their force from his earlier work within a Marxist framework and the problems arising from this.

These connections are taken up in detail in the chapters devoted to individual authors which follow. However, we do not wish to argue that the perspective that we adopt here is the only one which can usefully be taken with regard to these thinkers, or that the depiction of them as post-critical political economists provides an exhaustive account of their work. Rather, we believe that to see them as grouped together in this way provides one particular way of approaching their writing, which leads to important insights. Other approaches are possible which would complement this one, and might well lead to alternative affiliations between the various theorists considered, as well as emphasising different aspects of their analyses.

In this context it should also be emphasised that we have not tried here to cover the work of every writer who could be seen as a post-critical political economist. Our approach has been deliberately selective and we make no claim to be comprehensive, either in terms of the selection of authors or in terms of our coverage of the work of those authors we do consider. We have concentrated instead on particular thinkers and analyses which appear to us to be especially significant in terms of the debates to which we wish to draw attention. Our justification for this is twofold.

Firstly, we wish to consider the various accounts which we examine in some detail and to give full attention to their inherent complexity. One of the criticisms we raise in what follows of much post-critical writing is that it tends to neglect the internal tensions and nuances contained in the work of Hegel and Marx and to treat them in a rather summary fashion. In a number of cases their work is rejected in total on the basis of arguments carrying a particular emphasis, which might well be contradicted by other elements of their writing. We have tried to avoid doing this with the post-critical theorists who we discuss, but this has necessitated considering various points at length at the expense of other areas and writers.

Secondly, our main concern in this book is not to provide a full account of every aspect of post-critical thinking but to argue for the coherence of the notion of post-critical political economy as a distinct entity and to delineate the main features of its relationship to critical political economy. Until this is done it seems premature to aim for a fully comprehensive account of post-critical thought.

We have chosen to concentrate on this particular group of six thinkers because they appear to us to exemplify especially clearly the main concerns of post-critical thought, particularly with regard to the nature of the criticisms they raise of critical political economy. There are a number of other writers who could have been included. These fall into two main groups.

The first group consists of theorists who have raised a number of the same criticisms of Hegel and Marx as those whom we examine and who have investigated many of the same issues, notably the validity of grand narratives, the nature of historical progress and the epistemological foundations of critique. The earliest of these writers was Theodor Adorno, who we would see as an important influence on much post-critical thought. Other names that could be included here are Judith Butler, Jacques Derrida, Fredric Jameson and Slavoj Žižek. We have not analysed these authors because they do not seem to us to have the same kind of close involvement with questions of political economy as those we discuss. Their work centres more on cultural and philosophical issues which provide an important background to the post-critical approach but which are not centrally implicated in it.

This raises the question of the relationship between our account of post-critical political economy and more general studies of the relationship between Marx and Hegel on the one hand and schools of thought such as poststructuralism and deconstruction on the other. We see our work as complementary to such studies and would hope that a close examination of post-critical writings could help in the future in examining such broader questions. However, what we are attempting here is less ambitious than the provision of a general characterisation of this relationship; a task which would go well beyond the limits of the study of political economy.

The second group of writers who might well have been considered includes those who have attempted to rejuvenate the tradition of critical political economy either through the exploration of new theoretical perspectives or through linking it with empirical insights derived from other areas of radical thought, notably historical or geographical analysis. Notable names here include Giovanni Arrighi and David Harvey and, from an earlier generation, Henri Lefebvre. Again, such writers have focused on many of the issues which we consider here in the context of post-critical thought. However, we have not discussed their work precisely because it is conceived as a renewal of critical thought rather than as an attempt to provide an alternative basis for social theory, as is the case for the writers we analyse. Just as in the previous case we see our account of post-critical thought as complementary to analyses of the success or failure of attempts to renew the tradition of critique from within. We would hope that such analyses could draw, for example, on comparisons of such attempts with the work of thinkers we discuss such as Negri and Gorz.

The most obvious absence from our list of post-critical theorists is probably Jürgen Habermas. The influence of Habermas on notions of the nature of critique itself has been so pervasive in many quarters that his omission demands explanation (see, for example, the crucial role played by Habermas in the argument of Benhabib (1986)). In addition, Habermas has himself discussed a number of the thinkers we consider and there are important similarities and contrasts between his thought and some post-critical approaches, notably that of Foucault (Habermas 1987; Honneth 1991). Our principal reason for not dealing in detail with Habermas' writing is that, as his work has developed and has increasingly diverged from the framework provided by Hegel and Marx, it has also become less concerned with political economy as such and more centred upon questions of language, ethics and communication. At the risk of caricaturing what is a complex and developing body of ideas, we would argue that in his early work Habermas is participating in a renewal of critical political economy from within the tradition, while in his later work he moves away not just from critical political economy but from political economy altogether. Consequently, while his work raises crucial questions for the analysis of social theory in general, these questions are broader and more general than those we have chosen to focus on in our discussion of post-critical writings.

In addition to Habermas, a notable omission from our list of thinkers is Georges Bataille. Bataille not only directly influenced a number of the writers we discuss, notably Foucault and Baudrillard, he also wrote a substantial treatise dealing with issues of political economy from a dramatically different standpoint to that of Hegel and Marx (Bataille 1988). A more detailed consideration of post-critical political economy would of necessity involve an account of Bataille's thought. Here we do not consider Bataille, partly because his ideas on 'general economy' are so closely intertwined with his general philosophical approach, which we do not feel competent to assess, and partly because we feel that many of the issues raised by Bataille's writings on economic questions are also highlighted by the work of Baudrillard.

As the above discussion indicates, we do not see this book as providing a definitive account of post-critical writing. In contrast to such an account, what we wish to do here is to highlight important affinities between the writers we do consider in the hope that this can help in exploring broader questions concerning the relationship between critical political economy and other approaches to social theory.

1.5 Conclusion

It remains to say something briefly about the structure of the chapters which follow. We begin with two chapters setting out the nature of critical political economy, the first of which deals with Hegel and the second with Marx. These chapters are not intended to provide general overviews of the thought of these writers but rather to elucidate their standpoints with regard to political economy and to investigate the notions of critique which they employ. Following this outline of critical political economy we move on to six chapters analysing the post-critical approach, each dealing with one representative thinker. The concluding chapter investigates in more detail the common features of post-critical thinking, analyses the differences and similarities between such thinking and the tradition of critique inaugurated by Hegel and Marx and attempts an evaluation of the relative merits of the two approaches.

In our view much of the reception of post-critical thought in the English-speaking world has tended to be misplaced in one of two opposed ways. The first of these involves over-ready acceptance of the arguments put forward by post-critical writers, and in particular of their attacks on dialectical thought and the critical tradition. Examples here include the enthusiastic adoption of Foucault, and later Baudrillard, as providing keys to almost all aspects of social theory in the 1980s, and some of the current responses to the work of Hardt and Negri. We argue that such a response both neglects key internal tensions within post-critical thought and also accepts too easily the post-critical account of the work of Hegel and Marx. This account both oversimplifies the analysis of those writers and elides key commonalities between their thinking and post-critical thought. Such a response also ignores the continuing relevance of Hegel and Marx to the understanding of aspects of social reality which remain recalcitrant to post-critical analysis.

However, we also wish to avoid a second common response to post-critical political economy which we find problematic. This consists of straightforward rejection of the idea that the post-critical writers have identified anything of interest which was not already contained in critical thought. In contrast, we believe that post-critical thinking has both made a genuine attempt to deal with questions of real importance and also highlighted important issues which critical political economists must confront if the tradition in which they work is to be renewed and rejuvenated for the future.

This book, then, attempts to steer a middle course between uncritical acceptance and dogmatic rejection of post-critical claims. This does not mean, however, that we believe that elements of critical and post-critical political economy can simply be uprooted from their original context and combined in an eclectic mixture. Rather, we have tried to adopt an approach here based on a careful exploration of the underlying logic of post-critical arguments, highlighting both their implications for notions of critique and their internal consistency. Our conclusion is that while post-critical thought provides important insights which can be of benefit to critical political economy, the use of those insights requires in many cases a radical reworking of the conceptual structure provided by post-critical theorists. The argument which follows is intended as an initial contribution to such a reworking.

References

Bataille, G. (1988) *The Accursed Share: An Essay on General Economy. Volume 1 Consumption*, translated by R. Hurley. New York: Zone Books

Becker, G. (1976) *The Economic Approach to Human Behavior*. Chicago: University of Chicago Press

Benhabib, S. (1986) *Critique, Norm and Utopia: A Study of the Foundations of Critical Theory*, Columbia University Press

Colletti, L. (1973) *Marxism and Hegel*, translated by L. Garner. New York: New Left Books

Drazen, A. (2000) *Political Economy in Macroeconomics*. Princeton, NJ: Princeton University Press

Eagleton, T. (2000) *The Idea of Culture*. Oxford: Blackwell

Elster, J. (1978) *Logic and Society*. Chichester: Wiley

Fine, B. (1999) 'A Question of Economics: Is it colonizing the Social Sciences?', *Economy and Society*, 28(3) pp. 403–25

Fine, B. (2001) *Social Capital versus Social Theory: Political Economy and Social Science at the Turn of the Millennium*. London: Routledge

Habermas, J. (1987) *The Philosophical Discourse of Modernity*, translated by F. Lawrence. Cambridge, MA: MIT Press

Honneth, A. (1991) *The Critique of Power: Reflective Stages in a Critical Social Theory*, translated by K. Baynes. Cambridge, MA: MIT Press

Levitt, S. and Dubner, S. (2005) *Freakonomics: A Rogue Economist Explores the Hidden Side of Everything*. London: Allen Lane

Ray, L. and Sayer, A. (1999) 'Introduction' in L. Ray and A. Sayer (eds), *Culture and Economy After The Cultural Turn*. London: Sage

2
Hegel and the Political Economy of Modernity

Hegel develops a critical political economy, which is critical because he takes no aspect of the world to be discrete or impervious to revisionary re-reading in the light of its relationship with other spheres. Hence, for Hegel, the modern political economy is not accepted at face value; it is to be criticised in the light of a deeper philosophical reading of social and political developments. Hegel's philosophy is critical and holistic. Within its perspective, the economy is not detachable from a wider set of social relationships. Hegel accepts that a modern political economy operates for the most part via self-interested utility-maximising behaviour, but he qualifies this acceptance by emphasising the need for wider social and political values and commitments to limit the autonomy of the market and the impact of economic individualism. Hegel highlights the wider web of social relationships within which the economic is situated. In achieving the prime objective of an overall rational organisation of the social world, the economic goals of producing and distributing goods and services are subordinated to the goals of securing an overall harmony between social practices and of establishing ethical relationships between members of a community. Again, for Hegel, political economy does not transcend time, for the modern market economy is part and parcel of the distinctively modern world.

Throughout his career, Hegel reflected upon the problems and possibilities of community. In his earliest writings, he invoked the holistic political cultures of Ancient Greece as a counterpoint to the divisive individualism and alienation he diagnosed as afflicting the modern world. Yet from his Jena writings onwards, and notably in the *Philosophy of Right*, Hegel turned his back on nostalgia, aiming to frame an inclusive and realistic conception of the social world in which the modern development of individualism would be incorporated within a wider community that

14

restrained its disruptive tendencies. The mature Hegel is a realist, who reckons that the modern world is not to be wished away. Individualism and the individualistic tendencies sponsored by the market must be accepted and their rational evocation of the freedom native to the individual mind is to be endorsed, but political economy's obscuring of universal ties of reason and community must be remedied.

Hegel's philosophy aims to equilibrate theory with practice, comprehending and accepting significant historical developments rather than dismissing them due to nostalgia for abandoned social forms or to fanciful imagining of prospective ideals. The market and the developing modern political economy, whereby individuals aim to maximise self-interest and to enhance their own productive capacities, are central features of the modern world. Hegel accepts them as devices permitting and promoting individual freedom. They are to be conceptualised as forms of modern social architecture, in which individuals can be at home. At the same time, they are not to be treated uncritically. Hegel is critical of political economy insofar as it tends to absolutise individualistic self-interested behaviour. Hegel, like Marx, sees market behaviour as a historically developed social practice rather than as deriving from an unmodifiable elemental individualism. Its value is determined by assessing how it contributes to the overall value and purposes of social life. Arthur remarks on this affinity between Hegel and Marx in their readings of political economy, 'Both Hegel and Marx grasp very well that the deficiency of the "atomic theory" is that it absolutises the standpoint of the individual in civil society without grasping the fact that it is the social relations that create such forms of individualism rather than the other way round' (Arthur 1987, p. 105).

What Hegel values about the sphere of modern political economy is that it allows modern men (but for Hegel, not women!) to determine their individuality and particularity. A political economy represents the set of activities, whereby human beings express their freedom by enacting their particular powers and satisfying individual needs. For Hegel, human nature is not fixed. The powers and capacities of human beings are infinite, developing in particular ways in a variety of social contexts. A crucial site of this development is the sphere of political economy. While slavery or feudalism are economic systems, circumscribing human freedom by limiting the freedom of economic actors to work and to own materials, a modern political economy removes barriers to activity, enabling the infinite potential of mankind to be realised. The modern economy promotes freedom and releases mankind from restrictions, but Hegel observes how the modern economy is also a locus of alienation and disempowerment.

Hegel maintains that the modern political economy tends to promote an excessive regard for self-interest and to undermine common values and commitments. Hegel values the modern economy for releasing the infinite powers of mankind to work on and mould nature, but he also insists that economic activities should respect supervening ethical obligations. As Walton suggests, 'In a rational community (for Hegel) economic activity is informed by a sense of common values and ideals which are not reducible to rational self-interest' (Walton 1984, p. 258). Hegel is at pains to relate the modern political economy to differing historical social practices, such as the family and the state. In so doing, Hegel appraises the practices of political economy by relating them to wider social needs and values and sets them in the context of historical development. Likewise Hegel sees the emerging science of political economy as arising in tandem with actual market-based economies, and developing by focusing upon the increasingly unrestricted individualistic market behaviour of modern economic agents. It analyses the intricate social patterns that are yielded by seemingly random individualistic behaviour. Hegel respects this discrimination of patterns; nonetheless he is critical of the science of political economy because it tends to be uncritical towards the underlying assumptions of modern economic life. The science of political economy takes at face value the individualistic behaviour with which it deals. It does not recognise the countervailing and overriding need for human beings to express and affirm their social identity.

Hegel's philosophy as a whole is marked by his reading of the provenance and character of the modern world. In his analysis of modernity Hegel recognises the importance of political economy, appreciating how in the modern world individuals develop particular powers and satisfy ever more refined needs and wants in a complex system of production and exchange, in which individuals freely exploit nature. Free economic activity negates the naturalistic premises of human activity, but Hegel recognises that the modern development of this economic side of life exerts a strain upon human communities. The development of markets and concomitant fluctuations in wealth create cleavages in society. The extensive cultivation of diverse capacities and wants and the concurrent prevalence of extremes of wealth and poverty undermine social solidarity. The economic and ideological unleashing of self-interest subverts concern for the fate of others. Hegel draws upon the work of the Scottish economists such as Sir James Steuart and Adam Smith in conceptualising the operation of modern political economy. In his lectures on the *Philosophy of Right* Hegel cites Adam Smith on the division of labour, and draws upon Steuart's recognition of the need for an administrative supervision of economic arrangements (see Wasczek 1988, pp. 180–204).

Hegel's interpretation of modernity turns crucially upon contemporary developments in actual political economies and his reading of political economists. Nonetheless, his philosophical perspective on political economy is distinctively critical. Its critical force derives from Hegel's sensitivity to the fragmentation of experience and to the underlying links between apparently disconnected and disunited phenomena. Hegel is critical of political economy because he refuses to allow economic categories either to be divorced from other social categories or to be read as dominating the entire ensemble of social relations. Lukács in *The Young Hegel* recognises this *philosophical* dimension of Hegel's work as a political economist. Notwithstanding his deference to Marx's highly elliptical and controversial critique of Hegel, Lukács remarks perceptively,

> Hegel did not produce a system of economics within his general philosophy, his ideas were always an integral part of his general social philosophy. This is in fact their merit. He was not concerned to produce original research within economics itself (for this was not possible in Germany at the time), but instead he concentrated on how to integrate the discoveries of the most advanced system of economics into a science of social problems in general. Moreover – and this is where we find the specifically Hegelian approach – he was concerned to discover the general dialectical categories concealed in those social problems. (Lukács 1975, p. 319)

Hegel's philosophy is dialectical precisely because he tracks connections between apparently discrete and discordant aspects of reality. The human world in its theoretical and practical guises is a socially constituted one, in which its various activities are to be grasped by discerning their interconnections. Hegel's focus upon modernity and the transactions of economic activity is inspired by his apprehension of how connections between people and activities appear attenuated. It is motivated, further, by a determination to register the freedom and unity of social activity. Hegel's earliest writings disclose a profound engagement with what he took to be the alienated, fragmented character of modernity. His early theological writings reveal an image of modern Christian culture in which attenuated faith, divorced from political and economic engagements, contrasts with the requirements of a folk religion that would unite the various elements composing the life of a people (Hegel 1971). The Ancient Greek world, in which religion is integrated into a common political culture, contrasts pointedly with a pessimistic reading of the modern world. Hegel's critique of an alienated contemporary culture is accompanied by his yearning for an inclusive reconciliatory religion that could unite dissonant fragmentary elements. The goal of modernity, for Hegel, is to achieve a balanced inclusive cultural and social perspective that unites alienated individuals (see Plant 1973, pp. 15–41). At Jena, Hegel attended closely to the development of economic life and the study of political economy. Hegel's essay on natural law, *On the Scientific Ways of Treating Natural Law, on its Place in Practical Philosophy, and its Relation to the Positive Sciences of Right* rejects perspectives on law and politics presuming an atomistic reading of the social world. He conceives of social and political life as demanding an infinite perspective, uniting separate elements in an integrative, well-ordered whole (Hegel 1999a). In his later Jena writings, Hegel highlights the pressing need to unite economic practices within an integrative, socially responsible community. This perspective, in which a supervening ethical community resolves the divisiveness of economic particularism, is consonant with Hegel's philosophical critical urge to unify seemingly disparate elements. The practical political task of dealing with discordant economic phenomena is of a piece with Hegel's entire dialectical project of uniting concepts. In the *Philosophy of Right* Hegel depicts reason as the rose in the cross of the present, taking the project of philosophy to be one of reconciling mankind to actual, apparently disturbing developments (Hegel 1967, p. 12). This project of critical philosophical reconciliation is what constitutes the dialectical philosophical task in considering the historically crucial but problematic working of the modern economy.

Hegel understands political economy within a holistic reading of the interconnected character of the world; the world for Hegel is a social world that is to be understood in terms of connected patterns of thought (Lukács 1975, p. 319). Hegel admires Smith as a political economist, because he traces connections between apparently discrete and disordered phenomena (Hegel 1967, p. 127). Hegel, though, in conceiving of the world as an interconnected whole and in aiming to achieve reconciliation with an apparently refractory world, recognises that the merely given cannot be equated with what is rational. The rational for Hegel is the actual (*wirklich*) rather than the merely existent. Hegel perceives rationality to constitute the underlying essence of phenomena, and it is to be apprised by criticising appearances. Even at the end of his career, when he is taken by many commentators to be ultra-conservative, Hegel disparages the 'common prejudice of inertia' which he attributes to diehard conservative opponents of the English Reform Bill (Hegel 1999b, p. 237). Hegel recognises how the social world may require practical reform as well as philosophical clarification and endorsement.

Hegel's approach to political economy reflects a dialectical method that connects and critiques concepts. For Hegel, brute particularity is unspecifiable. Any particular aspect of the social world affirming a localised identity presupposes an informing unity. Particularity presupposes universality and dialectical thinking reveals connective associations. This is not to say that the universal subsumes the particular. Just as particulars cannot be maintained as simply distinct, so unity cannot overreach itself so as to destroy particularity in a revolutionary transformation of particular things. Hegel considers that a modern political economy is constitutive of a complex, internally differentiated identity, accommodating the generic, social nature of human beings *and* the particularities of individual self-expression.

Hegel sees the modern world's very amenability to the expression of man's particularity and its susceptibility to the development of robust self-interest as superseding previous social formations. Mankind is inherently free and rational but the social conditions of freely exercised individual identity are only nurtured by modern institutions, which allow the market to enable the free development of needs and work. Hegel sees the refinement of human capacities and tastes as positive features of a modern political economy, developing productive and consumptive powers, but the egoism and particularism that are promoted by market activities disturb him. Hegel specifies negative features or contradictions of the market that tend to incubate social divisiveness and alienation. He diagnoses major failings of market practices, including overproduction, involuntary unemployment and poverty amidst wealth, and prescribes remedies that are to be applied by government or civil institutions. Hegel's ambivalent reading of political economy is matched by his ambivalence on how government should respond to its negative features. Rather than recommending a wholesale transformation Hegel prescribes a number of specific remedies.

Hegel's realistic appraisal of the human condition militates against a disavowal of significant historical developments. His realism entails a concern to conserve the core ingredients of a modern political economy. The core factors to be conserved are those promoting the development of individuality and freedom. They are not to be overturned, because they shape the very character of human identity itself. Indeed, Hegel's overall reading of history implies a necessary working out of reason within historical development. Hegel's teleological conception of history, however, is relatively open in that the end of history is the development of reason and freedom and their development is intrinsic to the concept of human action itself. To assume the development of freedom and reason in history is a presumption harmonising with the presuppositions of the very study of history, because there could be no study of history, which is based on rational reconstruction of human action, unless some degree of freedom and rationality are assumed to be operative in historical events. Moreover, Hegel does not affect to anticipate the course of history, because his notion of freedom means that history is determined by free, contingent action. Hegel's teleological reading of history functions as a retrospective review of past developments in the light of mankind's rational and free nature (see McCarney 2000, Part 1).

Hegel recognises that the sphere of political economy, civil society, must be monitored and regulated according to a broad set of social requirements. Hegel considers how political economy should not be assessed simply on its capacity to satisfy welfare demands. He identifies the 'economic' as comprising a significant element in a wider social setting, and hence it is subject to a wide set of social concerns. 'Economic man', for Hegel, is an abstraction, constituting a distorted reflection of mankind's identity insofar as the merely economic ignores the more general interests and conditions of a free, social and political community. In criticising the practices of political economy, when taken in abstraction from the integrity of social life, Hegel operates as a 'critical' political economist. From a Hegelian perspective, the practice of political economy and its study warrant critical attention, because the assumptions of civil society, the sphere of economics and the corresponding 'scientific' categories of political economists are partial, respecting neither the many-sidedness of human beings nor the integrity of social life. In themselves, civil society and the standpoint of political economy do not provide a unifying sense of social identity.

Hegel's critique of the modern political economy focuses upon the dehumanising effects of the division of labour, the egoism engendered by market activity and the generation of extreme poverty amidst great wealth. The human cost is seen in the formation of an alienated rabble. Hegel's remedies for these maladies remain relatively constant over the course of his career. Like Steuart, he looks to state officials to monitor what takes place and to take action so as to correct market failures and to ensure that vulnerable economic actors are insulated from sudden changes in market conditions (see Wasczek 1988, pp. 180–204). Throughout his career, Hegel also identifies the potential for enhancing social integration that is shown by organisations such as estates and corporations. These institutions cater for the welfare of economic actors and provide a source of identity, superseding individual self-interest, as they are concerned for the welfare of social groups. Class allegiance contributes to a civic identity. A class unites otherwise disparate individuals, framing a practical expression of the conceptual operations underpinning the logic of Hegel's metaphysics. Civic identity flourishes, for Hegel, in the context of citizens appreciating the general concern for the community that is displayed in the structures and conditions of the political state that supersedes and regulates the sphere of political economy. Hegel identifies civic identity as being fostered, in particular, by the universal class of civil servants, which directly undertakes the work of the state.

Hegel's style of critical political economy differs from that of Marx. While Marx diagnoses capital as being unreservedly problematic in alienating mankind from the possibility of free social living and combines exploitation with the promotion of commodity fetishism, Hegel perceives a persisting rationality within a sphere dedicated to the maximisation of individual resources and the satisfaction of particular, multiplying wants. Hegel's critique of political economy is neither wholesale nor undiscriminating. It focuses upon the tendency of political economy to promote a one-sided sense of human identity when it is not integrated within an encompassing ethical, social framework. For Hegel, mankind's social co-operative nature is threatened by the egoism unleashed by marketised behaviour. The social consequences of market failure and the divisiveness of egoistic behaviour need to be rectified and modified by supervening social and political institutions. Hegel's critical perspective on political economy is more accommodating to the market than that of Marx. Hegel and Marx, however, are united by their common acceptance that the modern political economy is not a free-standing arena instantiating elemental drives and ahistorical forms of activity. Hegel and Marx take political economy to be a sphere that has a history and to be intelligible in the context of mankind's overall social activities. They are both critical dialectical theorists in that they connect and critique the several activities of political economy by relating them to wider social and historical developments.

2.1 Hegel: Jena

At the University of Jena (1801–07) Hegel considered and wrote on the subject of political economy in the context of developing his own systematic conception of reality. *On the Scientific Ways of Treating Natural Law, on its Place in Practical Philosophy, and its Relation to the Positive Sciences of Right* (1802–03) provides a revealing insight into Hegel's developing sense of how politics is to be comprehended and how political economy and the affiliated science of political economy fit into the enterprise of comprehending an ethical form of social life. In this seminal work, Hegel criticises formal and empirical approaches to the determination of natural law and in formulating his own sense of a developmental absolutist reading of ethical life, he recognises the place of political economy in the overall life of a community. He sees political economy and the science of political economy, however, as partial, in that all the assumptions and goals of practical economic life require to be criticised in the light of the overall goal of achieving an integrated, ethical political community.

The notion of natural law, for Hegel, is misleading in that it tends to posit the rational of political life in ostensibly primitive laws of human behaviour, whereas Hegel takes the essence of a rational law for the community to be one that develops in history. The truly rational for Hegel does not precede the intricacies of social development but is to be understood as being entwined in historical development. Hegel criticises empirical and formal approaches to the science of right, for these approaches tend to isolate relations or attributes from the whole manifold of social and political activities and to fix abstract identities rather than seeing them as being connected dialectically. In the first part of the book Hegel notes how even sophisticated scientific empirical standpoints share this partiality with formal approaches. He observes,

> And the more scientific (kind of) empiricism is in general distinguished from this pure empiricism not by having relations rather than qualities as its object, but by fixing these relations in conceptual form and sticking to this negative absoluteness (though without separating this form of unity from its content). We shall call these the *empirical sciences*; and conversely, we shall describe as purely *formal* science that form of science in which the opposition (of form and content) is absolute, and pure unity (or infinity, the negative absolute) is completely divorced from the content and posited for itself. (Hegel 1999a, p. 106)

Hegel's critique of formal and empirical approaches to the science of right yields to his own positive reading of a developmental absolutist and inclusive way of conceiving of an ethical community. In articulating the complex conditions of an ethical community Hegel observes that the community includes a practical realm, in which needs and pleasures are satisfied. This sphere of political economy allows for the development of individual tastes, but it should not dictate the overall shape of right; an ethical community is one in which the good of the whole supersedes the mere generalisation of the satisfaction of needs. Hegel observes,

> In the practical realm, these realities in their pure formlessness and simplicity – i.e. the feelings – are feelings which reconstruct themselves

out of difference, and which proceed from the supersession of undifferentiated self-awareness to restore themselves through a nullification
of the intuitions. They are physical needs and pleasures which, in turn
posited for themselves in their totality, obey one single necessity in
their infinite complications, and form the system of universal mutual
dependence with regard to physical needs and the labour and accumulation (of resources) which these require as a science, this system is
what is known as political economy. Since this system of reality is
(rooted) entirely in negativity and infinity, it follows that, in its relation to the positive totality, it must be treated wholly negatively by the
latter and must remain subject to the dominance of this relation. . .
(Hegel 1999a, p. 141)

Hegel identifies the sphere of political economy as playing a role, amongst
other practices, in contributing to the order of an ethical community. It
allows for the development of individuality in satisfying needs and in
incubating particular skills, but its very focus on particularity disqualifies
it from directly delivering the wider ambition of establishing an ethical
community. Hegel highlights the imperative for the political will of the
state to override merely economic goals. In so doing he articulates a political community that is composed of three classes. Members of the first
class, who defend the state, are absolved from economic responsibilities.
The other classes consist of a class that is engaged in free economic activity and a peasantry which is tied to the land. The three classes contribute
differentially to the community, offering, respectively, free universal commitment to the principles of the community, the development of particular economic resources and steadfast loyalty to the requirements of the
community.

In the *System of Ethical Life* (*System der Sittlichkeit*), which was written in
the early years of the nineteenth century but remained unpublished in his
lifetime, Hegel elaborated on his conception of the role of political economy in an ethical community. Pinkard observes how Hegel in this work,
makes critical use of the notion of mutual recognition and the social bases
of human consciousness (Pinkard 2000, pp. 171–177). As in his preceding
study on natural law, Hegel highlights how the true basis of an ethical community resides in the rational articulation of social practices, including
those of political economy. Hegel sees the shared social life of mutually
recognising agents as forming the social basis for individual autonomy,
and as providing the foundations for the standards of judgement that are
applied critically to the entire fabric of social life. Hegel constructs a powerful non-reductionist constructivist account of human experience; men are
natural creatures but they inexorably inhabit a social world, in which

they develop patterns of judgement and forms of entitlement that provide normative foundations for their social world. All categories for Hegel are interlinked; hence the natural and the social are mutually implicated.

In the *System of Ethical Life* human beings master nature in developing their freedom via socially constructed patterns of judgements and norms. A naturalistic recognitive encounter between human beings is presented as constituting a struggle, yielding the unbalanced relationship between a master and a slave. This dichotomous relationship fails to deliver equilibrated mutually supportive norms of conduct that are constitutive of human freedom. To be free human beings need to recognise them as being free. The family operates as a key transitional social institution, mediating between naturalistic ties and thoroughly socialised patterns of behaviour expressing the supra-naturalistic character of free agency. Hegel sees the economy and its development of a system of intricate needs and concomitant sophisticated forms of production as superseding the family, but the economy is not an absolute standpoint, for it does not provide an ethical framework accommodating all aspects of freedom.

Hegel imagines the absolute ethical life of a people (*Volk*) to provide the encompassing structure of freedom, allowing individuals to act freely and to develop their particular skills in the economic sphere. Absolute ethical life is maintained in a political association, containing subordinated economic forms that are developed and modified. The absolute ethical life of a people achieves a marked advance in the freedom of its peoples. It is inclusive and independent in its establishment of norms and practices expressive of human freedom. Hegel understands all the practices of a community as being united by their expression of freedom, consisting in the provision for the self-determination of individuals in a social context, acknowledging the mutuality of self-determination. Hegel imagines the symbolism of a community's religion as testifying to the divine spirit of freedom animating the life of all peoples.

The economy in the *System of Ethical Life*, as in Hegel's earlier treatment of it in his study on natural law, is not a discrete, detachable set of practices, in which a market mentality might flourish but has no bearing on the several aspects of human identity. Hegel is critical of a narrowly conceived political economy in that he takes economic behaviour to bear upon and to demand revision in the light of other social norms and institutions. In the Introduction to the *System of Ethical Life* Hegel maintains that the absolute character of ethical life consists in a form of infinity, in which the relational character of standpoints and attributes is recognised in and through a dialectical society. In this social dialectic subjects mutually recognise one another and their institutions to be united by the ethical standards and practices to which they adhere. Hegel deploys this notion of a self-related form of infinity throughout his career to capture an integrated, inclusive philosophy and social system, combining subjectivity and objectivity. He observes that the subjectivity of individuals in invoking and transgressing against norms highlights how an individual can supersede the finite limitations of empirical objects. Absolute ethical life in developing a universal set of ethical norms by which a people should live does not cancel individual subjectivity in requiring obedience and in punishing transgressions.

Absolute ethical life directly cancels the individual's subjectivity by nullifying it only as an ideal determinacy, as an antithesis, but it lets his subjective essence persist quite unaffected And he is allowed to persist, and is made real, as subject precisely because his essence is left undisturbed as it is. In ethical life intelligence remains a subjectivity of this kind. (Hegel 1979, p. 131)

By his conception of an absolute ethical life of a people, Hegel aims to articulate the structures of a finely balanced holistic regime that is genuinely self-sustaining and free. It encompasses a range of institutions and practices relating to political economy.

For Hegel, the ethical life of a self-sustaining and free community supersedes the standpoint of the family and its particular, naturalistic characteristics (Hegel 1979, pp. 127–9). Absolute ethical life consists in the supersession of all fixity and individuality and in 'absolute unselfishness, for in what is eternal nothing is one's own' (Hegel 1979, p. 147). While recognising that fixity and absorption in the particular is to be overcome, Hegel observes that ethical life must rest in distinctions that form parts of the whole. Within the absolute ethical life of a people, Hegel distinguishes economic activities as forming a system of needs that is an interlocking network of reciprocal needs and concomitant productive activities. Hegel understands economic activity as superseding nature, because enjoyment and its modalities are endless and are not to be restricted by natural limits. Labour, for Hegel, works upon and alters the merely natural (Hegel 1979, pp. 116–18). Human beings, for Hegel, in their social activities transcend the merely natural. Needs are refined endlessly in market transactions, and the productive processes, labouring and the use of tools mediate the given, natural world.

In recognising the developmental, socialising aspect of economic activity, Hegel observes the socially discordant features of a modern political economy. He notes that its system of interdependence renders individuals dependent upon what appears as an alien power (*Macht*) for the satisfaction of their own needs, and for the determination of the value of their own labour. Hegel observes that the value of an individual's labour and his needs, given the socially mediated character of the system of political economy, are determined by an elaborate process of market exchange, which an individual neither perceives nor comprehends. Hegel recognises how the scale and velocity of social transactions in a modern political economy undermine individual autonomy. He remarks, 'For this reason it is just as little the single contributor who determines the value of either his surplus or his need, or who can maintain it independently of its relation to everything else, as there is anything permanent and secure in its value' (Hegel 1979, p. 109).

Hegel also perceives how inequality is central to the operations of a market economy, in which individuals pursue their own particular interests and maximise their own holdings. All natural differences are accentuated by the inequalities of the market. Given the limitless character of social needs and enjoyment there is no natural barrier to the pursuit of personal wealth and concomitant social inequality. This generates an ideology of self-interested acquisitiveness, disturbing the unity of society. The inequality of the system of needs leads to extremes of wealth and poverty and a stark contrast between the reflective organising work of entrepreneurs and the mechanical, barbaric work of those operating machines in factories. Hegel notes,

> Next, great wealth, which is similarly bound up deepest poverty (for in the separation [between rich and poor] labour on both sides is universal and objective), produces on the one side in ideal universality, on the other side in real universality, mechanically . . . the unmitigated extreme of barbarity. (Hegel 1979, pp. 170–1)

Hegel sees the overall system of absolute ethical life as transforming the particularism and egoism of the economy. Membership of a social class provides individuals with identities that extend beyond a narrowly individualistic horizon. The government, whose members are drawn from the absolute class, acts upon economic life to remedy its deficiencies. Hegel distinguishes a class of absolute ethical life, a class of honesty and a class of unfree or natural ethical life. The military is the absolute class because its work does not serve particular or subordinate ends, but instead resides in the defence of all interests. The bourgeoisie, the class of honesty, is constituted by those who recognise a legal code and invoke universal standards in the regulation of their business, but who do not directly identify with the universal. It displays universality in its economic activities. Though its members focus on the satisfaction of particular needs, a general economic system develops via their activities, and money, the universal medium of exchange, represents this formal universality. This class respects formal legal norms that supersede individual reaction to injuries. The peasantry is the class of crude ethical life, absorbed in the process of satisfying physical needs. Unlike the class of honesty, its labour is bound up with nature and its labour neither supersedes the given, nor develops man's potentialities. It does maintain an ethical trust in the first class, thereby contributing to the achievement of a self-confident self-ruling community. This system of classes recalls the scheme that Hegel designated in the preceding *On the Scientific Ways of Treating Natural Law, on its Place in Practical Philosophy, and its Relation to the Positive Sciences of Right.*

In the *System of Ethical Life,* the government, which attends to the norms that maintain the absolute ethical life, is drawn from the absolute class. Supreme governing power is vested in its elders and it supervenes upon the activities of all classes whose differences are vital for the composition of an infinite, internally varied ethical whole. Hegel sees it as the task of government, which is representative of the entire community, to rectify the oscillations of the market that undermine the capacity of individuals to satisfy their needs, and to promote the universal perspective of the community rather than the particular egoistic perspective generated by market activity. More specifically, its object is to mitigate the extremes of wealth and poverty derogating from the ethical conditions, which would recognise the freedom of all. The government, for Hegel, works against the grain of divisive self-interest by deploying tax revenue to guard against fluctuations that destabilise the ability of individuals to satisfy their welfare. It ensures the provision of basic needs and the supply of non-market goods. The government also regulates the system of justice, ensuring that rights in the community are articulated and maintained. Absolute ethical life is achieved in a community, in which political rule transforms the practices of a political economy, and in which all classes, though mindful of their particular concerns, recognise their commonality in an absolute ethical life.

Hegel's sense of the significance of political economy and of its contribution to a wider notion of ethical life informs his *Third Jena System Draft: Philosophy of Nature and Philosophy of Spirit.* These are condensed lecture notes, in which Hegel emphasises the developmental character of Spirit; taking human beings to assert themselves by moulding nature to their purposes. Hegel points to the educative value of economic tools, noting how they are employed to shape nature to human purposes. He highlights, though, that human beings require recognitive encounters with other human beings to register their character as conscious free agents, and in these lectures he renders these crucial recognitive encounters sexual, in that recognitive encounters that develop human consciousness emerge out of the natural attraction of the sexes. These sexual encounters lead to the setting up of families and a struggle for recognition between heads of families, in which the very identity of each is put at risk. The prospect of mutual destruction inspires a form of recognition, which bestows property rights and enables the conduct of economic activity.

These Jena lectures on ethical life rehearse Hegel's ambivalent reading of political economy. On the one hand, he sees freedom as realisable only in a modern commercial society, in which individuals can freely pursue economic ambitions. On the other hand, an advanced form of political economy, generating extremes of wealth and poverty and relying on machines, threatens to undermine the social conditions of freedom. Hegel highlights the need for the state to intervene in economic affairs to mitigate the suffering of the worst off. He also advances the case for a holistic conception of social life, whereby political economy is integrated into the wider social and political life of a people. In this process of integration Hegel again points to the significance of differing estates, which undertake distinct functions but nonetheless contribute to the overall process of integrating economic actors to the normative conditions of a community. He now distinguishes between estates of peasants, of trade and law and of merchants as well as a universal estate composed of soldiers, businessmen who trade internationally and state officials. The universal estate plays a crucial and critical role in ensuring that economic freedoms are combined with social responsibility for ensuring that problems and deficiencies that are posed by modern economic practices are mediated and mitigated.

2.2 *Philosophy of Right*

Hegel's mature thinking on political economy is set out in his *Philosophy of Right* and in associated lecture courses in Heidelberg and Berlin. They reflect the standpoint of the Jena writings. Dickey and Nisbet (1999, p. xxviii) remark, 'His (Hegel's) youthful project of assimilating economics to politics undoubtedly culminates in PR (the *Philosophy of Right*)'. Hegel, in the *Philosophy of Right*, as in his earlier writings, elaborates upon the modern political economy and the correlative scientific understanding of modern political economy within the context of wider reflection on human society and culture. The *Philosophy of Right* theorises the economy in the context of the historical development of modernity.

Hegel conceives of political economy as constituting the core network of activities and practices that compose civil society. Civil society is an essential component of the modern ethical state, constituting the sphere of the market, where individuals can freely satisfy and develop particular needs and skills. Hegel considers, however, that this sphere of individual freedom requires monitoring and intervention on the part of the police or administrative arm of government, to ensure that market failures are corrected or mitigated. He operates with what Wasczek has termed *'an acceptance of the* principle that unites Smith and Steuart: *market failure* is the cause and condition of any intervention (Wasczek 1988, p. 203). Hegel relates political economy to the overall configuration of an ethical political community, and the complex of integrative structures, requisite for the equilibration of free social living within a community.

In the *Philosophy of Right* Hegel begins with the concept of the will, and the notion of freedom to which it is correlated. He invokes freedom as the core of human identity, to explain the logic of social activity. The *Philosophy of Right* also assumes a historical understanding of society and politics, because the freedom at the core of human identity is developed historically. Famously, Hegel states in the Preface to the *Philosophy of Right* that 'What is rational is actual and what is rational is actual' (Hegel 1967, p. 10). This *Doppelsatz* (double dictum) implies that to understand what is rational, philosophy must recognise the development of the actual world. Hegel does not endorse all aspects of existing states. In his *Lectures on Rechtsphilosophie* Hegel adopts an expressly critical perspective in that the *Doppelsatz* highlights how philosophical understanding engages critically with actual historical developments. (see Henrich 1983, pp. 9–39). Hegel conceives of the modern political community as achieving a marked advance over preceding political forms in respect of the freedom of its members, both extensively and intensively. Extensively, because the modern state allows for the freedom of all its members, and intensively due to its accommodation of the particular interests and individualistic moral conscientiousness on the part of individuals. Hegel's mature thought reflects his early engagement with political economy, showing an ambivalent attitude to the modern freedom of economic life. Hegel welcomes the unleashing of human capacities to satisfy wants and to develop particular skills, but worries over the divisiveness and particularism that are engendered simultaneously. The *Philosophy of Right* maintains a balance between recognising the positive features of a free market society and criticising its divisive and problematic aspects.

In the *Philosophy of Right* and in his *Lectures on Rechtsphilosophie*, Hegel contrasts the freedom and individualism maintained in the modern state to the unmediated, undifferentiated unity of the Ancient Greek polis. Hegel identifies the distinctively modern incorporation of the principle of individual, subjective freedom. He remarks on how Plato, in reasserting the authority and unity of the polis, excludes individualism and particularism from his ideal state.

> In his *Republic* Plato displays the substance of ethical life in its ideal beauty; but he could only cope with the principle of self-subsistent particularity, which in his day had forced its way into ethical life by setting up in opposition to it his purely substantial state. He absolutely excluded it from his state, even in its very beginning in private property and the family, as well as in its more mature form as the subjective will, the choice of a social position and so forth. (Hegel 1967, p. 124)

The modern state, for Hegel, incorporates the principle of self-subsistent particularity, via private property, through specific forms of family life, as well as by increasing opportunities for consumption and diverse forms of production in modern civil society. Indeed, Hegel takes civil society, the sphere of political economy, to allow for the modern expression of individual subjectivity and particular interests.

The pursuit of particular interests, admitted by modern civil society, constitutes but one aspect of the complex unity of the modern ethical state. Hegel does not envisage civil society as operating independently from other social spheres. Correlatively, Hegel comprehends the scientific tracking of the operations of civil society by the science of political economy to constitute an explanation of social phenomena that requires to be supplemented by conceptual exploration of other domains of social intercourse. Social life is more than a market; it requires commitment to integrative ethical forms of life. Hegel envisages that the decisive critical role of mapping civil society's links with other forms of social practice, such as the family and political structures, is to be played by systematic philosophical thinking. Philosophy, for Hegel, is critical and dialectical. A dialectical examination of the complex social world of ethical life abstracts from its thick processes and practices so as to arrive regressively at fundamental general concepts. These abstractions are then criticised so as to develop a concrete and worked-out understanding of the complete set of interrelated conditions that compose an ethical community. This ethical community expresses what Hegel takes to be the conditions of right.

In the *Philosophy of Right* Hegel provides a critical reconstruction of an ethical community by developing it from the foundational concept of the freedom of the will. This presupposition demands the ascription to individuals of rights and thereafter moral agency, because the maintenance of rights and contractual transactions derives from a commitment to moral conscientiousness. However, Hegel maintains that the modern focus on individual moral agency, in itself, cannot resolve the problems that are encountered in social experience. Indeed, the individualism of modernity complicates the process of social interaction. For instance, the securing of rights and contracts and the entire project of establishing and maintaining rules of social practice cannot be delivered merely by an individual's conscientious striving. Conscientious striving by discrete individuals promotes discord rather than unity. Social cohesion demands settled social practices and the acceptance of conventional, shared ways of doing things, as well as a commitment to accept a form of political organisation in which designated authorities oversee and adjust social processes. Modern social unity implies the practices of family life and civil society, but also an overarching political structure that guarantees the good of all society's members. Just as in his early work, *System of Ethical Life*, Hegel sees the modern sphere of political economy and its heightened individuality as necessitating an overarching political structure to secure the universal good. Hegel's dialectical development of the conditions of freedom thereby affirms the necessity of social practices, and a supervening political structure for the secure expression of individual freedom.

Hegel takes the family to be a social practice resolving the immediate primal dilemmas posed by pure individualism. Moral individualism in itself does not establish social relations of trust and love. The natural and affectionate ties of family life provide a social practice, in which children are nurtured, and in which adults can feel the support of reciprocal loving relationships. The relations of family life provide a context in which individuals recognise common ties and express their sociality. The family, though, does not allow for specifically modern expressions of individuality and particularity, and Hegel circumscribes its role so as to allow individuality to flourish outside the confines of family life. Hegel assumes that *male* children will relinquish the security of family life to develop and express their particular interests in civil society. Hegel's patriarchalism is emphasised by his assumption that female children do not participate in civil society, but transfer from their family of origin to a new family, to which they will devote their lives as wives and mothers.

The world of modern civil society that young men enter is a sphere in which particular interests and egoism flourish. It is the sphere of political economy, in which there is an intricate system of needs and complex ways of satisfying these needs. Hegel remarks, 'It [civil society] is the system of the ethical order, split into its extremes and lost, which constitutes the Idea's abstract moment, its moment of reality. Here the Idea is present only as a relative totality and as the inner necessity behind this outward appearance' (Hegel 1967, p. 123). Hegel recognises how civil society's focus upon particularity admits of no internal limit: 'Particularity by itself, given free rein in every direction to satisfy its needs, accidental caprices and subjective desires. . .' (Hegel 1967, p. 123). This sphere of civil society, that is political economy, threatens to dissolve into disorder, in that there is no logical limit to the expansion of individualised needs and the creation of particular forms of pleasure. Nonetheless, Hegel perceives the science of political economy as tracing the mediated, universal patterns of human exchange amidst the maelstrom of individuality and particularity. Hegel recognises the significance of Say, Smith and Ricardo as practitioners of a science, observing the universal ties amidst diversity and particularity and which arise 'out of the conditions of the modern world' (Hegel 1967, p. 127).

Hegel's mature analysis of the political economy of modernity reflects his earlier writings in recognising political economy to possess positive and negative sides. He sees the increasing complexity of economic life, and the developing complexity of products and needs, as betokening a richer, freer humanity, whereby natural determination is superseded by a social, purposive development of the human world. Likewise human labour becomes ever more complex and universal in its practice and organisation, as it is divided into more precise functions so as to maximise its efficiency. Products are humanised so as to reflect the determinations of human thought and imagination. In this social process of production and consumption human beings develop and assert their particular talent and interests, demonstrating the power of active, conscious thought over the unconscious processes of nature. Hegel recognises how work operates as a powerful force of education, because human beings maintain discipline and develop a range of skills in the processes of production.

While Hegel appreciates how a sophisticated modern political economy allows for human control over nature and the complexification of human development, he remains mindful of negative features of the economy of modernity, noting the effects of the increasing division of labour that renders work increasingly mechanical and abstract (Hegel 1967, p. 129). In the *Philosophy of Right* and more emphatically in his *Lectures on Rechtsphilosophie* Hegel also highlights the severe problems that are generated by the conditions of modern poverty, observing how periodic bouts of overproduction give rise to endemic conditions of involuntary unemployment that undermine the capacity of a resultant rabble of paupers to satisfy their wants (Hegel 1967, pp. 147–51 and Hegel 1983, p. 186). Their condition is seen to be all the more disturbing because they are enmeshed within a system of extreme inequality, in which destitution is juxtaposed to immense wealth and consumption of luxury products.

Hegel's analysis of the reciprocal determination of poverty and luxury in the modern world invokes a notion of infinity with which he operates throughout his career (Hegel 1967, p. 150). Hegel sees the pursuit of more and more refined needs and the reciprocal inexorable increase of dependence and want as endlessly infinite, bearing the character of what his *Logic* terms a bad infinite of the 'determinate void', that posits infinity as what lays beyond the finite (Hegel 1969, p. 137). Hegel sees the bad infinity of the endless pursuit of subjective welfare and its concomitant endless dissatisfaction as a heightened expression of the entire mindset of civil society that assumes a relentless and unquenchable egoism in the pursuit of unlimited self-interest.

Hegel does not advocate the abolition of the negative features of civil society, for he is a realist, whose *Logic* conceives of the good not as a determinate, ideal outcome, but as the continual process of combating difficulties in attempting to achieve it (Hegel 1969, pp. 818–25). Hegel does not underplay the problems of civil society; they are intrinsic to its functioning. The problems cannot be eradicated, but they are to be mitigated, and civil society is to be complemented and completed by political institutions and practices, adopting an expressly ethical and universal perspective. Hegel sees the activities of civil society as generating classes and corporations, assuming wider perspectives than the narrow forms of self-interest that are generally promoted by the economic pursuits of civil society. In his discussion of classes, Wasczek notes how Hegel emphasises their 'spiritual quality or "*Gesinnung*" ' (Wasczek 1988, p. 179). In the *Philosophy of Right*, Hegel distinguishes three classes, the agricultural class, the business class and the universal class of public servants, all of which engender a social perspective, superseding mere individual self-interest. They embody solidarity in the pursuit of corporate interests. Within the business class, Hegel observes how corporations arise, which cater for the interests of particular trades and industries. Like Steuart, Hegel accords corporations a role in mediating the effects of market fluctuations and catering for the welfare needs of their members (Hegel 1967, pp. 189–90).

While all classes play a role in offsetting the narrow particularism which is engendered by the individualism of civil society, the universal class of public servants, by focusing expressly on the universal interests of society, contributes directly to achieving the conditions of an ethical community. This class of public servants attends to the problems of civil society and corrects the market, so as to redress the effects of its fluctuations, to mitigate poverty and alienation. They ensure the supply of public goods and to raise the consciousness of members of civil society so that there is a general concern for the overall good of the community. Hegel's deep-seated realism entails that he anticipates that the activities of this class of public servants will not resolve the problems of the modern economy. Indeed, Henrich, (1983), McCarney (2000) and McGregor (1998) highlight the intractability of the problem of poverty in Hegel's thought. Yet if Hegel diagnoses modern poverty as being ultimately intractable, he also prescribes a number of remedies that include welfare provision by corporations and the government and the exploitation of colonies to ameliorate conditions at home. The plethora of measures that Hegel prescribes indicates that there is no systematic solution to poverty, but his standpoint should not be dismissed on this account, because he is a realist and he does not anticipate the elimination of all difficulties. As Wasczek (1988, p. 204) observes, 'However, what may appear a weakness, that Hegel is silent about specific rules and regulations, points to the decisive strength of his position: he is extremely flexible, allows for a great variety of circumstances and never falls into the trap of changing "ad hoc" measures into doctrines'. Hegel's interventionist measures are designed to ameliorate specific problems that are generated by structural economic conditions and to alter public consciousness so that the state's ethical nature is appreciated.

Sensitivity to the public good is promoted in the Hegelian state by its political institutions, representatives and administration. Hegel urges the rationality of a constitutional monarchy, a feature of which will be a legislature, in which classes are represented, and whose debates are publicised. Hegel recommends representation on a class and corporate basis, because he sees representation as being most effective when it arises out of the actual activities of civil society and builds upon freely formed interest groups. Hegel envisages that representatives will oversee state administrators acting to ameliorate the problems generated by an individualistic market economy. Hegel imagines there will be continuing problems, such as poverty, insecurity and particularism in a modern political economy that will not be eradicated, but he considers that the overall structure of a modern state, allowing for family love and political identification with the general good, can provide a context in which citizens can freely pursue individual interests while recognising reciprocal social ties. Ultimately, Hegel takes the modern state to express a coherent organisation of activities, whereby freedom is neither a negative rejection of social ties nor a relishing of individual satisfactions but consists in the uncoerced acceptance of universal ties, allowing individuals to develop in particular ways.

2.3 Conclusion

Hegel aims to connect political economy to a wider web of social relations and practices. Winfield (1987), in 'Hegel's Challenge to the Modern Economy,' emphasises how classical political economy identifies economic activity as dealing with the needs of individuals, whose identity and wants are seen as social. Hegel, in contrast, is seen to be their critic and a critical political economist precisely because his conceptions of political economy, and economic man are developed by mapping their connections to wider social phenomena. (Winfield 1987, p. 32). Hegel's connective explanatory strategy is to adopt a dialectical mode of thinking, mirroring the dialectical, connected character of social life. Hegel comprehends political economy to be ambiguous due to its positive and negative features. His critical perspective registers this ambiguity and aims to counter the negative features. Hegel recognises the hidden hand of universality lurking behind ostensibly self-interested actions of market behaviour, observing how the play of particular egoistic interests allows for the immense cultivation of powers, wants and needs within the dynamic economic system by which mankind dominates nature. In early and late work he highlights the role of labour in actively shaping a specifically human environment, and appreciates how the modern study of political economy observes general regularities within the ebb and flow of individual transactions.

While Hegel recognises positive features of the modern political economy he is also critical of its peculiar problems associated with a modern political economy, notably market failures such as overproduction and involuntary unemployment, and he is overtly sensitive to the tendency towards selfishness and egoism that is engendered by the dominant perspective of economic actors. In critiquing modern political economy Hegel is alive to the need of human beings to identify with supervening norms of community and for them to recognise the ties of mutuality binding them to one another. Plant highlights Hegel's recognition of 'the need for human beings to have a sense of identification with their own central life-activities and a sense of solidarity and significance within the broader society of which they are members' (Plant 1984, p. 231). For Hegel, the standpoint of modern political economy needs to be integrated within the normative structures of a community, possessing political institutions with which citizens can identify. The pursuit of individual purposes and the development of particular skills are to be aligned with civic purposes and a supervening community identity. The specific failures of the market also require corrective measures so as to mitigate their consequences. Involuntary unemployment and structural poverty invoke a number of responses. Hegel's prescriptions for market failures in early and late writings display a striking consistency. Plant observes, 'In all of his writings from *Jeneser Realphilosophie 1* to the *Philosophy of Right* he [Hegel] is insistent that the market has to be controlled by some kind of state intervention' (Plant 1984, p. 229). At times of crisis Hegel envisages the state controlling prices and production, supplying welfare, and encouraging colonisation as well as generally regulating and supervising the conduct of economic transactions. Social institutions such as corporations are also to attend to the welfare of members. He does not expect all imperfections will be remedied, but imagines that these expedients will contribute to a political atmosphere in which citizens will appreciate their social connections with others. Hegel is most concerned that a well-structured set of political institutions will enable citizens to recognise normative social obligations that underpin the individualistic conduct of market operations.

Hegel offers a distinctive, dialectical and critical perspective on political economy. The modern political economy is seen as a historical phenomenon, a crucial and defining aspect of modernity. The modern world is distinct from the Ancient world. At first blush modernity signals regress as much as progress. The solidarity of Ancient communities contrasts with the social divisions and egoistic preoccupations of modern bourgeois producers and consumers. Hegel, however, comprehends the modern world as possessing a complexity that demands complex analysis. The particularism and egoism advanced by modern political economy contribute to the progress of human freedom, because individuals are the agents of freedom and in enhancing their capacities to satisfy their particular needs and to develop their specific talents in the marketplace, they express their freedom. So Hegel understands the modern political economy historically and dialectically by seeing its distinctiveness in relation to preceding forms of economic and social organisation.

Hegel's dialectical perspective also connects political economy and other aspects of social life. He observes how economic activity presupposes the general capacity of agency, the attribution of property rights and contracts, the ascription of moral conscientiousness and the nurturing of individuals in families, and requires a supervening normative framework organised by and within the political state. This dialectical reading of political economy supplies Hegel's critical perspective. In itself the modern political economy is seen to be contradictory and unsustainable, and fundamentally skewed in its orientation. Its express and bloated individualism runs counter to mankind's social nature and cannot supply a suitable normative framework for social living. The individualism of the marketplace is a contradiction in that it requires social norms and ameliorative political action to be sustained. The modern economy needs to be complemented and completed by a supervening political state, which attends to the rights and welfare of all. Hegel's critical political economy is less radical in its critique than that of Marx. Where Marx critiques capital wholesale, identifying its particularism and egoism as entirely negative and accenting its wholly self-destructive character, Hegel identifies good and bad features and aims to restrain its particularism and to modify its destructive character.

Hegel and Marx, however, share a dialectical framework that is holistic in locating the economy in a general framework of social interaction and in identifying the present within the overall directionality of history. Hegel's standpoint on political economy is challenged by Marx, and, like Marx's critical political economy, is challenged either explicitly or implicitly by a number of subsequent theorists. Marx's critique of capital is itself an express challenge to Hegel. In his *Critique of Hegel's Doctrine of the State* Marx denies Hegel's contention that the state is capable of modifying and restraining the particularism of political economy. Marx imagines that the particular interests, which are promoted in the political economy, determine the state and the normative framework of the community. Classes are congealed interests dominating political institutions rather than allowing for the development of social perspectives. Marx takes the directionality of history to signal the ever-clearer dominance of the sphere of political economy; particular interests predominate and increasing productivity and control over nature means increasing divisiveness, alienation and exploitation rather than the freedom of a rationally organised and balanced ethical community, which contains and restrains the particularistic freedoms of the marketplace.

Hegel's reformist take on political economy is challenged by Marx's radicalism but the endurance of capital and the persisting historical significance of individualism, markets and commodification point to a persisting significance attaching to Hegel's critical accommodation to the structure of a capitalistic political economy. Subsequent theory presents further challenges to the Hegelian paradigm. A number of theorists have questioned the reach and power of dialectical theory on epistemological grounds. Postmodernism is but the loudest voice in questioning the power of dialectical social inquiry. Hegel's assumptions about the independence and integrative capacities of the state have also been questioned. Theorists of identity politics, cultural diversity and the capillary nature of power challenge the Hegelian assumption that the state can be the author of an integrative normative structure. The Hegelian emphasis upon the effectiveness of the modern political economy in expressing human productive powers and in satisfying human needs is also vulnerable to questioning of the value of productivity and consumption. Global theorists such as Hardt and Negri also deny the autonomy of the state in the current global context. Hegel's critical perspective, however, like that of Marx, remains of value in the contemporary situation. Hegel's historical reading of the modern economy relates its practices to wider social and political spheres, and thereby establishes a critical pathway for tracing and assessing the problems and possibilities of the economic sphere.

References

Dickey, L. and H.B. Nisbet (1999) 'General Introduction', in G.W.F. Hegel, *Political Writings*. Cambridge: Cambridge University Press.

Hegel, G.W.F. (1983) *Hegel and the Human Spirit: A Translation of the Jena Lectures on the Philosophy of Spirit (1805/6) with Commentary* trans. Leo Rauch. Detroit: Wayne State University Press.

Hegel, G.W.F. (1967) *The Philosophy of Right*. Oxford: Oxford University Press.

Hegel, G.W.F. (1969) *Hegel's Science of Logic*. London: George Allen and Unwin.

Hegel, G.W.F. (1979) *System of Ethical Life (1802/3) and First Philosophy of Spirit* (Part 111 *of the System of Speculative Philosophy* (1803/4) edited and translated by H.S. Harris and T.M. Knox. Albany: State University of New York Press.

Hegel, G.W.F. (1983) *Philosophie des Rechts: Die Vorselung von 1819/290 in einer Nachhschrift*. Frankfurt am Main: Suhrkamp.

Hegel, G.W.F. (1999a) *On the Scientific Ways of Treating Natural Law, on its Place in Practical Philosophy, and its Relation to the Positive Sciences of Right* in G.W.F. Hegel, *Political Writings*. Cambridge: Cambridge University Press.

Hegel, G.W.F. (1999b) 'On the English Reform Bill', in G.W.F. Hegel, *Political Writings*. Cambridge: Cambridge University Press.

Hegel, G.W.F. (1999c) *Political Writings*. Cambridge: Cambridge University Press.

Henrich, D. (1983) '*Vernunft in Verwirklung*', Introduction in G.W.F. Hegel, *Philosophie des Rechts: Die Vorselung von 1819/290 in einer Nachschrift*. Frankfurt am Main: Suhrkamp.

Lukács, G. (1975) *The Young Hegel*. London: Merlin Press.

Marx, K. (1992) *Critique of Hegel's Doctrine of the State* in K. Marx *Early Writings*. Harmondsworth: Penguin.

McCarney, J. (2000) *Hegel on History*. London: Routledge.

McGregor, D. (1998) *Hegel and Marx After the Fall of Communism*. Cardiff: University of Wales Press.

Pinkard, T. (2000) *Hegel: A Biography*. Cambridge: Cambridge University Press.

Plant, R. (1973) *Hegel*. London: George Allen and Unwin.

Plant, R. (1984) 'Hegel on Identity and Legitimation', in Z.A. Pelczynski (ed.), *The State and Civil Society (Studies in Hegel's Political Philosophy)*. Cambridge: Cambridge University Press.

Walton, A. (1984) 'Economy, Utility and Community in Hegel's Theory of Civil Society', in Z.A. Pelczynski (ed.), *The State And Civil Society (Studies in Hegel's Political Philosophy)*. Cambridge: Cambridge University Press.

Wasczek, N. (1988) *The Scottish Enlightenment and Hegel's Account of Civil Society*. Dordrecht: Martinus Nijhoff.

Winfield, R.D. (1987) 'Hegel's Challenge to the Modern Economy', in W. Maker (ed.) *Hegel on Economics and Freedom* (Macon, GA: Mercer University Press, 1987).

3
Marx and Critical Political Economy

3.1 Introduction

Like Hegel, Marx criticises political economy both for failing to relate its insights to a broader set of social concerns and for failing to recognise its nature as a historically grounded system of thought and practice. Also, like Hegel Marx sees these two failures as interlinked. Classical economic thought was unable adequately to conceptualise the relationship between economic developments and political and social factors because of the way in which it viewed relationships and categories specific to capitalism as having wider historical validity. Conversely, the inability of classical political economy to recognise that its insights were temporally bounded arose from its lack of attention to the context in which those insights were embedded.

Marx's critique of political economy is also similar to Hegel's in combining both an internal and an external element. Marx writes partly from within the tradition of political economy, arguing in detail with writers like Smith and Ricardo about problems which are clearly defined within the framework of analysis arising from tradition. He seeks to exploit the contradictions and lacunae which he finds in the work of the classical political economists. However, he also criticises classical economic thought from the outside, questioning the entire basis on which political economy has been conceived and posing a radically different alternative.

The simultaneously internal and external nature of Marx's criticisms has given rise to extensive debate concerning the extent to which his work can be assimilated to classical political economy and questioning the extent to which he can be seen in any sense as an 'economist'. One the one hand, writers like Maurice Dobb, Paul Sweezy and Ronald Meek, who played an important role in sustaining discussion of Marx's work in the politically difficult period between the 1920s and the 1960s, discuss his writing principally with reference to the economic approach inaugurated by Quesnay and Smith (Dobb 1937; Sweezy 1942; Meek 1973). At the same time, however, more philosophically oriented assessments of Marx tend to emphasise the external nature of his relationship to political economy. For example, Tony Smith writes

> I argue that Marx's success in establishing his perspective thus stands or falls with his use of dialectical logic. This, of course, is not to deny that in *Capital* and elsewhere Marx made numerous and profound contributions to economics, political science, sociology, history, anthropology, and so on, that can be considered independently of dialectical logic. But ignoring dialectical logic ignores the architectonic of *Capital*. It ignores what makes the work a whole, as opposed to an aggregate of separate empirical studies. (Smith 1990, p. x)

In Smith's account, then, political economy becomes one among several systems of thought which Marx analyses on the basis of the dialectical method he developed, in large part through his reading of Hegel. The implication is that to describe Marx as a critical political economist is to give an unwarranted privilege to his relationship to economic thought, as compared to his critiques of other aspects of social theory.

The disjunction between these two views of Marx's project has caused some concern to recent commentators on his work, especially those who have attempted to explore the implications for his thought of the work of the post-critical theorists who are the subject of this book. For example, Terrell Carver takes up this question in detail (Carver 1998, Chapter 4) with particular reference to the claim by Jean Baudrillard that Marx is unable to mount a truly radical critique of capitalist society because of the way in which his thought is imbued with the concepts of political economy. He begins by claiming that

> The opening chapters of *Capital* make better sense if they are read as the work of a student of natural philosophy, logic, history and political economy, rather than as a work of 'economics', Marxist or otherwise. 'Marx's economics' seems to me a misnomer. (Carver 1998, p. 63)

He goes on to develop this point with reference to the distinction drawn by Dominick La Capra between a 'single voiced' critique based on the assertion of propositions within the framework of political economy and a 'double voiced' critique which involves exhibiting the problematic nature of that framework. When examining Marx's approach to the labour theory of value Carver outlines Marx's acceptance of three propositions: firstly, that equal exchange of commodities means equal exchange of some kind of value substance; secondly, that this value substance must be labour; and thirdly, that as a result different sorts of labour can be 'reduced' to some kind of simple labour. Consequently,

> Smith suggested that commodities *contain* value, and Ricardo used equivalent expressions. Marx rejected that view only insofar as it made value itself sound like an inherent substance or material property of labour-products. But his own view, in my reading was only slightly different, though much more complicated. (Carver 1998, p. 79)

As a result, with regard to the debates around the labour theory of value: 'He (Marx) and the political economists speak in La Capra's 'single voice', despite the analytical, historical and political distinctions that Marx introduced into the genre' (Carver 1998, p. 82). However, Carver goes on to argue, partly following the work of Patrick Murray (1993), that Marx's analysis also has a 'double voiced' aspect:

> This is because it raises the question what is presupposed when a useful labour-product is treated as a commodity, something valuable solely or largely in terms of what can be obtained in exchange for it, or might be obtained in exchange. (Carver 1998, p. 83)

This aspect of Marx's analysis allows him to develop a theory of money, which is for Carver his central conceptual innovation in *Capital*, and which allows him to go decisively beyond the framework provided by classical economic thought.

Carver's account of Marx shows the difficulties involved in characterising his relationship with political economy. Carver begins very much in the same way as Smith, by wanting to emphasise the differences between Marx and preceding economic thought. However, as his analysis continues he recognises that there are also strong elements of continuity, which have to be accommodated. As a result he concludes that Marx's critique has a dual aspect, being both 'single' and 'double' voiced. However, he is unable to show how these two elements of Marx's work are connected, and simply presents them as existing side by side. Consequently, he is unable to answer the criticisms of writers like Baudrillard, who see Marx's attempt to provide a 'double voiced' critique of political economy from the outside as being fatally compromised by the extent to which he remains within the boundaries set down by Smith and Ricardo.

The argument of this chapter is that Marx's critique of political economy operates at several different levels and that obtaining a full understanding of the way in which these interact can be helped by seeing his work as part of the tradition of critical political economy, as outlined in the introduction to this book, and by regarding Hegel also as standing within this tradition, as described in the previous chapter. In response to this it could be argued, again following Carver, that Marx's relationship to Hegel is too complex and differentiated for them to be seen as part of a single approach of this kind. Carver claims that many of the affiliations which have been seen as binding Marx and Hegel together were in fact part of a story told in retrospect by Engels, which significantly oversimplified the historical reality (Carver 1998, Chapter 9).

There are two answers which can be made to this kind of criticism. Firstly, the concept of critical political economy employed here does not require ignoring salient differences between writers standing in this tradition. Clearly, Marx does differ from Hegel in important respects. In particular, his engagement with the detail of classical economic thought was much closer and more sustained than that of Hegel. Further, while for Hegel the state is put forward as an institution which can, at least in part, resolve the contradictions generated within the arena of civil society, in which economic conflicts become manifest, this is not the case for Marx. Marx regards such conflicts as irreconcilable within capitalist society and as indicating the necessity for the practical overthrow of existing social relations. However, the claim here is that, despite these differences, the thought of both Marx and Hegel can be illuminated through seeing them both as critical political economists. Further, doing this allows us also to understand more clearly the issues involved in the post-critical response to both Marx and Hegel.

Secondly, as Carver and others have argued, Marx's work is sufficiently complex to allow for a variety of readings: 'there have always been multiple Marxes, and each one is a product of a reading strategy' (Carver 1998, p. 234). We are not arguing here that the interpretation of Marx which we put forward is the only one possible, simply that it provides one productive way of thinking about his work. In fact the value of post-critical political economy is in part that it licenses an interpretive pluralism in considering Hegel and Marx. There is a dialectical relationship between critical and post-critical political economy in that while post-critical perspectives open up Hegel and Marx to new interpretations the worth of the accounts they generate depends in part on the extent to which they help subsequently in assessing post-critical thought.

3.2 Marx's critique of political economy

Marx's critique of political economy takes four main forms, which will be discussed below. In what follows we will start with the aspect of his critique which is closest to the internal structure of classical economic thought and move through the different modes of criticism, towards a more external approach in which political economy is viewed from the outside. Each kind of criticism will be illustrated with examples. These examples are not meant to provide a comprehensive review of Marx's work on political economy; they simply show the nature of the critical approach employed. What is noticeable, however, is that all four versions of critique raise questions of method, which relate back to the philosophical presuppositions of Marx's work, including his relationship to Hegel.

A Solving inherited problems

First, Marx tries to show how his theory solves various problems which are left unsolved by his predecessors. In this sense his criticisms are entirely within the framework of the questions posed by political economy, it is simply the answers which differ. One example of this is the famous 'transformation problem' which opens volume 3 of *Capital*. Here Marx takes a problem which had been recognised by Ricardo, that of the incompatibility between the exchange of commodities in a ratio proportional to their values on the one hand and the existence of an equal rate of profit for enterprises with different ratios of capital to labour, on the other. Ricardo's answer to this was to assert, as an empirical claim, that prices (exchange ratios) would not diverge too far from labour values in practice, so that such values could still be used as an approximation for such prices. However, he did not really have a compelling theoretical rationale for this assertion.

Marx provides a solution to the problem by differentiating between values and prices of production. When capital intensities differ, commodities exchange at their prices of production (long-run average prices), rather than at their values. The capital intensity of a particular sector or industry determines whether the price of production for that area of the economy will be above or below the value. Profits are equalised between different sectors. However, Marx argues that the total mass of profit produced will equal the total surplus value generated in production through the exploitation of labour. This provides the basis for the claim that profits depend on such exploitation.

In this way, Marx tries to provide a solution to a problem generated from within political economy; one which had baffled earlier classical economists. However, later debate on the characteristics of Marx's argument here has underlined the extent to which it depends upon a particular methodological approach. This approach is based on dialectical reasoning and on Marx's position as a critical political economist, rather than simply as a writer within the tradition of classical economics.

The key element of dialectical thought in this context is the movement from the abstract to concrete with different concepts relating to different levels of abstraction. This movement is crucial here because without it there is no clear reason for continuing to employ the concept of value, once it is recognised that in the world of competing capitals commodities do not exchange at value ratios. If analysis takes place simply in terms of the concrete issue of price formation in the market then there is no need for an underlying concept of value, as critics like Ian Steedman (1977) have argued. Answering such criticisms requires a concept of dependence which is not merely mathematical dependence and which can capture Marx's notion of the dependence of concrete phenomena on abstract relationships (Fine and Harris 1979; Fine 1986).

Marx's solution to Ricardo's problem is not then simply a question of presenting an alternative quantitative relationship between commodities, but is based on the argument that Ricardo failed to distinguish adequately between levels of abstraction and thus attempted to map the concept of value directly onto empirical reality in a way which obscured the true articulation between production and exchange. Marx's claim is that by seeing the movement from values to prices as part of the transition from the abstract world of 'capital in general' to the concrete analysis of competition between capitals one can understand this articulation clearly, and that this is part of the motivation for basing prices on the more fundamental value magnitudes. It can thus be seen that even the approach to critique employed by Marx which is most closely entwined with the concepts of classical political economy necessarily involves a dialectical approach which places him within a critical tradition.

B Uncovering hidden derivations

Marx's second mode of criticism is to take concepts which are regarded as fundamental by classical economists, and to show how they can both be derived from more basic notions, and also how this derivation illuminates hitherto unnoticed problems in the classical view of such concepts. A key example here is his account of the division of labour. In *The Wealth of Nations* Adam Smith begins his analysis with the growth of the division of labour, which is seen as resting on a trans-historical psychological principle, the innate human propensity to 'truck, barter and exchange'. The implications are clear: first, that the division of labour is the fundamental mainspring of economic growth and development and second, that it plays this role across human history regardless of social and institutional settings. In Smith the growth of the division of labour is essentially an un-contradictory process insofar as the main limitation of this growth springs not from something internal to it, but from an external constraint, the size of the market.

In *Capital* the account of the division of labour is very different. Marx does not begin his analysis with the growth of the division of labour, rather it is shown both as resulting from the pressure of capitalist competition and as dependent on a number of prior conditions such as generalised wage labour, monetary exchange and so on. Hence, his analysis of the division of labour does not occur until chapter 14 of volume 1 of *Capital*. Further, Marx's analysis allows him to see that Smith conflates two very different concepts under the heading of the division of labour: the division of labour within the manufacturing firm (or technical division of labour) and the division of labour within society (or social division of labour). These are governed by different principles; the technical division of labour within a capitalist enterprise is ruled by the hierarchical command of the owner or manager of that enterprise, while the social division of labour between enterprises is ruled by the anarchy of the market:

> In the society where the capitalist mode of production prevails, anarchy in the social division of labour and despotism in the manufacturing division of labour mutually condition each other. (Marx 1976, p. 477)

It is the conflict between these two principles, rather than the external limitation of the division of labour by market size, which is the chief barrier to the growth of that division:

> The division of labour within manufacture presupposes a concentration of the means of production in the hands of one capitalist; the division of labour within society presupposes a dispersal of those means among many independent producers of commodities. While, within the workshop, the iron law of proportionality subjects definite numbers of workers to definite functions, in the society outside the workshop, the play of chance and caprice results in a motley pattern of distribution of the producers and their means of production among the various branches of social labour. It is true that the different

spheres of production constantly tend towards equilibrium. . . . But this constant tendency on the part of the various spheres of production towards equilibrium comes into play only as a reaction against the constant upsetting of this equilibrium. (Marx 1976, p. 476)

While for Smith there is a single concept of the division of labour applicable to all societies, for Marx the social division of labour is a transhistorical concept which, however, takes very different forms throughout the course of human development. All societies have to allocate labour to different activities in some way, but only capitalist society does so through generalised market exchange of commodities. The technical division of labour, on the other hand, is for Marx a concept applicable only to capitalism. Yet, while Marx demonstrates the way in which Smith's concept of the division of labour wrongly conflates the technical and social aspects of the concept, he does not simply establish a distinction between these two aspects but also demonstrates the connection between them, and the contradiction resulting from this connection.

It can be seen then that this particular approach to the critique of political economy is largely based on what we have identified as a central element of critical political economy; the recognition of the historically bounded nature of economic categories. On the basis of this Marx is able both to show the dependence of the division of labour on prior historical conditions and to re-conceptualise it in illuminating ways.

Another example of this kind of critique within Marx's work is his theory of the tendency of the rate of profit to fall. The notion that profit rates tend to fall was a commonplace in classical political economy, but the reasons given for such a tendency differed between different writers. In Ricardo's case the declining rate of profit was seen as the result of the gradual movement towards taking less and less fertile land into calculation as the economy grows. Again, as with Smith's account of the division of labour, the fall in the profit rate was seen essentially as a natural, rather than a social phenomenon, and as a trans-historical necessity rather than a specific characteristic of capitalism.

For Marx, on the other hand, the fall in the rate of profit was rooted in factors unique to capitalism; the dependence of profit on the exploitation of living labour in the production process coupled with the pressure on capitalists to invest in machinery and expel labour from that process in order to gain a temporary competitive advantage. The result of these two opposing imperatives is a situation where what is individually rational from the point of view of a single capitalist potentially lowers profitability for the capitalist class as a whole.

Marx's criticism of earlier theories of the falling rate of profit exemplifies two important aspects of his general approach to the critique of political economy. Firstly, as with the account of the division of labour, what was previously seen as a trans-historical necessity is now located firmly within the social relationships specific to capitalism. Secondly, as with his analysis of the transformation problem, the theory of the tendency of the rate of profit to fall depends upon a movement through different levels of abstraction towards the determination of concrete situations. Marx does not argue that profit rates will inevitably fall, but that the factors outlined above create a tendency for them to fall which is located at a higher level of abstraction than that governing observable movements in the profit rate in a particular economy. Other countervailing factors, such as the cheapening of labour power or the opening up of new markets, may mean that the tendency of the profit rate to fall may not become manifest at an empirical level for considerable time periods; indeed profit rates may actually rise in practice. Thus, again Ricardo is criticised for mapping abstract concepts on to empirical reality in an unjustified way. His attempt to produce a deterministic law of falling profit rates is both unconvincing in itself, and also fails to show how visible movements in the rate of profit are dependent on more fundamental, unobservable factors (Fine and Harris 1979).

Marx in fact makes a very similar criticism of previous theories of the wage level, not just by political economists but also by that wing of the socialist movement influenced by Lassalle. Against Lassalle's 'iron law of wages' he argues that, while wages are ultimately regulated by the cost of reproduction of labour power, that cost of reproduction is itself further determined by social and historical factors. Empirical movements in wages are not the starting point for his account, but again the result of more fundamental factors.

C Developing new concepts

The third version of critique to be found in Marx's work involves the introduction of completely new concepts into the framework of political economy, which then decisively modify the other concepts with which they interact in his analysis. An example here is the concept of abstract labour. For many years Marxist economists tended to assume that the term 'abstract labour' in Marx meant roughly the same thing as 'embodied labour' in Ricardo and to assimilate Marx's labour theory of value to that of Ricardo as a result. Increasingly, however, the differences between the two concepts of labour have come to be seen as fundamental to the understanding of Marx's work. In particular, the distinction drawn by Marx between concrete and abstract labour has been regarded as central and Marx himself writes that 'I was the first to point out and examine critically this twofold nature of the labour contained in commodities . . . this point is crucial to an understanding of political economy' (Marx 1976, p. 132).

Recent accounts of abstract labour follow Rubin in viewing it as the basis for describing a process by which individual isolated acts of concrete labour are made social. The underlying assumption here is a trans-historical necessity for the distribution of labour between different branches of production. Under capitalism, this task is carried out in a specific way, through the process of exchange. As exchange brings the products of labour in relation to one another it also creates abstract labour, not as a mental abstraction but as the result of a real process: 'it is only by being exchanged that the products of labour acquire a socially uniform objectivity as values, which is distinct from their sensuously varied objectivity as articles of utility' (Marx 1976, p. 166). Producers do not carry out exchange because they are aware of labour as abstract; 'the reverse is true: by equating their different products to each other in exchange as values, they equate their different kinds of labour as human labour. They do this without being aware of it' (Marx 1976, pp. 166–7). Consequently,

> something which is only valid for this particular form of production, the production of commodities, namely the fact that the specific social character of private labours carried on independently of each other consists in their equality as human labour and, in the product, assumes the form of the existence of value (Marx 1976, p. 167)

appears as a trans-historical natural process. Thus Sayer argues that

> abstract labour, then, is neither a trans-historical category nor a mere 'mental generalisation'. It is a historical category which seeks to grasp that reduction of labour which Marx conceives as *actually* taking place within the *specific* conditions and relations of commodity production. (Sayer 1979, p. 24 his emphasis)

Labour in general, which is a trans-historical category based on a process of mental abstraction, also undergoes a process of abstraction in reality by becoming abstract labour. As abstract labour it necessarily manifests itself in a particular form, the form of value, so that Rubin regards 'abstract labour as labour which possesses a determined social form, and value as the unity of content and form' (Rubin 1978, p. 138). Chris Arthur underlines the way in which Marx's account here is radically different from that of classical political economy:

> Marx's exposition, which looks superficially the same as Ricardo's, provides, in reality, an answer to a different question. The classics attempted to find a common denominator in terms of which all values can be made commensurable and the fractional distribution of the total value between classes examined. . . . Marx advances his law of value as a hypothesis designed to show how labour is allocated qualitatively, and expended with economy, over the branches of the division of labour, in commodity-producing society. (Arthur 1979, p. 95)

Another example of this kind of critique in Marx's work is the development of the concept of labour power. Marx argued that previous political economists, while recognising the existence of surplus value at one level, had been unable to understand its nature and origin because of their assumption that capitalists purchased labour in return for wages. The problem here was that if the value of wages itself represents a certain number of hours of labour, and if it is assumed that all exchange is the exchange of equivalents, then the exchange of a certain quantity of labour for wages having the same value, measured in labour time, does not appear to allow for the generation of profit. Marx's solution to this problem was to claim that wages are not exchanged for labour but for labour power, the ability to labour. The labour required to produce a certain quantity of labour power, which is what is exchanged as an equivalent for the wage, is not the same as the amount of labour expended by the worker and the difference between the two represents the origin of surplus value and so of profit. Once the distinction between labour and labour power was recognised the key to the understanding of the nature of surplus and exploitation became available. Marx describes the confusions of the classical economists in the following terms:

> Because they were concerned with the difference between the market price of labour and its so-called value, with the relation of this value to the rate of profit and to the values of the commodities produced by means of labour etc, they never discovered that the course of the analysis had led not only from the market prices of labour to its presumed value, but also to the resolution of this value of labour itself into the value of labour-power. Classical political economy's unconsciousness of this result of its own analysis and its uncritical acceptance

of the categories 'value of labour', 'natural price of labour', etc. as the ultimate and adequate expression for the value-relation under consideration, led it into inextricable confusions and contradictions. (Marx 1976, pp. 678–9)

Marx thus provides a criticism of classical political economy through the introduction of new concepts which either replace or transform the concepts used by writers like Smith and Ricardo. The ramifications of these concepts run throughout his work, for example the analysis of abstract labour provides the foundation for Marx's theory of money, which is again significantly different from that of the classical tradition (Carver 1998, Chapter 4).

D Ideology and fetishism

The fourth, and most far-reaching, mode of critique employed by Marx involves not merely trying to solve the problems posed by political economy, reformulating concepts or even developing new concepts. Rather, at this level Marx attempts to provide a more general characterisation of the kind of thinking involved in classical economics and to exhibit its similarity to the structure of thought found in society more generally, particularly in justifications of the capitalist social order. In this way, this approach to criticism involves at least implicitly a theory of ideology and of the ideological nature of political economy.

Marx's account is set out in his theory of the fetishism of commodities. In part this provides a further statement of the historically grounded nature of economic categories. Rather than expressing a natural necessity valid across all historical periods such categories are specific to capitalism, so that Marx can write that

> The categories of bourgeois economics consist precisely of forms of this kind. They are forms of thought which are socially valid, and therefore objective, for the relations of production belonging to this historically determined mode of social production, i.e. commodity production. The whole mystery of commodities, all the magic and necromancy that surrounds the products of labour on the basis of commodity production, vanishes therefore as soon as we come to other forms of production. (Marx 1976, p. 169)

However, the account of commodity fetishism is not simply limited to indicating the way in which the propositions of political economy are historically dependent but goes beyond this in an important way. Just as

Hegel highlights the perspectival distortion involved in viewing the economy as a discrete, self-contained entity, so Marx is also concerned to show how the whole project of a science of political economy based on specifying quantitative relationships governing production and exchange can be seen as mystifying and as obscuring the underlying social relationships on which capitalism is founded. This is summarised most sharply in the statement that under capitalism social relations between producers 'do not appear as direct social relations between persons in their work, but rather as material relations between persons and social relations between things' (Marx 1976, p. 166).

This raises the question of the extent to which classical political economy is a source of real insights into the nature of capitalist production or whether it is inherently ideological. Here again, the dialectical approach which we have taken to be central to critical political economy becomes important. It is on the basis of this approach that Marx is able to argue that classical economic thought is simultaneously the expression of genuine truths about social reality and also fetishises aspects of that reality. For example, in the same footnote (Marx 1976, pp. 174–5) he writes that

> By classical political economy I mean all the economists who, since the time of W. Petty, have investigated the real internal framework of bourgeois relations of production, as opposed to the vulgar economists who only flounder around within the apparent framework of those relations

and that

> It is one of the chief failings of classical political economy that it has never succeeded . . . in discovering the form of value which in fact turns value into exchange-value. . . . The value-form of the product of labour is the most abstract, but also the most universal form of the bourgeois mode of production; by that fact it stamps the bourgeois mode of production as a particular kind of social production of a historical and transitory character. If then we make the mistake of treating it as the eternal natural form of social production, we necessarily overlook the specificity of the value-form.

Classical economic thought is seen both as investigating the 'real internal framework' of capitalism but also as overlooking the 'most universal form' of that system, which is the basis of its 'historical and transitory' nature. Marx's critique of political economy thus stresses the way it both illuminates and mystifies the world.

3.3 Marx and post-critical thought

It can be seen then that Marx's critique of political economy works at a number of different levels, which are closely interwoven in his analysis, and which all depend upon fundamental presuppositions in large measure common to both Marx and to Hegel. The complexity of this critique means that any characterisation of Marx's work being governed by one overriding principle would appear to be an oversimplification. Yet it is precisely this kind of characterisation which is offered by many of the post-critical theorists, as is outlined in detail below. Lyotard's view of Marx as offering an overarching grand narrative, Gorz's criticisms of Marx's concept of labour, the accounts of Foucault and Baudrillard which in different ways place Marx within the framework developed by Smith and Ricardo; all of these accounts claim to find a single key element in Marx's work and go on to pose this as a reason for rejecting that work either as a whole, or, in the specific case of Gorz, in large measure. In contrast, the analysis given here stresses the differentiated nature of Marx's engagement with classical economic thought.

It might, however, be claimed that to argue in this way risks emptying Marx's work of any determinate content. To stress the variety of ways in which Marx's critique operates is to run the risk of losing sight of any unifying basis for this critique and to reduce it to a set of disparate observations without underlying coherence. It is here that the notion of critical political economy becomes important. The coherence of Marx's criticisms of political economy arises from his standpoint as a critical political economist, and in particular from the central aspects of this standpoint, which in turn are shared with Hegel – the recognition of the historically limited nature of economic concepts and of the impossibility of adequately conceiving the economy in isolation from broader social and political factors.

By seeing Marx as a critical political economist in this sense it becomes possible to assess both the extent to which his work is governed by an overall set of principles and the way in which this also allows for differentiation and complexity. This does not mean arguing that all aspects of Marx's writings are compatible with each other. It does, however, necessitate careful analysis of where the tensions in his writing occur as opposed to summary statements.

These points can be illustrated by looking at an important issue in Marx's approach to the critique of political economy, and one where his views changed over time – namely the question of the appropriate starting point for that critique.

In the introduction to the *Grundrisse* (Marx 1973), Marx addresses this question. He begins with the following statement

> The object before us, to begin with, *material production*.
> Individuals producing in society – hence socially determined individual production is, of course the point of departure. (Marx 1973, p. 83, emphasis in original)

He then goes on to analyse such production. At this point, while he recognises that production always takes place within a definite social context, he continues by arguing

> It might seem, therefore, that in order to talk about production at all we must either pursue the process of historic development through its different phases, or declare beforehand that we are dealing with a specific historic epoch such as e.g. modern bourgeois production, which is indeed our particular theme. However, all epochs of production have certain common traits, common characteristics. *Production in general* is an abstraction, but a rational abstraction in so far as it really brings out and fixes the common element and thus saves us repetition. (Marx 1973, p. 85 emphasis in original)

Having then criticised the accounts of production in general in various classical economists, notably Mill, Marx concludes the opening section of the introduction as follows

> To summarize: There are characteristics which all stages of production have in common, and which are established as general ones by the mind; by the so-called *general preconditions* of all production are nothing more than these abstract moments which no real historical stage of production can be grasped. (Marx 1973, p. 88 emphasis in original)

Later in the introduction, in a section entitled 'The Method of Political Economy', Marx goes on to consider labour in general, or 'labour as such'. He makes the point that the development of a general concept of labour as an undifferentiated category is the result of a long period of historical development, and in particular depends on the generalised ability of workers to move from one job to another, which emerges only with capitalist society. However, this does not mean that the analysis of economic developments cannot start with such a general concept of labour

> It would therefore be unfeasible and wrong to let the economic cat-
> egories follow one another in the same sequence as that in which
> they were historically decisive. Their sequence is determined, rather,
> by their relation to one another in modern bourgeois society, which
> is precisely the opposite of that which seems to be their natural order
> or which corresponds to historical development. (Marx 1973, p. 107)

In the *Grundrisse* Marx follows a progressive process of conceptual exploration having arrived at a highly abstract general concept by regressive
analysis, just as Hegel does in regressively identifying freedom as the
general explanatory concept in his *Philosophy of Right*. Hegel does this
while recognising that the meaning of freedom and the possibility of its
general conception is only developed in history.

What is notable here is that in the introduction to the *Grundrisse* Marx
sees the starting point for his criticisms of political economy as being
general concepts of labour and production arrived at through a process
of mental abstraction, albeit one which depends on prior historical
developments. The problem with this is that, as a succession of critics of
Marx beginning with Bohm-Bawerk have observed, any such starting
point appears arbitrary (Kay 1979). It may well be that a concept of
labour in general only arises under capitalism, but this does not imply
that this concept need play a privileged role explaining what the defining features and development of capitalism need be.

Consequently, as writers like Sayer and Kay have stressed, Marx begins
Capital in a very different way from the earlier *Grundrisse* introduction
(Sayer 1979). The starting point for analysis is now the commodity,
which is explicitly linked, in the first sentence of the work, not with a
general trans-historical category but with a specific epoch:

> The wealth of societies in which the capitalist mode of production pre-
> vails appears as an 'immense collection of commodities'; the individual
> commodity appears as its elementary form. Our investigation there-
> fore begins with the analysis of the commodity. (Marx 1976, p. 125)

In this way, the starting point for Marx's critique in *Capital* is explicitly
defined in terms of a key characteristic of critical political economy, the
acknowledgement of the historically specific character of economic
categories. It is the recognition of this character and his concentration

on the particularity of capitalism, through the study of its 'elementary form' that enables Marx to avoid the problems thrown up by his earlier attempts to find an initial standpoint for his analysis. This in turn shows the way in which Marx's critical approach endows his work with coherence.

Two possible criticisms could be made of this argument. Firstly, it could be claimed that the commodity is no less arbitrary a starting point than were general concepts of labour or production. Secondly, it is not clear how to reconcile the adoption of a single starting point with the differentiated nature of Marx's critique of the classical tradition.

The justification for the starting point chosen in *Capital* lies in the movement from abstract concepts to concrete determinations. The *Grundrisse* introduction also attempts to base the method proposed on such a movement, but it fails to do so effectively because Marx can find no suitable bridge between the abstract ideas of production and labour in general and the concrete analysis which he wishes to make. The reason why he is able to do this in *Capital* is that, through starting from the analysis of the commodity form, he is able to develop a different kind of abstraction from the mental generalisations used in the earlier work. As outlined earlier in this chapter, the concept of abstract labour, which Marx develops through his account of the commodity form, does not rest on a mental generalisation but on a real process which is taking place under capitalism. For Marx, it is the ability of an analysis which starts from the concept of the commodity to grasp this process and the concrete phenomena which result from it which justifies the initial standpoint of that analysis and stops it from being arbitrary. In turn, this initial standpoint is chosen on the basis of critical political economy, since it results from grasping the specificity of capitalist production.

It could be argued, however, that this account of Marx's notion of critique simply provides one more unitary account, based on a particular notion of dialectical progression, and so renders Marx vulnerable to the attacks of post-critical theorists. According to such a view, the above account portrays Marx as using a closed and deterministic framework which could be characterised as a 'grand narrative' imposed on a complex reality in an unjustified way. The claim here, however, is that to see Marx as moving dialectically from a starting point of real abstractions, which are generated by sensitivity to the historically bounded character of economic categories, is not incompatible with seeing his work as complex, open and differentiated.

The starting point of the commodity form is compatible with a variety of different modes of critique within the general framework of dialectical thought. To take one example, the accounts of Marx's approach in *Capital* given by writers like Sayer, who take a Kantian approach, differs quite strongly from more Hegelian writers. Sayer sees abstract categories as representing the essence of capitalism while concrete categories represent appearances. While appearances are illusory, they do have a 'practical' validity which explains their hold on people. This supposed validity is no accident, but arises from the nature of the essential relations of capitalism, which determine the form of appearances. Sayer writes that

> It is the nature of the forms in which the phenomena present themselves which explains the peculiarities of their conception, and the phenomenal adequacy of the conception which explains its tenacity. (Sayer 1979, p. 37)

while these forms can be accounted for 'in the final analysis, by the peculiarities of the relations which obligate this form of manifestation' (Sayer 1979, p. 37).

For Sayer, Marx's method of enquiry consisted of uncovering the hidden essence behind the world of appearances. He sees this as analogous to Kant's critical philosophy, with Marx asking what fundamental characteristics of capitalism make its phenomenal form a possibility. The approach used by Marx to do this is, for Sayer, a variant of the 'retroductive' method of scientific inquiry of Peirce and Hanson, while his account of the mechanisms by which this phenomenal form is produced owes much to the analysis of 'causal powers' by Roy Bhaskar and Rom Harré (Bhaskar 1975). While Marx's inquiries begin with phenomena and work backwards retroductively to the essential relations which make those phenomena appear, the presentation of his results begins with essence and progresses to concrete appearances.

This account of Marx contrasts with those writers who describe his approach in more overtly Hegelian terms. To take just one example here Jairus Banaji argues that rather than being a unilinear progression from essence to appearance the opening chapters of *Capital* can be seen as a 'spiral' in which 'the movement from abstract to concrete is not a straight-line process. One returns to the concrete at expanded levels of the total curve' (Banaji 1979, p. 40). For Banaji, these chapters are not to be understood in Kantian terms as a movement from essence to appearance but in Hegelian terms as a movement from being to essence or immediacy to mediation. As such

> the individual commodity forms the *analytic* point of departure. From this, however, we do not pass over directly to the concept of

capital. By analysing the commodity, drawing out its determinations, we arrive at the concept of *value* as the abstract-reified form of social labour. This as the ground of all further conceptual determinations (money, capital) forms the synthetic point of departure of *Capital*. (Banaji 1979, p. 40 emphasis in original)

Banaji does not see a self-sufficient abstract essence as somehow related to a concrete appearance. Rather, abstractions are by their nature incomplete, and this incompleteness forces them to develop, giving rise to the movement towards the concrete:

> it follows that the 'abstraction of value' cannot by itself 'reflect nature . . . truly and completely' as Lenin supposes. As the abstract universal, it is something simple and undeveloped, this form of simplicity is its one-sidedness, it remains a principle that has still to 'realise itself', to become 'active'. And this it can only do by 'entering into appearance', determining itself in appearance or in the whole 'wealth of developed form'. (Banaji 1979, p. 22)

The aim here is not to adjudicate between these particular accounts of Marx, or to take a stand more generally on the relative merits of interpretations of his work which are influenced by either Kant or by Hegel, or indeed by other thinkers or approaches. It is simply to indicate that to see Marx's critique of political economy as starting from a point defined by the standpoint of critical political economy, and as moving from there towards the determination of concrete phenomena, is compatible with a wide range of different conceptions of how that critique progresses. Indeed, rather than choosing between the two above characterisations of Marx's work, it is important to recognise that each of them captures particular aspects of his thinking, and that they can do so precisely because that thinking, and the critique which results from it, is complex and differentiated. However, this does not mean that Marx's conception of critique is so open-ended as to allow any kind of critical approach to claim validity. Both Sayer and Banaji concur in seeing the starting point of the commodity form as crucial and thus in rejecting a notion of critique which is based simply on mental generalisations. Thus, their contrasting interpretations of Marx bear witness to the possibility of a conception of critical political economy which has content and so provides an overall standpoint within which critique takes place but which also allows for variety and complexity.

3.4 Conclusion

This chapter has attempted to show that Marx's relationship to classical political economy combines a variety of modes of critique which do not simply coexist side by side but are given an underlying coherence by the standpoint which he adopts as a critical political economist. The key elements of this standpoint are his recognition of the historically specific nature of the categories used in political economy and of the way in which the economic realm is embedded within a broader social and political context. In this sense Marx and Hegel are working within the same tradition, and as a result Marx's critique has a number of common elements to that of Hegel, in particular the movement from abstract to concrete concepts through a dialectical process. However, the way in which post-critical theorists have tended to characterise Marx's work as governed in all essentials by a single rigid principle is an oversimplification of what is a complex and multilayered analysis.

While the differentiated nature of Marx's critique of political economy can be set against the claims of post-critical theorists and used to question their notion of the closed and deterministic nature of critical political economy, this of course does not answer their more substantive arguments against the conceptions of capitalism put forward by Marx and Hegel and their questioning of its adequacy as a basis for contemporary social theory. These issues will be taken up in detail in the following chapters.

References

Arthur, C. (1979) 'Dialectics and Labour' in J. Mepham and D. Hillel-Ruben (1979) (eds.), *Issues in Marxist Philosophy: Volume 1 Dialectics and Method*. Hassocks: Harvester Press.

Banaji, J. (1979) 'From the Commodity to Capital: Hegel's Dialectic in Marx's *Capital*', in D. Elson (ed.), *Value: The Representation of Labour in Capitalism*. London: CSE Books.

Bhaskar, R. (1975) *A Realist Theory of Science*. Leeds: Leeds Books.

Carver, T. (1998) *The Postmodern Marx*. Manchester: Manchester University Press.

Dobb, M. (1937) *Political Economy and Capitalism*. London: Routledge and Kegan Paul.

Fine, B. (ed.) (1986) *The Value Dimension: Marx versus Ricardo and Sraffa*. London: Routledge.

Fine, B. and L. Harris (1979) *Rereading Capital*. London and Basingstoke: Macmillan.

Kay, G. (1979) 'Why Labour is the Starting Point of Capital', in D. Elson (ed.), *Value: The Representation of Labour in Capitalism*. London: CSE Books.

Marx, K. (1973) *Grundrisse*, translated by M. Nicolaus. Harmondsworth: Penguin.

Marx, K. (1976) *Capital: Volume 1*, translated by B. Fowkes. Harmondsworth: Penguin.

Meek, R. (1973) *Studies in the Labour Theory of Value*, 2nd edition. London: Lawrence and Wishart.

Murray, P. (1993) 'The Necessity of Money: How Hegel Helped Marx Surpass Ricardo's Theory of Value' in F. Moseley (ed.), *Marx's Method in Capital: A Re-examination*. Atlantic Highlands, NJ: Humanities Press International.

Rubin, I. (1978) 'Abstract Labour and Value in Marx's System,' *Capital and Class*, no. 5.

Sayer, D. (1979) *Marx's Method: Ideology, Science and Critique in 'Capital'*. Hassochs: Harvester Press.

Smith, T. (1990) *The Logic of Marx's Capital: Replies to Hegelian Criticisms*. New York: SUNY Press.

Steedman, I. (1977) *Marx After Sraffa*. London: New Left Books.

Sweezy, P. (1942) *The Theory of Capitalist Development*. Oxford: Oxford University Press.

4
Foucault and Political Economy

4.1 Introduction

Michel Foucault differed significantly in his relationship to Marxism, and to the critique of political economy initiated by Hegel and Marx, from many of the other thinkers considered here, notably Lyotard, Baudrillard and Gorz. The intellectual and political formation of these writers, and of other contemporaries such as Castoriadis, was in revolutionary political activity – for example, in the *Socialisme ou Barbarie* group for Lyotard and Castoriadis, in the circles around Sartre and *Les Temps Modernes* for Gorz and to a lesser extent Baudrillard, and with the *Utopie* collective for Baudrillard. For Gorz and for Lyotard the Algerian War was a crucial political experience and all these writers were deeply affected both by enthusiasm for (and in some cases participation in) the events of May 1968 and by the subsequent failure of the movement inaugurated by those events. The failure of this movement contributed to a more general questioning of the theoretical and political tradition which had previously influenced them, and in particular to a critique of the adequacy of Marxism as a guide to radical theory and practice. This questioning, in the cases of Gorz and Baudrillard, drew on writers who had influenced them during their earlier Marx-inspired work: Sartre, Illich and ecological thought in the case of Gorz; Durkheim, Marcuse and the sociological critique of consumption in the case of Baudrillard. However, instead of trying to incorporate insights from such writers into a Marxist critique of contemporary society, Gorz and Baudrillard increasingly used them to elaborate an alternative theoretical standpoint, not just counterposed to Marxism, but to Hegelian dialectics and to the project of a critique of political economy founded on dialectical thought.

Foucault's trajectory was quite different. Following his early studies with Jean Hyppolite he identified himself as a Marxist in a general sense.

However, before 1968 he was never politically involved in the way that Gorz, Baudrillard and Lyotard were, and he was never a member of the revolutionary left. The main part of Foucault's political activity came after 1968 and in a different context; that of the newly emerging struggles for gay liberation and for the rights of prisoners and mental patients. Intellectually, the central influences on Foucault differed from those on Baudrillard and Gorz. Sartre was inescapable but Foucault's response to him was notably ambivalent (see Miller 1994, pp. 44–5). The influence of the Frankfurt School and of Lefebvre, Barthes and the critics of consumption was largely absent. More central for the young Foucault were phenomenology, as expressed through the work of Merleau-Ponty and Heidegger, and structuralism.

Foucault's analysis of political economy was strongly affected by the structuralist tradition in French philosophy of science, as expressed in the work of Bachelard, Canguilhem and Cavaillès. This tradition was also a central influence on the work of Louis Althusser, who in part introduced Foucault to this way of thinking and who praised Foucault's early work in this context: 'I feel bound to acknowledge the obvious or concealed debts which bind us to our masters in reading learned works, once Gaston Bachelard and Jean Cavaillès and now Georges Canguilhem and Michel Foucault' (Althusser and Balibar 1970, p. 16). Such structuralism emphasised the way in which theoretical schemas necessarily stand between observers and reality and the radically differing nature of such schemas. The work of both Bachelard and Althusser also stressed the sharpness of the transition from one schema to another, as encapsulated in the concept of the 'epistemological break'. Implicitly in the work of earlier writers, and explicitly in Althusser's case, this account of the relationship between theory and the real and of theoretical change, was contrasted to Hegelian models of dialectical development and immanent critique.

Foucault's critique of Marxism and of the Marxist account of political economy was not, then, rooted in the experience of a political crisis as it affected a politically engaged intellectual. It was fundamentally an intellectual critique, based on a distinctive philosophical standpoint. The political positions taken up by Foucault were in large measure the consequence rather than the cause of his divergence from the Marxist tradition. The validity of Foucault's rejection of Hegel and Marx can only be assessed against this background.

4.2 Foucault and Marx

Foucault's discussion of Marx takes place at three distinct levels, which in the past have tended to be confused. Firstly, there is the epistemological critique outlined above, in which dialectical thought is rejected in favour of an alternative conception of theoretical change. In *The Order of Things* this conception was expressed through the notion of an *episteme*, however this idea was modified and developed in later work. In Foucault's earlier work the method adopted in place of dialectics is described as 'archaeology'; again this changes as his work develops, and in his later writing is replaced by the concept of 'genealogy', a term which refers back to Nietzsche's *Genealogy of Morals* and which signifies the increasing importance of Nietzsche in Foucault's work from the late 1960s onwards.

The second level at which Foucault criticises Marx is that of social theory in general. Here the conception of a social totality rooted in the material conditions of production (even if only in 'the last instance') is rejected in favour of an approach which sees society as held together by power relations. These relations of power are not hierarchical in the sense of emanating from a central locus of oppression but are omnipresent in all human relationships, weaving such relationships together into a kind of network. As Foucault puts it:

> The state is superstructural in relation to a whole series of power networks that invest the body, sexuality, the family, kinship, knowledge, technology and so forth. True, these networks stand in a conditioning-conditioned relationship to a kind of 'meta-power' which is structured essentially round a certain number of great prohibition functions; but this meta-power with its prohibitions can only take hold and secure its footing where it is rooted in a whole series of multiple and indefinite power relations that supply the necessary basis for the great negative forms of power. (Foucault 1980, p. 122)

In his later work Foucault came increasingly to root forms of knowledge in forms of power, so that the account given of power relations became increasingly linked with his account of theoretical change.

The third strand to Foucault's critique of Marx is his detailed discussion of the formation of political economy as a discipline in the late eighteenth and early nineteenth century. His initial account of this is contained within *The Order of Things*, and its implications for the evaluation of Marx's radicalism are most succinctly summed up by the statement that

> the alternatives offered by Ricardo's 'pessimism' and Marx's revolutionary promise are probably of little importance. Such a system of options represents nothing more than the two possible ways of examining the relations of anthropology and History as they are established by economics through the notions of scarcity and labour . . .

[such] controversies may have stirred up a few waves and caused a few surface ripples; but they are no more than storms in a children's paddling pool. (Foucault 1970, pp. 261–2)

Before proceeding to examine this third aspect of Foucault's discussion of Marxism in more detail, it is worth assessing the relationship between the three levels of his critique.

Foucault's historical account of the emergence of political economy can be seen as an application of his general archaeological method. Yet there is nothing in that method in itself which necessarily leads to the conclusion that the differences between Marx and Ricardo are relatively insignificant, or that Marxism is fundamentally structured by the same categories as classical political economy. One could imagine an archaeological account of the development of economic thought in which Marx's work marked a rupture between two *epistemes*, rather than being contained within one. Thus, the first and third levels of Foucault's criticism of Marx are largely independent of one another.

The second level of critique can also be said to be independent of the other two. Foucault links his account of theoretical change to a social theory of power. Yet it is not at all clear that this is a necessary link. Power relationships could be said to ground knowledge claims without such claims being characterised by the kind of radical discontinuity suggested by the archaeological method. Conversely, an archaeological account of theoretical frameworks does not have to invoke a theory of power, and, indeed, such a theory is largely absent from *The Order of Things*.

This in turn, however, raises a further issue in the interpretation of Foucault's thought; that of the relationship between his early 'archaeological' and later 'genealogical' analyses. Foucault sees the recognition of the centrality of power as marking the key divide between these two periods

It was these different régimes [of power] that I tried to identify and describe in *The Order of Things*, all the while making it clear that I wasn't trying for the moment to explain them, and that it would be necessary to try and do this in a subsequent work. But what was lacking here was this problem of the 'discursive régime', of the effects of power peculiar to the play of statements. I confused this too much with systematicity, theoretical form, or something like a paradigm. (Foucault 1980, p. 113)

However, he does not spell out the extent to which the shift from an archaeological to a genealogical method affects the validity of the earlier archaeological writings. The result of this is that genealogy comes to be seen simply as archaeology plus power relations, without any deeper consideration of the links between Foucault's account of power and his discussion of the presuppositions of theory. This has implications for Foucault's account of Marxism.

When writing about power Foucault tends to criticise Marxism from a very different standpoint to the archaeological account of the similarity between Marx and Ricardo quoted above. His later critique is largely founded on a political stance in which Marxism is seen both as adhering to a misleading identification between power and the state and as neglecting the most important sites of power relations, in particular the body:

> One can say that what has happened since 1968, and arguably what made 1968 possible, is something profoundly anti-Marxist. How can European revolutionary movements free themselves from the 'Marx effect', the institutions typical of nineteenth- and twentieth-century Marxism? This was the direction of the questions posed by '68. In this calling in question of the equation: Marxism = the revolutionary process, an equation that constituted a kind of dogma, the importance given to the body is one of the important, if not essential elements. (Foucault 1980, p. 57)

The question of the relationship between the different levels of Foucault's critique of Marx is then in large measure one of the relationship between this account of Marxism and power and the earlier account of the formation of political economy.

4.3 Foucault and the formation of political economy

Foucault's account of the emergence of classical political economy is brilliantly suggestive and iconoclastic. Conventional accounts of the history of economic thought, from both an orthodox and a Marxist perspective, essentially concur in identifying a small number of key turning points in the development of the discipline. Two such ruptures are common to both perspectives. The first of these is the formation of classical political economy in the mid-eighteenth century with the work of the physiocrats, especially Quesnay, leading on to the writing of Adam Smith. The second is the so-called 'marginal revolution' of the late nineteenth century, in which the classical tradition was supplanted by the 'neo-classical' or 'marginalist' economics inaugurated by Jevons and

Marshall in Britain and by Walras and Pareto in Continental Europe. Marxist writers tend to identify a third crucial break by differentiating Marx's work from the preceding classical writers, notably Smith and Ricardo, and from those following such as Mill, who can be seen as a bridge between the classical and neo-classical schools. In this they essentially follow the account given by Marx himself in the *Theories of Surplus Value* (Marx 1963, 1968, 1971). In contrast, orthodox writers locate Marx firmly within the tradition of classical political economy; a position expressed in its most extreme form in the description of Marx by Nobel laureate Paul Samuelson as a 'minor post-Ricardian'. However, some orthodox writers do identify a third key moment in the history of economic doctrine, the work of Keynes in the 1930s. For such writers Keynes' work marks both a 'revolution' comparable to the marginalist one half a century earlier and also an alternative fundamental criticism of neo-classical economics to that provided by Marx.

Economics is thus a discipline where there is both a general acceptance that progress has been marked by radical shifts in theoretical perspectives and also a fairly high degree of consensus about when such shifts have occurred, even amongst economists with widely differing viewpoints. Finally, despite emphasising such shifts, economists have tended to be in agreement about the essential underlying continuity of the subject area. The most radical change of perspective, that embodied in the marginalist revolution, is commonly seen as a change in the kinds of questions being asked, away from long-run growth towards the allocation of resources in a static framework, and as a change in the theories endorsed, away from the labour theory of value towards seeing price as based on utility, demand and supply. It is not seen as a change in the fundamental character of the discipline itself.

Foucault's work directly challenges both Marxist and orthodox approaches to the constitution of political economy as a discourse. It does so in two main ways. Firstly, it locates the crucial turning points in this constitution at different times to both the orthodox and radical approaches. Two key shifts are isolated, each of which parallels for Foucault a similar shift in the development of the discourses of biology and linguistics. The first is in the early seventeenth century with the transition from bullionist to mercantilist thought while the second is in the late eighteenth century between Smith and Ricardo.

Orthodox and Marxist historians of economic thought have tended to stress the similarities rather than the differences between bullionists and mercantilists. The former have been characterised as attaching a special importance to money in general, and gold in particular, over and above other commodities, and as seeing the accumulation of gold (*specie*) as the primary aim of national economic policy. The latter relaxed the emphasis on the building up of stocks of money as an end in itself but continued to emphasise the importance of a positive balance of trade resulting in an increase in national wealth as the central economic goal of any particular country. Conventionally, both schools of thought have been seen as mistaken in their emphasis on the hoarding of national 'treasure' and as superseded by the realisation which came with the classical political economists that such treasure is only of use if it is employed as capital; in other words, it must be temporarily 'given up' in order to generate returns at a future date.

Foucault in contrast sees the bullionist and mercantilist outlooks as fundamentally different. The bullionist theory is based on the notion of resemblance, which he regards as the basis of renaissance thought:

> Here, the monetary sign cannot define its exchange value, and can be established as a mark only on a metallic mass which in turn defines its value in the scale of other commodities. If one admits that exchange, in the system of needs, corresponds to similitude in the system of acquired knowledge, then one sees that knowledge of nature, and reflection or practices concerning money, were controlled during the Renaissance by one and the same configuration of the *episteme*. (Foucault 1970, p. 172)

The important change between bullionism and mercantilism is the move away from basing the value of the money commodity on its character as a precious metal, a way of thinking rooted in the notion of resemblance, towards the complex of ideas which later took form as the quantity theory of money, an approach based upon the very different concept of representation. It is representation, for Foucault, which is the organising idea of thought in the Classical Age from the mid-seventeenth to late eighteenth century.

> Whereas the Renaissance based the two *functions* of coinage (measure and substitution) on the double nature of its intrinsic *character* (the fact that it was precious), the seventeenth century turns the analysis upside down: it is the exchanging function that serves as a foundation for the other two characters (its ability to measure and its capacity to receive a price thus appearing as *qualities* deriving from that *function*). (Foucault 1970, p. 174)

Mercantilism inaugurates a system of thought described by Foucault as the analysis of wealth. The work of both the physiocrats and Smith is inscribed within this system of thought, so that the conventional break between mercantilism and the early stages of classical political economy becomes of little consequence. The analysis of wealth is founded on the ability of money to represent commodities in the process of exchange: 'for Classical thought in its formative phase, money is that which permits wealth to be represented' (Foucault 1970, p. 177). This in turn leads to such an analysis taking a tabular, spatial form with money connecting different commodities in an intricate web:

> And just as the entire world of representation covers itself with representations which, at one remove, represent it, in an uninterrupted sequence, so all the kinds of wealth in the world are related one to another in so far as they are all part of a system of exchange. (Foucault 1970, p. 179)

This linkage between the elements of wealth is compared with the Linnean classifications founding natural history during this period and with the systematisation of language in the *Port-Royal Logic*, which is seen by Foucault as the centrepiece of what he describes as general grammar.

Foucault's account of the analysis of wealth is designed to show the work of the quantity theorists, physiocrats and Smith as unified by this common approach based on representation. In doing this he continues to revise commonly accepted notions of the major turning points in the development of economic thought. However, he also emphasises the second important factor differentiating his approach from both orthodox and Marxist accounts of this development. For Foucault the analysis of wealth is not simply an earlier and more imperfect version of nineteenth- and twentieth-century political economy and economics; it is a system of thought governed by its own logic, which is radically discontinuous both from the monetary thought of the Renaissance which preceded it and from the approach stemming from Ricardo which replaced it. As Foucault states in his discussion of mercantilism:

> It is usual to characterize this [mercantilism] rather hastily as an absolute 'monetarism', that is, a systematic (or stubborn) confusion between wealth and coinage. In fact, it is not an identity – more or less confused – that 'mercantilism' established between these two things, but a considered articulation that makes money the instrument of the representation and analysis of wealth, and makes wealth, conversely, into the content represented by money. (Foucault 1970, pp. 174–5)

At the end of the eighteenth century, Foucault argues, the analysis of wealth was replaced by a radically different way of thinking about the exchange of commodities, the key exponent of which was Ricardo. This was part of a more general change, from the Classical Age to what Foucault describes as the Age of History. While the thought of the Classical Age was tabular and spatial, based on the tracing of intricate webs of connection, the thought of the Age of History was linear and developmental, with an emphasis on following a trajectory through time. Again, Foucault draws parallels between the world of political economy and the study of both the natural world and of language; highlighting the growth of the historical school of philology, particularly in Germany, and the beginnings of an evolutionary approach to the analysis of species in the work of Cuvier.

Contrary to both orthodox and Marxist accounts of classical political economy, Foucault sees the key theoretical breakthrough as coming between Smith and Ricardo, rather than with the work of Smith or of Marx:

> Whereas in Classical thought trade and exchange serve as an indispensable basis for the analysis of wealth (and this is still true of Smith's analysis, in which the division of labour is governed by the criteria of barter), after Ricardo, the possibility of exchange is based upon labour; and henceforth the theory of production must always precede that of circulation. (Foucault 1970, p. 254)

This breakthrough has, for Foucault, three main consequences. Firstly, reciprocal interaction is replaced by causal determination:

> This accumulation in series breaks for the first time with the reciprocal determinations that were the sole active factors in the Classical analysis of wealth. It introduces, by its very existence, the possibility of a continuous historical time, even if in fact, as we shall see, Ricardo conceives of the evolution ahead only as a slowing down and, at most, a total suspension of history. (Foucault 1970, p. 255)

Secondly, scarcity becomes a central organising concept within economic thought, as opposed to the work, for example, of the physiocrats, in which the key problem addressed was the ability of the economy to attain plenitude and to generate a surplus; an ability which they saw as rooted in the productivity of agricultural land. Thirdly, economics becomes historical in the sense that the finitude of resources which is the basis of scarcity develops over time, constraining the choices available to economic agents.

Foucault's argument is that Marx's thought is structured by the same underlying framework as that of Ricardo, in which causality, scarcity and history are crucial organising elements. Consequently, Marxism cannot be seen as a radical critique of the *episteme* which began in the early nineteenth century; it is rather a product of that *episteme*. While Foucault does not discuss Hegel in any detail in *The Order of Things* it is clear that many of his arguments concerning Marx could be extended to Hegel and to Hegelianism in general. In particular, the stress on historical development, and on the historically grounded nature of both theoretical and social developments, in both thinkers, is, for Foucault, not the mark of a radical critique of conventional social theory. On the contrary it simply marks both Hegel and Marx as typical exemplars of the Age of History and thus indicates that a critical social theory based on their work will fail to confront the questions which Foucault sees as of crucial importance.

4.4 Evaluating Foucault's account

Foucault's discussion of the formation of classical political economy is of great interest. In particular, his depiction of the analysis of wealth in the Classical Age is rich in insights about writers like Mun, Turgot and Galiani as well as more well-known figures such as Quesnay and Smith. His comparison of Smith and Ricardo is also illuminating. It should be noted, however, that emphasising the theoretical differences between Smith and Ricardo does not necessarily imply that the differences between Marx and Ricardo are lessened in importance. For example, the work of David McNally, written from a Marxist perspective, also stresses the fundamental nature of the change from Smith to Ricardo, but provides a very different interpretation of the significance of this change (McNally 1988). For McNally, the main elements of the divide between the two writers are firstly that Smith and the physiocrats are theorists of agrarian capitalism rather than industrial capitalism, and secondly that for Smith political economy was not a distinct discipline, but was rooted in a moral and philosophical framework which was largely absent from Ricardo's work. McNally also argues that these differences can themselves be explained in Marxist terms; for example, his development of the concept of agrarian capitalism draws heavily on the work of the Marxist historian and economist Robert Brenner. In this way, McNally claims that it is possible to provide an analysis of the break between

Smith and Ricardo which develops, rather than overturns, Marx's account of the course of classical political economy.

While Foucault's work provides a number of valuable analyses of individual thinkers, and draws suggestive parallels between economic thought and biological and linguistic concepts, there are, however, two major questions which can be raised about his approach to economic thought in general and to Marxism in particular.

The first question relates to the characterisation of the work of Marx and Ricardo. Here, Foucault's account should be distinguished from simplistic criticisms of Marx as wedded to historical teleology or as an economic determinist. However, he does argue that Marx's work is centrally structured around temporal development and an associated notion of causation, and that this displaces spatial relationships and reciprocal interaction.

It can surely be argued that this does not capture the full complexity of Marx's method. In *Capital* there are a number of key points at which such a pattern of interaction assumes primacy over linear development. Three in particular are crucial; the initial account of value and exchange in volume 1, the schemas of reproduction in volume 2 and the development of the theory of value to incorporate differing capital intensities and the associated divergence of prices from value in volume 3. These three analyses arise from the differing characters of the three volumes of Marx's work; volume 1 dealing with the production process in general, volume 2 with relations of distribution and exchange and volume 3 with the integration of production with distribution and exchange through the process of competition.

The case of the reproduction schemas provides a very clear example of the difficulties faced by Foucault's account of Marx. It could be argued that during the period of the 'Second International' before the First World War, and in the thought of some Marxist writers subsequent to this, such as Grossman (1992), the schemas were indeed interpreted in the way that Foucault describes. They were seen as accounts of the temporal course of capitalist development, analogous to the dynamic theory provided by Ricardo, and there was a lively debate about the extent to which they showed that the collapse of capitalism was inevitable. This debate was inconclusive, and more recent analyses of Marx's methodological approach have argued that the failure to derive unambiguous predictions of the course of capitalist development from the schemas was unavoidable, since the schemas are not in fact a model of economic growth or decline over time. Rather, they are a particular kind of construction through which Marx shows the conditions which would have to be fulfilled for an economy to be stable; either in static equilibrium in the case of simple reproduction or along a path of balanced growth in the case of expanded reproduction. As such, even in the case of expanded reproduction they are essentially timeless and ahistorical since they are precisely designed to show what would have to be the case for the economy not to be subject to disruptive change. They outline a network of exchanges between sectors which is very similar in many ways to that provided by Quesnay in his *Tableau Economique* (1972).

However, there is one important difference between Marx and Quesnay in this regard. The schemas are not meant to be a description of an actual economy, since Marx regarded capitalism as an inherently unstable system, so that any model of balanced equilibrium could not capture the key elements of its development over time. Rather they outline the relationships which characterise the economic system at a particular level of abstraction, one in which allowance is made for differences between sectors but not for the process of competition. This then provides the basis for movement to a lower level of abstraction at which, for example, the possibility opens for a theory of crisis and cycles in the economy. Thus, Marx does not replace the study of networks or tables of exchange with a theory of causal determination based on production. Both are present in his work and a succession of such spatial tables is provided, each at a different level of generality. These tables in turn impel the analysis forward to the next aspect of temporal determination, which in turn gives rise to a more detailed network of interrelationships. For example, the reproduction schemas are followed by the account of the interrelationship between capitals of differing intensities, through competition, which results in the formation of a uniform rate of profit and of prices of production. In some ways this movement from the abstract to the concrete can be assimilated to the path of the Hegelian dialectic, with each spatial representation of the structure of the economy a temporary resting place which is immediately undermined by its own contradictions.

It would, however, be possible for Foucault to counter this argument by pointing to the dependence of the whole edifice on the role of labour in production. While Marx's account combines both spatial and temporal perspectives, the temporal has been seen as having primacy through the ultimate determination of each moment in the process by productive conditions. As Foucault puts it in his account of Ricardo

> As they circulate through the market, while they are being exchanged for one another, values still have a power of representation. But this power is drawn from elsewhere – from the labour that is more primitive

and more radical than all representation, and that cannot, in consequence, be defined by exchange. (Foucault 1970, p. 254)

Here it is important to look at the first of the three examples of reciprocal interaction in Marx outlined above, the initial account of the role of value in exchange in volume 1 of *Capital*. As described above in Chapter 3 Marx's analysis here involves the introduction of a new concept, that of abstract labour, which had not previously existed within classical political economy. Recent discussions of Marx's value theory have stressed the differences between his concept of abstract labour and the notion of embodied labour on which Ricardo's value theory is based and the consequent difference between Marx's value theory and that of Ricardo. This discussion has partly been motivated, as discussed earlier, in the debates following the work of Piero Sraffa, which appeared to indicate that, interpreted in a Ricardian sense, value was a redundant concept since prices and profits were derived directly from the technical coefficients of production without the use of intervening value categories (Sraffa 1960). Worse, in the case of the joint production of commodities (which was particularly significant because in the neo-Ricardian analysis of Marx any production process involving fixed capital can be seen as a case of joint production) the use of the concept of value generated paradoxical results in the Sraffian framework. Specifically, it became possible in such cases to derive the existence of positive profits, but negative surplus value, thus detaching the existence of profit from the exploitation of labour on which Marx claimed it depended.

The key aspect of Marx's concept of abstract labour in the context of Foucault's characterisation of Marx is not just that it differs fundamentally from Ricardo's embodied labour, but also that it is linked to exchange and thus is not posed as prior to all representation in the way that Foucault describes. Three points have been stressed by those writers analysing abstract labour, largely following Isaac Rubin's work of the 1920s (Rubin 1978; Fine 1986; Moseley 1993). Firstly, only socially necessary labour can create value for Marx and labour can only be validated as socially necessary through the process of exchange. Thus exchange cannot be seen simply as secondary to production in Marx's account; value is created through the articulation of both production and exchange in an integrated process. Secondly, the validation of labour as necessary is achieved through exchange for money, so that the existence of a money commodity as the representative of value in general is intrinsic to a capitalist economy. This led to a detailed analysis of Marx's theory of money and the way it differed from Ricardo's use of the quantity theory.

Thirdly, the objective of Marx's theory of value is not simply to provide a theory of price formation and the rate of profit. It is also to show how qualitatively differing forms of labour can be brought into quantitative equivalence with one another, and in so doing to characterise the nature of labour within capitalism.

The significance of this approach to Marx's theory of value for Foucault's account was threefold. Firstly, it re-emphasised precisely the break, which Foucault had attempted to close, between Marx's work and that of Ricardo. Secondly, it re-connected Marx's theory of value with Hegel and with dialectical thought. The accounts given in this tradition both of the relationship between production and exchange and of the role of money were explicitly dialectical in a way which the conventional assimilation of Marx to classical political economy and to Ricardo's value theory was not. Thirdly, it made it more difficult to see Marx's work as determined by production in the way in which Foucault had suggested in his description of the Age of History. Hegelian accounts of Marx's value theory did not see value as determined simply, or primarily, by exchange, in the manner of neo-classical economics, or even of Smith. However, they also did not see value as formed entirely within production, as in Ricardo's work. Rather, value emerges for Marx through the dialectical interplay between production and exchange. The dual requirement for value-creating labour both of being employed in capitalist production and of being validated through exchange, can only be understood, it is argued, in a dialectical framework, which prevents the analysis collapsing back into a one-dimensional dependence either on production or exchange. Thus, in both the value theory which grounds his work and in the structure of *Capital* as it moves through different levels of analysis, Marx incorporates both spatial and developmental forms of analysis. The frameworks identified by Foucault as founding the *epistemes* of the Classical Age and the Age of History are both present in Marx's work, and dialectical thought enables us to understand their coexistence in his work and the tensions between them.

The second important question which can be asked about Foucault's analysis of the constitution of political economy as a discipline relates to the relationship between the thought of Ricardo and Marx on the one hand and neo-classical economics on the other. Foucault writes that 'Marxism exists in nineteenth-century thought like a fish in water' (Foucault 1970, p. 262). However, whatever the merits of his account of the compatibility between Marx and the classical political economy of Ricardo and others, this leaves open the issue of the supposed break between this tradition and the neo-classical thought initiated by Walras and Jevons.

Neo-classical economics not only explicitly refers back to Smith (much more so than to Ricardo), but is predominantly built around precisely those networks of exchange, which to Foucault characterise the Classical Age. Exchange is also seen as primary when compared with production, both at the level of the theory of value and price, where the existence of both depends upon the utility provided by a commodity, which can only be expressed through exchange, and in the depiction of the economy as a whole. The main approach to this depiction in the neo-classical framework, the general equilibrium theory originally developed by Walras, appears to provide a very similar model of balance between interlocking elements, viewed in a tabular perspective, to the writers of the Classical Age discussed by Foucault. In general equilibrium theory, at least in its contemporary version, production is very much secondary. For example, the mathematical version of the theory developed by Arrow and Debreu (Debreu 1959) which rigorously proved for the first time the existence of a simultaneous equilibrium point for the economy as a whole, did so in a model of pure exchange. Both production and accounts of movement to and from that equilibrium point (the so-called 'transition' question) were added in later.

It is true that some accounts of Walras' thought, notably that of Michio Morishima, do see important parallels between his work and that of Ricardo and Marx. Indeed, Morishima argues that Walras' general equilibrium theory was not developed for its own sake, but as a means towards an account of the accumulation of capital and evolution of the economy over time (Morishima 1977). On the basis of this interpretation Morishima sees Marx and Ricardo as twin inheritors of Ricardo's legacy, developing his analysis in different ways but dealing with the same fundamental problems. If true, this seems strikingly to confirm Foucault's observations. However, two things should be noted here. Firstly, Morishima's account of Walras remains controversial. More importantly, Morishima himself argues that later neo-classical economists have departed dramatically from Walras' work, precisely because of their focus on models of static exchange at the expense of developmental questions. Thus, even if we allow for a basic similarity between Ricardo, Marx and Walras, the question remains of the relation between Ricardian economics and later neo-classical writings.

4.5 The significance of Foucault's account

At this point it is worthwhile returning to the links between Foucault's detailed account of the formation of political economy and the more general epistemological and social themes, which he also wishes to high-light. His contrast between Ricardo and Marx, on the one hand, and the analysis of wealth prevalent in the Classical Age on the other, exemplifies his archaeological method in two ways. Firstly, a manner of thinking pre-viously regarded as a confused precursor of modern analyses is reclaimed and exhibited as a coherent and rational whole, structured around its own central organising concepts, which cannot be identified with those in operation today. Secondly, contemporary thought, even that which pur-ports to be radical critique, is shown as governed by fundamental con-cepts and assumptions of which it is unaware.

In this way, Foucault's archaeology attacks a crucial claim of both Hegelian and Marxist thought, that of being able to understand the conditions for its own emergence. Marx's analysis of the relationship between classical political economy and his own writing purports to explain both the economic and social reasons for the rise of political economy as the expression of the viewpoint of the nascent class of industrial employers and for its later collapse into so-called 'vulgar econ-omy' as this class increasingly came to depend on an ideological ration-ale in the face of working class resistance. He also claims to be able to show how his dialectical analysis of economic contradictions enables him to solve the questions which classical political economy was unable to answer, for example the coexistence of the labour theory of value with differing capital intensities across firms and sectors – a puzzle the solution to which had always eluded Ricardo.

Foucault's archaeology thus is posed very much as an epistemological alternative to the dialectical critique of political economy inaugurated by Hegel and Marx, and his specific account of the location of Marx's work within nineteenth-century economic thought attempts to demonstrate this general claim in detail. It is also important, however, to investigate the links between the archaeological approach adopted by Foucault here and his social theory of power.

This issue has elicited a wide range of responses among readers of Foucault. Three in particular, however, appear important when consider-ing the implications of Foucault's work for critical political economy. An example of the first interpretation is the view of Aijaz Ahmed, in the context of his analysis of the work of Edward Said, in *In Theory: Classes, Nations, Literatures*. Ahmed writes that

> Foucault certainly knew how to be allusive, but underneath all his mul-tiple enunciations one knows exactly what his agreements and disagree-ments with Marxism actually have been. His first and irreconcilable

difference is that he locates Marx firmly within the boundaries of what he calls the 'Western episteme'; in its epistemic construction, he says, Marx's thought is framed entirely by the discourse of Political Economy as this discourse is assembled within that episteme. From this purported philosophical difference, then, follows his equally clear disagreement with Marx over the principle that might govern historical narrativization; he radically denies that narratives of history can be assembled at the twin sites of the state and economic production, which he deems to be the exclusive originating sites of Marx's historical narrative. (Ahmed 1992, p. 165)

For Ahmed then, Foucault's archaeology determines his social theory. The founding of social and historical realities on multiple forms of power relations rather than on the state and the economy is the result of his epistemological critique of the presumptions of Marxism. However, as shown above, this critique is problematic both because it neglects the real differences between Marx's thought and classical political economy and because it adopts an oversimplified approach to the internal complexity of Marx's analysis. Rather than simply exemplifying the underlying assumptions of the age of history in contrast to those of the Classical Age, Marx's work exhibits elements of both systems of thought, integrated through a productive internal tension, which leads his account through a series of levels of abstraction. If the posing of power as the central concept of social theory by Foucault is simply a consequence of his archaeological account of Marxism then it could be criticised along with that account.

However, even if Foucault did base his theory of power on his epistemological criticisms of dialectical thought it is not clear that the problems with those criticisms necessarily invalidate his later social theory. That theory might itself have validity even if the basis on which it was developed was flawed. What becomes problematic, however, in such a case, is both assessing the scope of that validity and the factors on which it rests. These issues are taken up in the other two responses to Foucault's account of power.

A second approach takes Foucault's account of power both as primary and as incompatible with Marx's thought while the archaeological account of Marx is accorded much less importance. For such writers, the force of Foucault's work as an alternative to Marxism, and to dialectical thought in general, lies in the identification of a range of subject areas which the dialectical tradition is seen as having ignored. These particularly concern the body, both as related to sexuality and as related to techniques of imprisonment, medicine and psychiatry. Not only is Foucault seen as having uncovered aspects of social reality unexamined by Marx, he is also regarded as having identified forms of oppression based on power and related to these aspects, which are of more significance than the 'traditional' economic relations of exploitation highlighted by Marxists. He has also been seen as uncovering the potential of varying forms of resistance to such oppression, though this is more controversial given the notably pessimistic streak in much of Foucault's writing, and the fact that he tends to be sceptical about the possibility of escaping from the grip of power relations.

What is notable in such interpretations of Foucault is that the analysis of political economy tends to be omitted. While the account given by Ahmed may be extreme in seeing Foucault's concrete accounts of power relations purely as following, rather than as partly motivating, his archaeological critique of Marx, it is also surely one-sided simply to assume that the presentation of a social theory based on power and its application to particular historical instances is sufficient to justify sidelining the question of the significance of the economic.

To take one example of the potential problems involved in an approach which sidelines concerns of political economy, the account of the origins of the prison system given by Foucault himself has been criticised strongly by the Italian Marxists Dario Melossi and Massimo Pavarini. In their book *The Prison and the Factory* Melossi and Pavarini present a very different analysis to that outlined by Foucault; one which relates it much more closely to the growth of capitalism and to changes in the economy. While Foucault's *Discipline and Punish* (1977) was published after the bulk of their book was written, Melossi does discuss it in an appendix, where he observes that Foucault's book exhibits 'almost total disinterest in the relationship between discipline and the capitalist organisation of work' (Melossi and Pavarini 1981, p. 192). He goes on to write that

> The 'birth of the prison' is not merely a much earlier phenomenon than *Surveiller et punir* implies, but one intimately connected with efforts to get nascent capitalist industry under way by national monarchies operating within a mercantilist framework. (ibid.)

Melossi does not deny the importance of Foucault's book, but he regards it as primarily a philosophical, rather than an historical work. As such, it is centrally not concerned with a concrete account of prison within its social and economic context, but with an account of the formation of certain modes of thought:

> Thus the place for *Surveiller et punir* is within a Foucaultian *genealogy of morals*. The origins of moral sentiments, of the sense of guilt, of

subjection, of the 'too human'; Nietzsche's mnemotechnics are made specific in the *disciplines* of *Surveiller et punir. . .* Thus it is right that within the debate on Foucault's book, prison as such fades into the background and the struggle over the use of disciplinary techniques – over power, over the political – constitutes the real focus of discussion. (ibid.)

Viewed in this context, Foucault's social theory becomes not so much an alternative to Marx and to the critique of political economy, but something concerned with a very different set of questions. It appears that, in the case of prisons, there can exist parallel narratives; one concerned with the operation of the institution and resistance to it, within a precisely located economic context, and one concerned with the way in which the institution acts as an instance of a more general transformation in ways of looking at the world. However, this immediately raises the question of the relationship between these two kinds of account. If Foucault's account of power is to be seen not as substituting for a Marxist account of institutions but as complementing it, then the way in which this is to be done needs to be specified.

This leads to the third response to Foucault's theory of power. This interpretation views Marx and Foucault as essentially providing complementary analyses of capitalist society, each of which captures a particular aspect of modern social reality. This viewpoint is argued particularly strongly by Richard Marsden, who writes that 'the more I read of Marx and Foucault, the more they seemed to explore a common problem, albeit in very different ways' (Marsden 1999, p. 26). For Marsden, while Marx can explain 'why' particular aspects of capitalism arise, Foucault's work is necessary to explain 'how' they actually take shape in a concrete way and to analyse the techniques and practices necessary to instantiate them and to ensure that they persist. The particular area of capitalist reality which concerns Marsden most is labour regulation within the workplace. Jonathan Joseph provides a rather similar account of the compatibility between aspects of Foucault's work and that of Marx, though he is more critical of Foucault than is Marsden (Joseph 2004).

Both Marsden and Joseph argue that the critical realism developed by Roy Bhaskar can be used as a means to bridge the separate analyses of Marx and Foucault. Their approach is to reinterpret Foucault's notion of power in terms of Bhaskar's concept of causal powers. Such causal powers embody the influence of underlying social structures on surface phenomena. Joseph and other writers who are sympathetic towards trying to link Foucault's work with Marxism in this way have also pointed to Foucault's later work in which he modified some of his stronger statements about power and allowed more of a role to the individual subject in expressing resistance (Foucault 2001). In this work on governmentality Foucault analysed the way in which the disciplinary techniques used in managing people as the modern state emerged, in particular the stress on self-management and self-control, laid the basis for the emergence of liberalism. In turn this liberalism laid the basis for classical political economy

> Out of the problems of population, territory and wealth a new science of political economy emerges. The science of political economy establishes itself by separating out the state and civil society and the political and legal order, and establishing the importance of the realm of self-interested market-based activity. (Joseph 2004, p. 156)

Joseph argues that this approach

> Is important in maintaining an economic focus, but it adds to Marxism by emphasising that economics takes place within a wider social context and that the development of society is not exclusively economic, but that the economic is interwoven with other social factors. (ibid.)

The work of writers like Marsden and Joseph is important in indicating some of the ways in which Foucault's work could be seen as being compatible with critical political economy. However, it does also raise certain problems. Three in particular seem important. Firstly, it is not clear how the later work of Foucault is to be linked with the alternative, archaeological account of the emergence of political economy set out in *The Order of Things*. Secondly, it is not obvious that Foucault's account of power can simply be critically appropriated in this way and placed within a framework governed by a critical realist interpretation of Marxism. It could be argued that much of the force of Foucault's account of power comes precisely from its fragmented and dispersed, almost molecular, character and that this would be lost if it were simply seen as part of a stratified and hierarchical reality of the kind set out by Bhaskar. Thirdly, as Marsden in fact points out, such an approach may run the risk of missing some of the ways in which Foucault's challenge to dialectical thought actually highlights some of the real weaknesses of critical political economy. Foucault's work may simply be seen as showing the ways in which the market and the state bring about certain effects, with the result that his ideas are no longer used to rethink such concepts in a radical way.

Each of these three responses to Foucault's work contains certain difficulties. However, these difficulties, and the contradictions between the different responses, in large measure indicate the complexities of Foucault's thought. Like Marx and Hegel, Foucault's critical social theory is complex and multi-layered and consequently tracing the implications of his work for critical political economy requires also requires attending to the tensions within his own arguments.

4.6 Conclusion

Foucault's work poses three challenges to dialectical thought in general and to Marxism in particular. Firstly, it presents an alternative epistemological approach, based on the archaeology of knowledge. Secondly, it presents an alternative social theory based on the microphysics of power. Thirdly, it presents an analysis of Marxism as inscribed within, and determined by, nineteenth-century thought and as thus unable to provide the standpoint for radical social critique. From the analysis above it can be seen that the differences between Marxism and classical political economy are greater than allowed for by Foucault and that Marxism itself is more complex and internally heterogeneous than it appears in Foucault's account. Both of these characteristics of Marxism can be explained within a dialectical analysis more effectively than within Foucault's archaeological framework. Such an analysis offers the possibility of explaining the coexistence within Marx both of elements of Ricardo's thought and of radically anti-Ricardian concepts. It can also explain how static, tabular concepts, such as those Foucault identifies in the work of Smith and Quesnay, can be found in Marx in a dynamic tension with developmental ideas such as those located in Ricardo. Thus, a dialectical approach allows for a richer account of Marx's method than Foucault's archaeology.

To the extent that Foucault's account of power rests on this archaeology, then, it can also be questioned. If, however, Foucault's attempt to ground social theory on an analysis of power relations is independent on his archaeological critique of Marx then it requires further justification of its neglect of political economy. It cannot simply be assumed that an account of institutions based on power relations is superior to one incorporating an economic element.

However, this does not mean that Foucault's work can be discarded. On the contrary, it abounds in important insights. However, these insights, as expressed both through the archaeological account of successive *epistemes* and through the genealogical account of systems of power, are primarily either about structures of thought or about particular institutional changes or social developments which accompany economic changes.

Thus, what Foucault provides is not a substitute for a critique of society based on the critique of political economy but a depiction of changes in mentality or social practice which can accompany such a critique.

The unanswered question posed here, however, is that of the links between such changes and economic developments. In answering this, two pitfalls must be avoided. Firstly, what Foucault's work shows in a very valuable way is the inadequacy of simplistic views of systems of belief as ideological rationalisations of economic interests. This inadequacy is demonstrated both by the care with which Foucault shows the coherence of the ideas with which he is concerned, and by the nature of the transitions which he exhibits between different frameworks.

Secondly, however, it is important not to see Foucault's analysis as a self-sufficient theory of society. Either because of an adherence to his archaeological critique of Marxism, or for other reasons, Foucault and his followers have tended to present their analyses of belief structures and institutions as obviating the need for concrete analysis of changes at the level of political economy. Rather than seeing these analyses as opening up an important problem; that of relating changes in mentality and practice to economic changes, they have regarded them as concluding the debate and as providing the basis for setting the economy to one side. It is now surely possible to re-open this set of questions and to see Foucault's work, not as incompatible with dialectical thought, but as a possible instrument for its rejuvenation in the future.

References

Ahmed, A. (1992) *In Theory: Classes, Nations, Literatures*. London: Verso.

Althusser, L. and E. Balibar (1970) *Reading Capital*. London: New Left Books.

Debreu, G. (1959) *Theory of Value: An Axiomatic Analysis of Economic Equilibrium*. New Haven: Yale University Press.

Fine, B. (ed.) (1986) *The Value Dimension: Marx versus Ricardo and Sraffa*. London: Routledge.

Foucault, M. (1970) *The Order of Things*. London: Tavistock-Routledge.

Foucault, M. (1977) *Discipline and Punish: The Birth of the Prison*. London: Allen Lane.

Foucault, M. (1980) *Power/Knowledge*. Hassocks: Harvester.

Foucault, M. (2001) 'Governmentality', in M. Foucault, *Power: The Essential Works 3*, edited by J. D. Faubion. London: Penguin.

Grossman, H. (1992) *The Law of Accumulation and Breakdown of the Capitalist System*, translated and abridged by J.Banaji. London: Pluto Press.

Joseph, J. (2004) 'Foucault and Reality', *Capital and Class*, no. 82.

McNally, D. (1988) *Political Economy and the Rise of Capitalism: A Reinterpretation*. Berkeley and Los Angeles: University of California Press.

Marsden, R. (1999) *The Nature of Capital: Marx after Foucault*. London: Routledge.

Marx, K. (1963) *Theories of Surplus Value*, volume 1. London: Lawrence and Wishart.

Marx, K. (1968) *Theories of Surplus Value*, volume 2. London: Lawrence and Wishart.

Marx, K. (1971) *Theories of Surplus Value*, volume 3. London: Lawrence and Wishart.

Melossi, D. and M. Pavarini (1981) *The Prison and the Factory: Origins of the Penitentiary System*. Basingstoke: Macmillan – now Palgrave Macmillan.

Miller, J. (1994) *The Passion of Michel Foucault*. London: HarperCollins.

Morishima, M. (1977) *Walras' Economics: A Pure Theory of Capital and Money*. Cambridge: Cambridge University Press.

Moseley, F. (ed.) (1993) *Marx's Method in* Capital: *A Re-examination*. Atlantic Highlands, NJ: Humanities Press International.

Quesnay, F. (1972) *Tableau Économique*, edited with new material, translations and notes by M. Kuczynski and R. Meek. London and Basingstoke: Macmillan.

Rubin, I. (1978) 'Abstract Labour and Value in Marx's System', *Capital and Class*, no. 5.

Sraffa, P. (1960) *Production of Commodities by Means of Commodities: Prelude to a Critique of Economy Theory*. Cambridge: Cambridge University Press.

5
André Gorz and Critical Political Economy

5.1 Introduction

André Gorz may seem to differ at first sight from many of the other proponents of post-critical political economy considered in this book. While Lyotard, Baudrillard and, to a somewhat lesser extent, Foucault, tend to write at high levels of philosophical abstraction and sociological generality, Gorz is much more firmly grounded in empirical accounts of contemporary capitalist reality. The main body of his work is written simply and clearly, and, in perhaps an even more significant departure from much other recent French social theory, is centred on a set of defined policy proposals. These are ambitious (and have been described as utopian), but Gorz clearly sees them as a mobilising focus for a renewal of the left, around which practical political struggles can and should take place. In that way, the tenor of his work differs sharply both from the overarching pessimism of much of Baudrillard's writing and from the emphasis on local and particular resistance, as opposed to political activity at the level of the state, which can be found in Foucault's work.

However, recent interpretations of Gorz (in large measure following the pioneering work of Bowring 2000) have created the possibility for a new perspective on his work in which his intellectual trajectory appears to bear striking similarities to that of the other writers we have grouped together as post-critical political economists, notably Baudrillard, whose work Gorz cites favourably at a number of points (see Gorz 1980, p. 59; Gorz 1989, p. 48). Gorz's concrete social and economic analyses rest on an extensive philosophical framework, developing the work of Sartre, contained in writings from the 1950s which remain untranslated, and in some cases were only published decades after they were written. Thus, like Baudrillard and Foucault, Gorz moved towards social theory from an initial engagement with philosophical themes. More specifically, both Baudrillard and Gorz tried in their writings of the 1960s to produce an updated Marxist analysis of capitalist society, with a particular emphasis on the role of consumption. This can be seen as part of a general trend in French thought of the time, exemplified in Georges Perec's novel *Things: A Story of the Sixties* (Perec 1990). Both drew widely on non-Marxist sources in this quest, notably American sociology and anthropology, for example the work of Vance Packard, David Riesman and Marshall Sahlins (though there were important differences here with Baudrillard referring much more to the institutionalist economic tradition of writers like Galbraith and Veblen, while Gorz was heavily influenced by Ivan Illich). Both were influenced by the ecological activity of the late 1960s. Both subsequently came to be much more critical of Marxism and in particular of what they saw as the misguided attempt within Marxism to found radical social theory on an account of the revolutionary potential opened up by the status of labour under capitalism. However, the timing and determinants of their break with much of Marxism and adoption of a post-critical perspective differed. For Baudrillard this happened in the early 1970s, partly in response to what he saw as the failure of the movements of the late 1960s, especially the May 1968 events in France and the Black Power movement in the USA. Gorz's shift in position occurred almost a decade later and seems to have been the result of a variety of factors, of which the most important was the change in his analysis of the role of labour under capitalism which resulted from his detailed studies, with a range of collaborators, into the division of labour (Gorz 1977). Gorz's development thus opens up intriguing possibilities for understanding the development of a post-critical perspective in political economy and of investigating the resources which such a perspective might offer for the renewal of the left.

5.2 Gorz and the role of labour

The pivotal work in Gorz's development is his most influential one, *Farewell to the Working Class* (1982). Prior to this work Gorz had attempted to provide an analysis on which to base the renewal of the left, through two main avenues. The first was a discussion of strategic possibilities for the workers' movement, most notably set out in his book *Strategy for Labor: A Radical Proposal* (1967). The second, as provided for example in the journalism he wrote under the name of Michel Bosquet for *Le Nouvel Observateur* in the 1960s and 1970s (see Bosquet 1977), was the extension of radical analysis to cover a host of new issues thrown up by recent capitalist development and previously ignored by the left. Gorz looked at questions such as product safety, public transport, the role of the motor car, the impact of tourism on the developing world, migrant labour, multinational investment, the incorporation of worker militancy through 'new management techniques', education and schooling and ecological questions such as pollution and the limits to growth posed by the exhaustion of natural resources. The implication of Gorz's work at this time was that by taking up such issues in an energetic and committed way, and by framing demands around such issues imaginatively, the left could be rejuvenated, both through political parties and through trade unions, with the aim of mounting a coherent challenge to capitalist institutions.

In *Farewell to the Working Class* Gorz rejects this earlier perspective. Developing new strategies and incorporating new issues is not undesirable or insignificant in his later view, but it is not sufficient for renewal of the left. A precondition for such renewal is a re-conceptualisation of the role of work in modern society, which will lead inexorably to a demand for a radical reduction of the time to be spent in paid labour. This demand is now fundamental, in Gorz's view, to any effective left strategy, or indeed to almost any prospect of progressive social change whatsoever.

Gorz's advocacy of the centrality of reducing paid working time rests on three main arguments. First, technological change has made such a reduction necessary by dramatically raising both actual and potential labour productivity. This means that the alternative to reducing working hours for all is a dramatic increase in inequality with an elite of employed individuals combined with a dramatic increase in unemployment. In the absence of redistributing working time Gorz foresees

> the disintegration of society and the division of the working population itself into a number of occupational elites on the one hand, a mass of unemployed or casually employed people on the other and an even greater number of indefinitely interchangeable and replaceable workers in industry and, more especially, industrialized and computerized services, sandwiched between the two. (Gorz 1989, p. 92)

Secondly, developments in technology have also brought about greater interchangeability between workers, so that sharing of available work has become possible, since such work is no longer the specialist preserve of particular individuals (see Gorz 1989, pp. 76–8). Thirdly, and most fundamentally, the current organisation of work under capitalism systematically undermines the development of capacities for resistance among workers. Thus, the basis for encouraging such resistance must come from outside the workplace, rather than arising as a natural response to production conditions, as Gorz argues that Marx believed would be the case. This argument is set out in detail in the first half of *Farewell to the Working Class*. Gorz describes Marx's view as being that

> proletarianisation would replace particular producers and their 'limited interests' by a class of *producers in general* who would be immediately aware of their power over the world and conscious of their capacity to produce and recreate that world and humanity itself. With the advent of the proletariat, the supreme poverty of indeterminate power would be the seed of virtual omnipotence. (Gorz 1982, p. 24, emphases in original)

However, 'Marx's theory of the proletariat is not based upon either empirical observation of class conflict or practical involvement in proletarian struggle' (Gorz 1982, p. 16) and in reality

> More than anyone anticipated, capital has succeeded in reducing workers' power in the productive process. . . It has simultaneously increased the technical power and capacities of the proletariat as a whole and the impotence of proletarians themselves, whether as individuals, teams or work groups. (Gorz 1982, pp. 28–9)

The result of this is that

> the class that collectively is responsible for developing and operating the totality of the productive forces is unable to appropriate or subordinate this totality to its own ends by recognising it as the totality of its own means. In a word, the collective worker remains external to the living workers. Capitalist development has endowed the collective worker with a structure that makes it impossible for real, flesh-and-blood workers either to recognise themselves in it, to identify with it or to internalise it as their own reality and potential power. (Gorz 1982, p. 29)

The political conclusion which Gorz draws from this is that the Marxist conception that 'liberation *within* work . . . is the necessary prerequisite for liberation *from* work' (Gorz 1989, p. 95, emphases in original) is 'an unsustainable utopia' (ibid.). In contradistinction to this

> The emancipation of individuals, their full development, the restructuring of society, are all to be achieved through the liberation *from*

work. A reduction in working hours will allow individuals to discover a
new sense of security, a new distancing from the 'necessities of life' and
a form of existential autonomy which will encourage them to demand
more autonomy *within* their work, political control of its objectives and
a social space in which they can engage in voluntary and self-organized
objectives. (Gorz 1989, p. 101, emphases in original)

Much of Gorz's work since *Farewell to the Working Class* has been
devoted to outlining the details of how such a policy of reducing working hours could and should be implemented, countering what he sees as
misconceptions of his position, and describing his vision of the impact
of such a policy on society more generally. A number of key themes
emerge which are relevant to Gorz's conception of a critical basis for
political economy.

First, Gorz is not arguing for the abolition of waged labour or modern
industrial production. He sees these as functionally necessary for providing the material resources on which human liberation depends. Certain
kinds of goods, especially necessities, must continue to be produced in
as sophisticated and efficient a way as possible in what Gorz terms the
sphere of heteronomy. The aim is to maximise productivity in this
sphere in order to reduce the paid working time spent by individuals in
heteronomous production to the minimum. This will enable the maximisation of the time spent in autonomous production, outside the
modern industrial system. The sphere of autonomy encompasses, among
other things, the production of non-necessities using craft and other
techniques designed to provide fulfilment through work, artistic and creative activity which again promotes self-fulfilment and childcare and
other caring responsibilities.

Secondly, Gorz's proposals regarding income embody both rights and
responsibilities. Individuals will receive a guaranteed lifetime income, but
in return must work for a certain set period in the sphere of heteronomy.
In order to ensure as much flexibility for workers as possible Gorz argues
that this set period should be specified as much as possible in terms of the
responsibilities of a lifetime – allowing people, for example, to work six
months in every year followed by a 'sabbatical' for the remaining six
months, or to work all year for 20 hours each week, or a range of other
possibilities, as they choose. Broadly, Gorz sees a reduction in working
hours by roughly a half as necessary and feasible (see Gorz 1985, p. 53).

Thirdly, Gorz extends his analysis to a critique both of the modern
consumer and leisure industries and, perhaps more controversially, of

the welfare state. Both phenomena arise out of the pressures resulting from current levels of work intensity, in terms of simple lack of availability of time, personal distress arising from powerlessness at work and consequent feelings of lack of fulfilment. Reduction of working hours would remove the need for much of current mass consumption and state provision of welfare. Correspondingly, in the absence of such reduction, leisure, caring and the family are likely to become key arenas for further commodification of everyday life.

This analysis is exemplified in Gorz's discussion of childcare and domestic labour. He starts from a criticism of proposals to remunerate such activities through wages arguing that

> If the activities performed by women without any financial reward were to be given a wage, they would either not be done at all or would be done very differently. All the aspects of 'spontaneous offering', affective involvement and scrupulous care would not only become 'priceless', but could never in fact be expected of a male or female wage worker whose main concern was to exchange a certain number of working hours for market goods and services of an equivalent value. (Gorz 1982, pp. 83–4)

In addition, such a development would lead to the imposition of capitalist standards of standardisation and industrialisation on caring activities, through a process of what Gorz refers to as 'computerised socialisation'. Consequently 'the last enclave of individual or communal autonomy would disappear; socialisation, "commodification" and pre-programming would be extended to the last vestiges of self-determined and self-regulated life' (Gorz 1982, p. 84). In contrast to this, Gorz argues that the left should demand an expansion of time available for both men and women to carry out childcare and domestic tasks, thereby challenging both sexual hierarchies and the household division of labour. In this way 'far from being a relic of pre-capitalist society, women's activities and qualities prefigure a post-capitalist and post-industrial society, culture and civilisation' (Gorz 1982, p. 86) since 'wage labour no longer seems more "noble" or admirable than unpaid autonomous activity within the extended or nuclear family. People can find greater fulfilment in the latter than in the former' (ibid.).

Gorz extends his account from the specific case of childcare to a more general critique of state involvement in welfare and caring, arguing that this results from the disruption in people's lives caused by capitalist pressure for mass consumption and the territorial division of labour accompanying industrialisation. This weakens civil society so that

> Disconnected individuals call on the state to compensate, by an ever-greater social presence, for the disappearance of their capabilities to help each other, to protect each other, to care for each other, and to raise their own children. The extension of institutional responsibility promotes further professionalization, specialization, and the subversion of all activities – hence accelerating the decline of civil society. (Gorz 1980, p. 37)

As a result of this process

> The citizen is invited to behave primarily as a consumer, a customer, a client who is legally entitled to a series of services, facilities and forms of assistance. The citizen no longer consumes those goods and services which correspond to the autonomous needs which he or she feels, but those which correspond to the heteronomous needs attributed to him or her by the professional experts of specialized institutions. (Gorz 1980, p. 38)

Gorz thus argues for a reduction in state expenditure on welfare and its replacement by communal and voluntary provision. However, this requires a prior reduction in working time to make such provision possible. Such a reduction on its own, however, will not ensure human liberation, if it is not accompanied by the development of new forms of communal solidarity:

> For it will not help to enlarge the sphere of individual autonomy if the resulting free time remains empty 'leisure time', filled for better or worse by the programmed distractions of the mass media and the oblivion merchants, and everyone is thereby driven back into the solitude of their private sphere. (Gorz 1982, p. 87)

Gorz's arguments for replacing state welfare by communal provision are threefold. Firstly, as detailed above, he argues that the labour involved in such provision will actually be fulfilling for people, when carried out within the sphere of autonomy, rather than in the sphere of heteronomy. Secondly, again as outlined above, he claims that the care provided as a result of such provision will be qualitatively superior to that offered by the state. Thirdly, he argues that, at least in the case of medicine and education, state and professional provision can actually be harmful in itself (see Gorz 1980, pp. 149–95 for the case of health and Bosquet 1977, pp. 147–51 for the case of schooling). At various points since *Farewell to the Working Class* Gorz has provided refinements to his initial proposals. For example, in *Paths to Paradise* he develops the idea of small-scale co-operative or communal production as a third sphere, intermediate between those of autonomy and heteronomy (Gorz 1985, pp. 59–63). The motivation for this is the desire to find a propitious framework for the development of inventive creativity, since he argues that 'innovative ability . . . will be more freely deployed outside the constraints of a capitalist economy' (Gorz 1985, p. 61). Such refinements, however, do not significantly alter the substance of his analysis, with regard to either his proposals for the future or his criticisms of orthodox Marxism. Gorz's writings thus raise two central questions from the standpoint taken in this book. First, what is the relationship between his account and that given by the critical political economy inaugurated by Hegel and Marx? In particular, just how deep are his criticisms of Marxism? Secondly, how convincing is Gorz's post-critical position as a basis for developing a radical political economy and thereby renewing socialist practice? These questions will be the subject of the following two sections of this chapter.

5.3 Gorz and Marxism

Gorz actually presents many of his arguments as following from, and justified by, Marx's own analysis. Two passages from Marx are particularly important here. The first is Marx's account in the *Grundrisse* of the impact of machinery on the labour process (see Marx 1973, pp. 690–5). This provides Gorz with some of his most powerful descriptions of the oppressive effect of modern industrial production on working-class consciousness. The second is the passage towards the end of *Capital* volume 3, at the outset of Marx's description of 'The Revenues and Their Sources' where he distinguishes between the realm of freedom and the realm of necessity: 'the realm of freedom really begins only where labour determined by necessity and external expediency ends; it lies by its very nature beyond the sphere of material production proper' (Marx 1981, pp. 958–9). The realm of natural necessity expands with the development of society and the productive forces, which provide the wherewithal to satisfy expanding needs but

> Freedom, in this sphere, can consist only in this, that socialized man, the associated producers, govern the human metabolism with nature in a rational way, bringing it under their collective control instead of

being dominated by it as a blind power; accomplishing it with the least expenditure of energy and in conditions most worthy and appropriate for their human nature. But this always remains a realm of necessity. The true realm of freedom, the development of human powers as an end in itself, begins beyond it, though it can only flourish with this realm of necessity as its basis. The reduction of the working day is the basic prerequisite. (Marx 1981, p. 959)

In a similar vein Marx writes in the *Grundrisse* that the development of machine-based production makes possible:

The free development of individualities, and hence not the reduction of necessary labour time so as to posit surplus labour, but rather the general reduction of the necessary labour of society to a minimum, which then corresponds to the artistic, scientific etc. development of the individuals in the time set free, and with the means created, for all of them. (Marx 1973, p. 706)

Such writings by Marx might imply that Gorz's work is a straightforward development of the Marxist project of a critical political economy. However, Gorz argues that in many other places Marx's writings take a very different form. This is so both with regard to the impact of mechanisation on the labour process and with regard to the relationship between necessity and freedom. Gorz traces the way in which in *The German Ideology* Marx moves from the assertion that in order to safeguard their existence proletarians must transform the world to the second assertion that precisely because they have been radically dispossessed they are in a position to effect such a transformation (Gorz 1982, p. 25). The two assertions are very different yet Marx elides this difference. In a similar way other passages from the *Grundrisse* convey a very different message from the account of mechanisation referred to above, notably this one, which Gorz quotes:

Capital's ceaseless striving towards the general form of wealth drives labour beyond the limits of its natural paltriness and thus creates the material elements for the development of the rich individuality which is as all-sided in its production as its consumption, and whose labour also therefore appears no longer as labour, but as the full development of activity itself, in which natural necessity in its direct form has disappeared; because a historically created need has taken the place of the natural one. (Marx 1973, p. 325)

Gorz concludes that

> Marx's own works reveal a gross contradiction between his theory
> and his exceptionally astute phenomenological descriptions of the
> relation of worker to machinery: the alienation of the worker from
> the means of labour, from the product and from the knowledge
> embodied in the machine. (Gorz 1989, p. 95)

In addition to the tensions evident in Marx's account of the mechanisation of the labour process, Gorz argues that the recognition that labour,
even within a socialist society, will remain part of the realm of necessity,
and that true freedom will lie outside the world of work, requires significant revisions to much of Marx's writing. He claims that, for Marx,
socialist revolution was envisaged as leading to a transparent identity
between participation in social labour and personal development:

> It was assumed that there would be a continuum and an absence of
> conflict between individual activity and social production (and *vice
> versa*). The personalisation of social activity and the socialisation of
> personal activity were taken to be the two sides of communist devel-
> opment. (Gorz 1982, p. 76)

For Gorz on the other hand

> Contrary to what Marx thought, it is impossible that individuals should
> totally coincide with their social being, or that social being should
> encompass all the dimensions of individual existence. Individual exist-
> ence can never be entirely socialised. (Gorz 1982, p. 90)

The sphere of heteronomy is based upon a set of technical necessities
which are inescapable whatever the nature of social organisation. It
imposes an external constraint upon individuals which makes impossible any identity between personal and social being. What socialists
should aim for is the limitation of heteronomy to the minimum possible, rather than a utopian attempt to abolish it altogether, which will
only have the effect of suppressing individuality itself.

Gorz thus identifies an important tension within the project of critical
political economy around the concept of labour. In effect, what Gorz
denies is the dual role posited by Marx for labour under capitalism, as
both the locus of exploitation and the source of privileged possibilities for
theoretical insight and practical transformation. Gorz comes to identify

labour primarily with the former rather than the latter and to broaden the critique of labour from the specifics of exploitation to a more general concern with the imposition of external necessity on the individual. He sees the resolution of this tension as requiring not so much a rejection of Marx's writings *in toto* but rather a determined adoption of certain conceptions put forward by Marx in opposition to others. Marx's writings are contradictory and the renewal of political economy depends on resolving this contradiction by choosing between alternative visions implicit in his work.

Before evaluating Gorz's criticisms of Marx it is first necessary to examine the political and historical determinants of his movement towards a more radical critique of Marx's work. A key question here, as with Baudrillard, is that of whether the problems Gorz identifies with Marx's concept of labour have been inherent in Marxism for the start, or whether they have emerged with recent developments in capitalist society. Was Marxism always inadequate – or at least contradictory – as a conception of human liberation, or have the contradictions identified by Gorz come to assume a greater importance in contemporary capitalism as a consequence of the failure of Marxism to keep pace with current changes?

Again like Baudrillard, Gorz tends to be somewhat ambiguous here. The early chapters of *Farewell to the Working Class* present Marxism as flawed from the outset. The picture presented is one where Marx superimposed a Hegelian dialectic on the process of capitalist production, without due attention to empirical reality. Gorz's most scathing comments come in the first chapter of the book (entitled 'The Working Class According to Saint Marx'):

> Orthodoxy, dogmatism and religiosity are not therefore accidental features of Marxism. They are inherent in a philosophy structured upon Hegelianism (even if this structure was 'turned upon its feet'): the prophetic element it contains has no other basis than the revelation that came to the mind of the prophet himself. Any attempt to find the basis of the marxist theory of the proletariat is a waste of time... The philosophy of the proletariat is a religion. It acknowledges as much of reality as it finds reassuring. (Gorz 1982, p. 21)

Like a number of the thinkers considered in this book, in passages like these Gorz appears to be rejecting both Marx and Hegel as proponents of erroneous 'grand narratives' whose chief defect is the unwarranted imposition of an external philosophical framework on the contingency and complexity of lived experience.

However, at other points Gorz presents a very different account of the problems inherent in Marxism. Here the issue is not so much Marx's Hegelianism but transformations in contemporary capitalism. The developments Gorz is especially interested in are those resulting from technological change, in particular as this has affected the skilled and semi-skilled workers who, in his early work, he had seen as a possible basis for socialist practice. The domination of workers by the machine, and the consequent lack of validity of Marx's account of class consciousness, is here not an inherent feature of capitalism, but the outcome of a specific set of struggles

> The splits within trade unionism in the 1965–75 period came as a consequence of this fragmentation of the world of labour into a *class* of worker/producers and a *mass* of worker/consumers: semi-skilled workers who no longer identified with anything, especially not their work. (Gorz 1989, p. 87, emphases in original)

During this period Gorz argues that the revolt of semi-skilled workers against Taylorism caused massive industrial disruption and a sharp rise in wage costs. However, the demands of the workers were not limited to higher wages or similar negotiable trade union claims; 'a mass of workers withdrew from the class logic of the labour organizations as well as the attempts made by political parties and governments at mediation or repression. This was the period of wildcat strikes, mass absenteeism and sabotage' (Gorz 1989, p. 58, see also Gorz 1985, pp. 8–12). However, this revolt ultimately failed owing to a successful capitalist strategy combining the carrot of restructuring of the labour process around a veneer of more involving work practices with the stick of high unemployment resulting from technical change and economic crisis. It is this failure of the revolt of semi-skilled workers which has opened up the possibility for massively increased inequality and unemployment – described by Gorz as the 'long-term "South Africanization" of society' (Gorz 1989, p. 71) – a possibility which can only be countered by the radical reduction of working time.

Seen in this way, the necessity to reformulate Marxism arises not so much from the fundamental problems of Marx's method itself, but from the requirement to come to terms with modern capitalist developments, in particular the dramatic nature of technological change. However, the ambiguity in Gorz's work concerning the extent to which the weaknesses of Marxism arise directly from Marx's approach, or from changes in external reality, continues to make an assessment of the extent to which he has moved from critical political economy to a post-critical framework problematic. This also has implications for assessing the validity of the proposals put forward by Gorz, to which we now turn.

5.4 The strengths and weaknesses of Gorz's argument

Gorz's writings, at their best, have the capacity to be genuinely inspiring, in their sensitivity to empirical developments, their ability to draw together a wide range of insights from disparate sources and writers and, especially, the audacity of their vision of an alternative future. However, there are also a number of potential concerns which arise from his work. Four interconnected issues in particular will be considered here: the empirical status of his analysis, the basis of his conception of critique, the implications of his conception of labour, and his implicit rejection of a dialectical approach (for a more comprehensive discussion of various criticisms that have been made of Gorz, and a rebuttal of them see Lodziak and Tatman 1997, chapter 4).

Gorz has been widely criticised on straightforward empirical grounds, for exaggerating the tendency of capitalism to destroy jobs and create mass unemployment and for overemphasising the desire of workers for reductions in working time. An example of this is Alex Callinicos' claim that Gorz argues that 'the proletariat is in the process of being abolished by technological change. Empirically this assertion does not hold water' (Callinicos 1987, p. 187). Callinicos compares the absolute numbers employed in manufacturing in the USA in the 1980s with the 1960s and argues that the main development in this period is a fall in the relative share of manufacturing in employment rather than a reduction in employment generally. He concludes that

> The changes in recent years which have led Gorz and his like to speak of the tendential disappearance of the working class, and of which the contraction of manufacturing's share of output and employment in the Western economies is the most widely noted symptom, are best seen as a process which has occurred throughout the history of industrial capitalism, namely the recomposition of the proletariat in response to an altering structure of capital accumulation. (Callinicos 1987, p. 188)

Now at times Gorz does tend to present empirical data rather baldly to support his case, though often here he is reporting the projections of others rather than making them himself. For example he writes that

> The abolition of work is a process already underway and likely to accelerate . . . Keynes is dead. In the context of the current crisis and technological revolution it is absolutely impossible to restore full employment by quantitative economic growth. (Gorz 1982, p. 3, see also pp. 126–44)

It can also be argued that such predictions have proved inaccurate as a matter of empirical record, though this in turn opens up a debate about whether Gorz was absolutely wrong or whether (perhaps like Marx) the timescale of his predictions was excessively foreshortened. However, such a debate seems to miss the main point of Gorz's analysis for two reasons. First, it ignores the fact that the main burden of his criticism of Marx is not over the number of industrial workers but over the negative impact of the experience of labour in industrial capitalism on class consciousness and the possibility of social transformation, though, as detailed above, he is unclear about the extent to which this impact is a recent phenomenon. Secondly, in a number of places Gorz outlines ways in which capital can, at least temporarily, resolve its crisis and maintain employment (see, in particular, the essay 'Socialism or Ecofascism' in Gorz 1980, pp. 77–91 and the thesis on 'Reducing Social Costs: Exit Right' in Gorz 1985, pp. 24–8).

The strategy described here for capital has two main strands – the export of polluting technologies and manufacturing to the developing world and a shift in the industrialised countries towards the service sector, in particular the bringing of services currently insulated to some degree from the market fully under capitalist control. Here Gorz writes in a tone strikingly reminiscent of Baudrillard's critique of consumption

> In this way, individuals can be made to train themselves, maintain themselves and 'produce' themselves to fit a social norm which is pre-programmed by the autoproduction technology that they use. The desire for autonomy and free time is exploited and turned against its subject. What should be the material basis for our control over our own lives serves instead to imprison us in solitary autoconsumption. (Gorz 1985, p. 27)

The main difficulty with this strategy is the likely eventual automation of the service sector, which will reduce its ability to absorb the labour force 'released' by manufacturing. However, Gorz does not see this as an insuperable barrier for capital. Rather he hypothesises that the ruling class will organise the distribution of material resources, unrelated to work performed, to enable the continued consumption of the commodities produced.

> The provision of means of payment to enable people to consume particular commodities will mark the final triumph of the reign of commodities *and* the negation of commodity relations. . . . Commodities produce the people who are needed to get commodities consumed and produced. Individuals, consumers themselves, become commodities, produced or self-produced and sold at a profit. (Gorz 1985, pp. 27–8, emphasis in original)

If such a 'solution' to the crisis is adopted

> The remuneration of citizens assumes the *semblance* of the wage, products consumed assume the *semblance* of commodities, and social relations the *semblance* of market relations; but these are hollow appearances. What is being preserved *is not the capitalist system but capitalism's system of domination, whose chief instruments were the wage and the market.* (Gorz 1985, p. 39, emphases in original)

While Gorz refers in this context to Jacques Attali's writings, the analysis is also very close to that provided by Baudrillard (see the account of capital as a 'mode of domination', labour as 'one sign among many', the collapse of the sphere of production into the sphere of consumption and labour as a gift of capital in Chapter 1 of *Symbolic Exchange and Death* (Baudrillard 1993, pp. 6–49)). Gorz compares Baudrillard and Attali in Gorz 1980, pp. 55–64 and Bosquet 1977, pp. 166–72.

The key issue here is, however, that of the extent to which Gorz's critique of Marxist political economy depends upon an empirical argument and to what extent it is based either on ethical or conceptual concerns. In both of the cases outlined above, those of class consciousness and the possible strategies open to capital, the structure of Gorz's argument is based not on predicting what will inevitably happen, but on justifying his policy proposals by references to the kinds of alternatives which await if they are not followed. His claim is that without reductions in working time the left can rely neither on an upsurge of militancy within the workplace (because this is systematically frustrated by working conditions) nor on alternative paths to social renewal (because the strategies being prepared by capital to 'resolve' the crisis will close off such paths). Such a justification for his position by Gorz cannot simply be an empirical claim, but must rest on a prior ethical and political commitment. He takes a conception of liberation as given and then shows what, in his view, is required to achieve it. Empirical considerations are adduced as supporting evidence here, but they are not the primary motivation for the analysis. However, while this means that Gorz's analysis cannot simply be refuted by descriptions of the current reality of capitalism it is also the case that his approach depends on a certain conception of the critique of that reality and of the potential for human liberation which must itself be investigated.

As Bowring demonstrates, Gorz provides a 'person-centred social theory' based in large part on existential phenomenology. Continually, throughout his work, the touchstone for both his critique of capitalism and his proposals for the future is the lived experience of individuals. This is true in his early work such as *Strategy for Labor* where the concept of structural reform arises out of his concern not just with the objective development of society but with the subjective question of what will actually motivate workers to create a movement which can lead to social change. Again, as shown above, his critique of Marx's theory of class consciousness rests on an account of the experience for individual workers of industrial production and the division of labour. Gorz summarises this aspect of his position when he writes that

> The only non-economic, post-economic goals capable of giving meaning and value to savings in time and labour are ones individuals must discover within themselves. No historical necessity imposes on us the reflexive revolution which the defining of these goals implies. (Gorz 1989, p. 96)

In Gorz's earlier work the example of Sartre is obviously central here, in later analyses he also draws in particular on Habermas' contrast between the 'system' and the 'lifeworld'.

Gorz's reliance on individual subjectivity has been criticised for being utopian and voluntarist, however this seems unfair. He does not simply assume that individuals can exercise their subjective desires without constraint, rather, as shown above, the reverse. It is notable, however, that Gorz differs from a number of the post-critical theorists considered in this book – for example, Foucault, Lyotard and Baudrillard – in his emphasis on the autonomous human subject as a basis for liberating practice. The debates of the constitution of the subject in recent social theory, particularly in France, are too wide-ranging to consider in this context. There are two aspects to these discussions though which bear more directly on Gorz's account of political economy and need to be examined more closely. These are his conception of human needs and desires and the problem of relativism.

In his early work Gorz rejects any clear division between natural and artificial needs:

> The Marxist distinction between fundamental and historical needs thus becomes problematical and risks creating confusion in all cases where because of man's destruction or distortion of nature fundamental needs can no longer be satisfied – or even apprehended – except in a mediate manner. Between the natural origin of a need and its natural object, we note the interposition of instruments which not only are human products, but which are essentially social products. After the destruction of the natural environment and its replacement by a social environment, fundamental needs can only be satisfied in a social manner: they become immediately social needs; or more exactly, fundamental needs mediated by society. (Gorz 1967, p. 89)

The inescapably mediated nature of needs is a recurrent theme in Baudrillard's work, for example in chapter 2 of *For A Critique of the Political Economy of the Sign* (Baudrillard 1981) on 'The Ideological Genesis of Needs' where he writes that

> We must abandon the constitutive social structure of the individual, and even his lived perception of himself: for man never really does come face to face with his own needs. (Baudrillard 1981, p. 86)

If all needs and desires are socially constructed then it appears problematic to base a conception of human liberation entirely on individual subjectivity, and in his later work Gorz moves much more to a position where some needs are seen as more 'natural' and implicitly of higher priority, than others. He writes

> What do we need? What do we desire? What do we lack in order to fulfil ourselves, to communicate with others, to lead more relaxed lives, and establish more loving relations? Economic forecasting and political economy in general have nothing to offer here. . . Deliberately and systematically, they supply use with new wants and new scarcities, new types of luxury and new senses of poverty, in conformity with capital's need for profitability and growth. (Gorz 1982, p. 120)

The implication is that individuals can reach behind the veil of misleading desires constructed by capital to uncover genuine needs which can form a subjective basis for liberation. Yet this claim appears vulnerable both to the arguments put forward by writers like Baudrillard and also to those propounded by Gorz himself in his earlier work.

Even if such needs could be uncovered by particular individuals, however, there appears no guarantee that they would be similar enough across workers as a whole to provide the basis for a coherent movement. This is the problem of relativism, in the context of Gorz's attempt to base social transformation on individual subjectivity. How can the disparate experiences of individuals be brought together in a common project? It is here that Gorz's criticism of Marx's conception of the status of labour becomes potentially problematic. For the importance attached to labour in Marx's theory is not simply accidental, or the result of a refusal to face empirical realities, as Gorz sometimes seems to assume. Rather, labour plays a crucial epistemological role within Marx's account. It is the commonality of the experience of labour under capitalism which provides a shared basis for the development of theory and practice within the workers' movement broadly conceived. If the experience of labour is removed as a possible basis for transformation and resistance to capital is based on individual experience outside the workplace then there is no clear sense of how separate experiences can be combined in a common project.

Gorz appears to realise this in a rather unsatisfactory passage in the *Critique of Economic Reason* where he argues that, after all, there is some scope for autonomy within the capitalist labour process and that this might prove to be a basis for workers' resistance:

> Nevertheless, the element of autonomy within heteronomy which a growing percentage of occupations entail is sufficient for existential autonomy to be seen as a *possibility that is thwarted* by the way society is organized. The limited autonomy work and modes of socialisation offer individuals is sufficient to make a growing number of them aware of their potential and *of the limits of the autonomy conceded them.* (Gorz 1989, p. 98, emphases in original)

The problem here is that to the extent that such limited autonomy at work provides a basis for social transformation, Gorz's analysis seems to revert back to that of Marx, in which the experience of labour is the foundation of critique. However, if it is not such a basis, but only a phenomenon of limited impact, the problem of synthesising the differing experience of individuals into a basis for resistance remains.

The final potential problem with Gorz's account is his approach to dialectical thought. Marx's dialectical approach to capitalism is based on

two crucial features of capitalist reality: its invasive character and its contradictory nature. For Marx, capitalism by its nature resists limitation,
reaching into the most hidden pores of society through a process of
commodification and colonisation in terms of both geographical reach
and penetration of aspects of human experience. At the same time it is
deeply contradictory and its expansionary character rests not on a
smooth and untroubled development but on the necessarily temporary
resolution of the instabilities to which it is constantly subject. A number
of the post-critical thinkers in this book reject such a dialectical approach.
However, where Gorz differs from the others is that they tend, as for
example in the work of both Foucault and Baudrillard, to reject the conception of capitalism as contradictory while endorsing the account of it
as invasive, and even stressing this more than Marx himself. The result
is the pessimistic view of social change described at the opening of this
chapter. Gorz, on the other hand, believes that capitalism is, potentially
at least, subject to limitation. Rather than a dialectical overthrow of the
system, based on exploiting its contradictions, he advocates a radical
limitation of its reach by confining it to the sphere of heteronomy. Such
a limitation is, indeed, the only way to prevent capitalism resolving its
contradictions in a way which will decisively reduce the potential for
human emancipation.

The influence of Habermas seems important here. In a number of his
writings Habermas evolves a conception of socialism as the limitation of
capitalism (though in a more determined and far-reaching way than that
envisaged by traditional social democracy) rather than its overthrow. For
example, in an article written shortly after the East European revolutions
of 1989 he sets out a criticism of Marxism very similar to that offered by
Gorz (Habermas 1990, pp. 11–13) and then goes on to argue that

> The social and ecological *curbing* of the market economy is the inter-
> national formula in which the social democratic aim of the social
> curbing of capitalism was bound to be generalized. . . This is the basic
> issue around which argument today revolves. . . The solution . . . can
> lie only in changing the relation between autonomous public spheres,
> on the one hand, and the areas of activity governed by money and
> administrative power, on the other. (Habermas 1990, pp. 17–18,
> emphasis in original)

The key issue here is that of whether capitalism can be limited in this
way, even by the radical measures proposed by Gorz, or whether its invasive character is so inherent as to resist such restrictions. Here both

aspects of Marx's dialectical approach need to be borne in mind. Both Gorz and Habermas tend to assume that the sphere of heteronomy can at least in principle function in a way which is not crisis-ridden (despite Gorz's analysis of the current crises of capitalism). The main problem is that of creating a social force of sufficient weight to keep this sphere within its 'proper' bounds. If it is indeed reproducing itself smoothly then this might well appear to be possible, at least in theory. However, if the heteronomous world is subject to inevitable disruptions, which themselves are the source of its need to expand into all areas of social life, as Marx believed, then Gorz's policy faces the problem of ensuring the limitation of this world.

Gorz recognises this issue and places great stress on the argument that, when working hours are limited, working-class assertiveness within the sphere of heteronomy will increase as a consequence. In this context he quotes Simone Weil's remark that 'no one would accept being a slave for two hours a day' (Gorz 1982, p. 87). This argument appears to have some plausibility. However, it does not appear sufficient on its own to outweigh the theoretical and historical strength of the analysis put forward by Marx and others concerning the necessarily expansionist character of capitalism as a system.

5.5 Conclusion

The affinities and differences between Gorz and the other post-critical thinkers considered in this book are complex. Gorz differs from the majority of them in his optimism about a potential future and the specific nature of his policy proposals. Yet he is similar to them in his rejection of a dialectical approach, though for different reasons. In his critique of Marx's conception of labour and of the role of consumption in modern capitalism he is reminiscent of Baudrillard. He also resembles Baudrillard in expressing a certain ambiguity about the extent to which his analysis involves a rejection of Marxism as a whole, or whether it relates more to the failure of Marxism to grasp contemporary developments.

Gorz's work provides an important basis for the renewal of a critical political economy, through the range of topics it considers, in particular its ecological perspective and through the crucial issues about the role of labour and consumption in modern society which it poses. However, there are a number of unresolved issues which need to be confronted in using his analysis; in particular the extent to which it is dependent on a particular empirical account and the epistemological and political basis on which its conception of critique is founded.

References

Baudrillard, J. (1981) *For A Critique of the Political Economy of the Sign* translated by C. Levin. St Louis: Telos Press.

Baudrillard, J. (1993) *Symbolic Exchange and Death* translated by I. Hamilton Grant. London: Sage.

Bosquet, M. (1977) *Capitalism in Crisis and Everyday Life* translated by J. Howe. Hassocks: Harvester Press.

Bowring, F. (2000) *André Gorz and the Sartrean Legacy: Arguments for a Person-Centred Social Theory*. Basingstoke: Macmillan – now Palgrave Macmillan.

Callinicos, A. (1987) *Making History: Agency, Structure and Change in Social Theory*. Cambridge: Polity Press.

Gorz, A. (1967) *Strategy for Labor: A Radical Proposal* translated by M. Nicolaus and V. Ortiz. Boston, MA: Beacon Press.

Gorz, A. (ed.) (1977) *The Division of Labour: The Labour Process and Class Struggle in Modern Capitalism*. Hassocks: Harvester Press.

Gorz, A. (1980) *Ecology as Politics* translated by P. Vigderman and J. Cloud. Boston, MA: South End Press.

Gorz, A. (1982) *Farewell to the Working Class: An Essay on Post-Industrial Socialism* translated by M. Sonenscher. London: Pluto Press.

Gorz, A. (1985) *Paths to Paradise: On the Liberation from Work* translated by M. Imrie. London: Pluto Press.

Gorz, A. (1989) *Critique of Economic Reason* translated by G. Handyside and C. Turner. London: Verso.

Habermas, J. (1990) 'What does Socialism Mean Today? The Rectifying Revolution and the Need for New Thinking on the Left', *New Left Review* (September/ October) 183, 3–21.

Lodziak, C. and J. Tatman (1997) *André Gorz: A Critical Introduction*. London: Pluto Press.

Marx, K. (1973) *Grundrisse* translated by M. Nicolaus. London: Penguin.

Marx, K. (1981) *Capital: Volume 3* translated by D. Fernbach. London: Penguin.

Perec, G. (1990) *Things: A Story of the Sixties/A Man Asleep* translated by D. Bellos and A. Leak. London: Harvill.

6
Baudrillard, Dialectics and Political Economy

6.1 Introduction

For around a decade, from the mid-1980s to the mid-1990s, Jean Baudrillard was regarded as a leading figure in the world of cultural studies, whose work was also of general significance in philosophy and social theory. Today Baudrillard is distinctly unfashionable and his recent work appears deliberately to avoid claiming to be more than a series of random jottings and dislocated thoughts. For example, in the recent survey by Gary Gutting of twentieth-century French philosophy (Gutting 2001), Baudrillard's name does not appear.

This chapter will argue, however, that Baudrillard's work represents an important contribution to post-critical political economy, with significant affinities to a number of the other thinkers considered in this book. To uncover those affinities though, Baudrillard has to be understood in a way which is rather different from much of the discussion of his work within the area of cultural theory. The epistemological statements which dominate much of that discussion, focusing on the apparent denial of objective reality beyond the world of discourse and on concepts such as hyperreality and the simulacrum, need to be seen not as a starting point for Baudrillard, but as the result of his engagement with critical political economy and the difficulties he identifies in the work of Hegel, Marx and their followers. As a result this chapter will focus on Baudrillard's early work up until the publication of *Symbolic Exchange and Death* in 1976, during which he pursued this engagement most thoroughly.

The following quotation from Baudrillard's first book, *The System of Objects*, sets out the situation which he tried to understand throughout the following decade:

> once we fall under the sway of this managed convergence, this planned flimsiness, this continually eroded synchrony – then all negation becomes impossible. There are no more overt contradictions, no more structural changes, no more social dialectics. For the tendency which seems, in accordance with technical progress, to mobilize the whole system in no way challenges that system's ability to remain unmoving and stable in itself. Everything is in movement, everything shifts before our eyes, everything is continually being transformed – yet nothing really changes. This is a society whose embrace of technological progress enables it to make every conceivable revolution, just so long as those revolutions are confined within its bounds. For all its increased productivity, our society does not open the door to one single *structural* change. (Baudrillard 1996, p. 155)

Baudrillard's initial concern, then, as it was for Gorz a decade later in *Farewell to the Working Class*, was to understand the specific characteristics of contemporary capitalism which make it resistant to the possibility of significant radical change, and to explore the implications of this resistance for social theory in general and Marxism in particular.

6.2 Baudrillard and the concept of labour

Many of the problems identified by Baudrillard in critical political economy are rooted in his account of the role of labour in that tradition of thought. His own attitude towards labour is determined by two main considerations, one historical and one ethical. Historically, he argues that the centrality of labour to theoretical understanding and social development was the outcome of a specific historical period, and thus cannot be taken as the basis for a more general critique. That period is now at an end. Drawing especially on the work of Marshall Sahlins on 'the original affluent society' (Sahlins 1974) he argues that pre-capitalist societies have no concept of 'work' or 'scarcity' in the industrial sense. Huntergatherers neither attempt to accumulate possessions or to generate a surplus for further investment. This is not because resources are too scarce for such accumulation, rather according to Sahlins the inhabitants of such societies spend less time working than we do. The difference is one of attitude, not of objective possibilities.

Not only has labour not always been central to society, it has now lost the centrality which it had in Marx's time. We have moved from the industrial era in which production was central to a new 'code-governed' phase in which simulation rather than production is key. However, the way in which labour has ceased to be central now is exactly opposite to that shown by Sahlins for pre-capitalist societies. Labour is less central now simply because it is so all-pervasive that it has ceased to have any specific character. When all human activity becomes work the concept of labour ceases to explain anything.

Consumption, leisure and pleasure have all become areas where the individual has to work. Baudrillard argues both that the individual and his or her needs are themselves produced by the social labour of the system and that the result of this is the generation of an ideology where the fulfilment of such needs becomes seen as a task of labour. Hence

> it is true: there has been no revolution of mores and the puritan ideology is still in force. In the analysis of leisure we shall see how it pervades all apparently hedonistic practices. We may assert that the puritan ethic, with all it implies in terms of sublimation, transcending of self and repression (in a word, in terms of morality) *haunts* consumption and needs. (Baudrillard 1998, p. 76)

This is explained by the fact 'that needs and consumption are in fact an *organized extension of the productive forces*: there is then nothing surprising about the fact that they should also fall under the productivist and puritan ethic which was the dominant morality of the industrial age' (Baudrillard 1998, p. 76 emphasis in original). As a result of this 'the alienation of leisure is more profound: it does not relate to the direct subordination to working time, but is linked to the **very impossibility of wasting one's time**' (Baudrillard 1998, p. 154 emphasis in original).

No aspect of the individual's life is free from this process, which applies as much to those areas thought to constitute 'free time' as to those in which the domination of capital is immediately apparent. Consequently, 'everywhere, we find in leisure and holidays the same eager moral and idealistic pursuit of accomplishment as in the sphere of work, the same **ethics of pressured performance**' (Baudrillard 1998, p. 155 emphasis in original).

Baudrillard's conclusion from this is that the Marxist account of labour has become a hindrance to the understanding of the social control exerted by capital through leisure and consumption, because it leads Marxists to identify labour with commodity production and to ignore the spread of labour throughout society. He writes that

> we must therefore formally recognise the disappearance of the determinate sites of labour, a determinate subject of labour, a determinate

time of social labour, we must formally recognise the disappearance of the factory, labour and the proletariat if we want to analyse capital's current and real dominance. (Baudrillard 1993, p. 18)

In a society where labour is omnipresent in this way the attempt to isolate one particular instance of labour, such as waged labour under the direct control of capital, and to use this as the basis of social criticism, is both counter-productive and self-defeating. It is counter-productive because, by privileging one aspect of a more general phenomenon, and hence obscuring that generality, it reinforces the mechanisms of domination which are making labour universal within society. It is self-defeating because if labour is everywhere and all human activity can be interpreted as work, then the concept of labour ceases to have the determinate content necessary to be a basis for critique.

The result of this is that the relationship between labour and production which is at the basis of Marxism has become reversed for Baudrillard. For Marx production ultimately depends on labour. For Baudrillard in the current period labour is something which has been produced by the system. This is so in two senses. First, labour power, the ability to labour, is now something which is created by capital: 'labour power is no longer brutally bought and sold, it is designed, marketed and turned into a commodity – production re-enters the sign system of consumption' (Baudrillard 1993, p. 14). Secondly, the opportunity to labour is produced by capital and offered to workers. Increasingly, according to Baudrillard, capital does not need labour to produce commodities – these can be made by machines. The function of labour is rather to provide a place in the system for workers: 'labour, like social security, has come to be just another consumer good to be distributed throughout society. The enormous paradox is that the less labour becomes a productive force, the more it becomes a *product*' (Baudrillard 1993, p. 28 emphasis in original). This is strikingly similar to some of the arguments put forward by Gorz.

In addition to this historical argument Baudrillard mounts an ethical critique of the primacy of labour within Marxism, arguing that this is a barrier to true human liberation. He argues that Marx's critique of capitalism and his uncovering of the hidden forces underlying the exchange values of commodities stopped short of a comparable examination and critique of the commodity of labour power. By failing to carry out such a critique Marx became implicated in precisely that mode of thought which he is trying to criticise:

in maintaining a kind of dialectical equilibrium between concrete, qualitative labor and abstract, quantitative labor, Marx gives logical priority to exchange value (the given economic formation). But in so doing, he retains something of the *apparent movement of political economy*: the concrete positivity of use value, a kind of concrete antecedent within the structure of political economy. He does not radicalise the schema to the point of reversing this appearance and revealing use value *as produced by the play of exchange value*. (Baudrillard 1975, pp. 24–5 emphases in original)

The result of this failure by Marx, in Baudrillard's view, is that social liberation becomes identified with the production of use values by human labour power. This conception of labour power as the fundamental human potential is itself produced by the system of political economy and thus plays a crucial role in the ideological legitimation of this system. Further

in this Marxism assists the cunning of capital. It convinces men that they are alienated by the sale of their labour power, thus censoring the much more radical hypothesis that they might be alienated as labour power, as the 'inalienable' power of creating value by their labour. (Baudrillard 1975, p. 31 emphases in original)

Baudrillard thus presents both historical and ethical arguments against the Marxist account of the centrality of human labour. These arguments do not just apply to Marxists sympathetic to a Hegelian approach, but also to the structural Marxists following Althusser. The reason for this is that Baudrillard, Althusser and his followers saw the role of labour in production as being just as central as did other Marxists. Their stress on the irreducible nature of theoretical practice did not change the fact that such practice was still viewed in terms of productive labour. Baudrillard points out that Althusser himself views the relationship between a 'scientific representation' and a 'real movement' as something to be analysed in terms of the production of a theoretical object, and argues that this is no accident. According to Baudrillard, Althusser is unable to think in terms other than those governed by the concept of production.

Baudrillard accepts Althusser's account of Marx's view of theoretical production. However, he sees this view as problematic in itself, because it forms the root of the illegitimate extension of the concept of production to societies in which it does not apply.

This argument is developed not through a direct criticism of Althusser himself, but through an analysis of the work of one of his followers, Maurice Godelier, on pre-capitalist societies. According to Baudrillard,

Godelier was led into insoluble contradictions by his attempt to reconcile the apparent determining character of non-economic relations in such societies with an underlying centrality of production: 'the theory results in a perfect sophism of recovery, undoubtedly the masterpiece of a structuralist materialism with "scientific" pretensions' (Baudrillard 1975, p. 72).

The key difficulty for Godelier is the necessity of explaining why pre-capitalist societies fail to produce a surplus when the means are available for them to do so. Since the explanations he provides for this failure rest on social and cultural factors, rather than economic ones, it appears that the economic is not determinant in such societies. In order to maintain the fiction that production and the economy are ultimately central, Godelier is forced into contortions such as the definition of kinship as an economic relation. Baudrillard argues, following Bataille, that such an explanation rests on a fundamental misconception:

> it is not the socio-cultural realm that limits 'potential' production; instead, exchange itself is based on non-production, eventual destruction, and a process of continuous *unlimited* reciprocity between *persons*, and inversely on a strict *limitation* of exchanged *goods*. It is the exact opposite of our economy based on unlimited production of goods and on the discontinuous abstraction of contractual exchange. In primitive exchange, production appears nowhere as an end or a means: the meaning occurs elsewhere. (Baudrillard 1975, pp. 79–80 emphases in original)

Structural Marxists such as Godelier and Althusser base their application of concepts such as production to pre-capitalist societies on Marx's famous passage from the introduction to the 'Grundrisse' in which he argues that earlier societies can be understood as a result of the development of bourgeois society in an analogous way to the understanding provided by human anatomy of the anatomy of the ape. Baudrillard argues that, while this represented a genuine advance over a naïve evolutionist model, it remained an ideological account in which the application of categories derived from capitalism to societies in which they have no validity is legitimated. Such societies must be analysed in their own terms and if this is not done and their specificity is not respected then 'Marxism contains a *miscomprehension* of a rupture far more profound than the one Althusser detects' (Baudrillard 1975, p. 86 emphasis in original). This is one area where Baudrillard's rejection of a dialectical approach is particularly apparent, since he does not countenance any possibility of an account

of such societies which both starts from their self-understanding but uses this as a basis for going beyond such understanding, as would be the case in an immanent critique of the Hegelian kind.
Baudrillard continues in similar terms:

> let us return to the central argument. Does the capitalist economy retrospectively illuminate medieval, ancient and primitive societies? No: starting with the economic and production as the determinant instance, other types of organization are illuminated only in terms of this model and not in their specificity or even, as we have seen in the case of primitive societies, *in their irreducibility to production*. The magical, the religious and the symbolic are relegated to the margins of the economy. (Baudrillard 1975, pp. 86–7 emphasis in original)

Not only does this miscomprehension render Marxism unable to understand pre-capitalist societies; by doing this it renders it unable to comprehend capitalism itself. Baudrillard writes that 'instead of exporting Marxism and psychoanalysis (not to mention bourgeois ideology, although at this level there is no difference) we bring all the force and questioning of primitive societies to bear on Marxism and psychoanalysis' (Baudrillard 1975, p. 49). This is necessary because 'the blindness about primitive societies is necessarily linked to a weakness in the radical critique of political economy' (Baudrillard 1975, p. 90). Put most strongly

> this miscomprehension is not a peripheral or secondary weakness. (The deepest racist avatar is to think that an error about earlier societies is politically or theoretically less serious than a misinterpretation of our own world. Just as a people that oppresses another cannot be free, so a culture that is mistaken about another must also be mistaken about itself. This is only another way of formulating Marx's equation between the level of the analysis of contradictions and the comprehension of the specificity of other societies). In effect, the miscomprehension, moving from societies 'without history' to archaic or feudal formations, nurtures a *theoretical, political and strategic miscomprehension of capitalist formations themselves*. (Baudrillard 1975, p. 107 emphasis in original)

It is important to highlight a particular tension which is apparent in Baudrillard's critique of the Marxist concept of labour, and which reoccurs throughout his discussion of Marxism. He tends to oscillate between two very different views of the validity of Marxist concepts.

The first, particularly exemplified in the historical argument outlined above, implies that, while Marxism was broadly valid for the era of production which has now drawn to a close, changes in society meant that it is no longer applicable. Thus 'production, the commodity form, labour power, equivalence and surplus-value, which together formed the outline of a quantitative, material and measurable configuration, are now things of the past' (Baudrillard 1993, p. 9). We have 'passed from the commodity law of value to the structural law of value, and this coincides with the obliteration of the social form known as production' (Baudrillard 1993, p. 10). As a result 'the structural revolution of value eliminated the basis of the "Revolution". The loss of reference fatally affected first the revolutionary systems of reference, which can no longer be found in any social substance of production, nor in the certainty of a reversal in any truth of labour power' (Baudrillard 1993, p. 10).

According to this view, then, Marxism was applicable but has now been superseded by historical events. This view, however, coexists with another standpoint adopted by Baudrillard, which is particularly implicit in the ethical argument described above, concerning the role of labour in human liberation. According to this standpoint, Marxism was never adequate as a theory of liberation. As outlined above, Baudrillard claims that Marxism was inescapably tied to its own object of critique, classical political economy, through its emphasis on labour and production. He also argues that this emphasis rendered it unable to understand the specificity of other societies, and that this in turn led it to misconstrue its own society.

Baudrillard appears then to adopt two incompatible approaches to the nature of the validity of Marxism. Many observers have analysed this in terms of a linear progression in his thought, arguing that as he moved from a critical Marxist standpoint in his first two books towards a rejection of Marxism he shifted from seeing Marxist categories as valid but only within a specific historical context to rejecting them altogether. This interpretation does not appear convincing. An immediate problem is that many of the passages where Marxism is rejected completely occur in *The Mirror of Production*, while in *Symbolic Exchange and Death* Marxism is seen as applicable to the era of production but not to contemporary society. Yet *The Mirror of Production* pre-dates *Symbolic Exchange and Death*. More seriously, the ambiguity concerning the standpoint from which Marxism is to be criticised runs through each individual text written by Baudrillard during this period. For example, the account of history in *Symbolic Exchange and Death* allots a validity to Marxism within a specific historical context. Yet the concept of symbolic exchange itself is central to

Baudrillard's argument that Marxism is generally inadequate as a theory of liberation. This is because Marxism has no place for what he sees as the most fundamental conceptual divide; that between symbolic exchange and the 'whole field of value' encompassing both the production of material goods and of signs:

> A critique of general political economy (or a critical theory of value) and a theory of symbolic exchange are one and the same thing. It is the basis of a revolutionary anthropology. Certain elements of this anthropology have been elaborated by Marxist analysis, but it has since proved unable to develop them to the critical point of departure. (Baudrillard 1981, p. 128)

Baudrillard thus tends to shift between a view of Marxism as applicable only within a particular temporal period, which has now come to an end, and a view of Marxism as inadequate in itself to the task of human liberation. The ambiguity between these two perspectives is of central importance for understanding the way in which he attempted to resolve the problems of radical social theory. In order to examine this ambiguity in more detail, however, it is necessary to look at Baudrillard's account of historical development.

6.3 History and periodisation

There are two key historical transitions for Baudrillard. The first is the transition which has recently been completed, in his view, between the era of production and what he calls 'the current code-governed phase' (Baudrillard 1993, p. 50). The second is between societies which are based on symbolic exchange and societies which are not. One way of viewing these, following from Mike Gane's reading of Baudrillard (Gane 1991), is to see the first kind of analysis as influenced by Marx and the second as stemming from Durkheim. However, this is too simple, especially if, as Gane tends to do, the Durkheimian Baudrillard is seen as superseding the Marxian Baudrillard. Firstly, the two accounts coexist in particular texts, notably in *Symbolic Exchange and Death*. Secondly, both accounts of historical ruptures can be argued to result from the same set of concerns, which are crucially connected to Baudrillard's response to Marxism.

Most of Baudrillard's first two books, *The System of Objects* and *The Consumer Society*, and a number of articles in his third, *For a Critique of the Political Economy of the Sign*, are devoted to analysing the nature of the first transition. These accounts are summarised and extended in the second chapter of *Symbolic Exchange and Death*, entitled 'The Order of Simulacra'. Baudrillard's account covers a range of areas of social life; the relation of individuals to objects, consumption, leisure, the media, art and design, ecological degradation; however, these are always presented as examples of an underlying trend which is broader than the individual case being analysed. The central element of this trend is the extension of social control and the rule of the system from the specific area of commodity production to colonise every aspect of peoples' lives. Now that this process is complete, he argues, there is no site within society which is not dominated by capital, and thus no possibility for resistance against the system. Indeed, any attempts to resist are doomed to be incorporated, and end up reinforcing the dominance of the established order. The most extreme case of this, analysed in some detail in the fourth chapter of *Symbolic Exchange and Death*, on the body, is that of sexual liberation: 'we can show how sexuality is reduced, *in its current mode of "liberation"*, to use-value (the satisfaction of "sexual needs") and exchange-value (the play and calculation of the erotic signs governed by the circulation of models)' (Baudrillard 1993, p. 115 emphasis in original). Similarly for women's liberation: 'we must also note, however, that woman can only be 'liberated' and 'emancipated' as 'force of pleasure' and 'force of fashion', exactly as the proletariat is only ever liberated as the 'labour force' (Baudrillard 1993, p. 97).

Baudrillard's account of this transition leads him to a number of very acute analyses of particular processes. To take just one example of this, his account of 'models' and 'series' shows how mass production of consumer goods, which ostensibly promises a democratisation of consumption possibilities, in fact leads to the opposite. Not only does the increased quantity of goods make minor differences between them more and more important in terms of the status they provide, but also each individual good is no longer appreciated in its own right but only as a derivation from an idealised model, which remains unattainable. Thus,

> we find that we are in fact, in our 'consumer society', farther and farther away from equality before the object. . . A seeming equality attaches to the fact that all objects obey the same 'functional' imperative. But, as we have seen, this formal democratisation of cultural status conceals other inequalities which are far more serious in that they affect the very reality of the object, its technical quality, its substance and its life-span. The privileges of the model are no longer institutional, it is true; they have, as it were, been internalised – but this has merely made them more tenacious. Just as, in the wake of the bourgeois

revolution, no other classes ever gradually acquired positions of political responsibility, so likewise, in the wake of the industrial revolution, consumers have never won equality before the object. (Baudrillard 1996, p. 154)

In the essay 'Gesture and Signature: Semiurgy in Contemporary Art' Baudrillard extends this analysis to art objects. The work of art becomes the model for a series based on its reproducibility. Consequently art 'is caught up in its subjectivity, in its very act, by that seriality against which it registers itself in the external world' (Baudrillard 1981, p. 108). The result is the incorporation of art into the dominant order, and the loss of any critical function for even that art which presents itself as the most radical and innovative.

On the basis of examples such as these Baudrillard argues that Marx's analysis of the exchange value of commodities is inadequate. Commodities do not just have exchange value and use value in his view, they also have a sign value. Consumption is centrally about sign value, the role of an object in a system of signification in which its value is defined not by its equivalence to other objects, as with exchange value, or by its individual character, as with use value, but by its difference from other objects. Thus, 'the definition of an object of consumption is entirely independent of objects themselves and *exclusively a function of the logic of significations*' (Baudrillard 1981, p. 67 emphasis in original).

This logic is a 'logic of differentiation' (Baudrillard 1981, p. 67). Consequently we need a 'differential logic of sign value' to parallel Marx's 'economic logic of exchange value' (Baudrillard 1981, p. 123). Such a logic can be developed through a corresponding critique of the political economy of the sign, which can match Marx's critique of classical political economy: 'the critique of the political economy of the sign proposes to develop the analysis of the sign form, just as the critique of political economy once set out to analyse the commodity form' (Baudrillard 1981, p. 143).

Through the range of examples he provides Baudrillard's account of the transformation of contemporary society acquires considerable force. However, there are a number of problems with his analysis. Three in particular seem especially important.

First, there is the question of the extent to which Baudrillard's critique of consumption has really gone beyond Marxism, or, for that matter, beyond the writings of critics of consumer society such as Veblen and Galbraith. With regard to the latter, Baudrillard stresses two aspects of his work; his rejection of any kind of fundamental human needs and his rejection of any attempt to base the analysis of consumerism on psychology.

However, his arguments here are not very convincing. He claims that

> psycho-social economics is a sort of near-sighted, cross-eyed hydra.
> But it surveys and defends something for all that. It exorcises the dan-
> ger of a radical analysis, whose object would be neither the group nor
> the individual subject at the conscious level, but social logic itself, for
> which it is necessary to create a *principle* of analysis. (Baudrillard
> 1981, p. 74 emphasis in original)

This leaves it unclear what such a principle might be, and how one can
analyse a social logic except through the workings of individuals and
groups. Baudrillard asserts that 'this is not a question, as should be clear by
now, of treating prestige, status, distinction etc., as motivations, a level
that has been largely thematized by contemporary sociology' (Baudrillard
1981, p. 74). However, when it comes to saying what would be an alternative approach he writes that

> there is no doubt that individuals (or individuated groups) are con-
> sciously or subconsciously in quest of social rank and prestige and, of
> course, this level of the object should be incorporated into the analy-
> sis. But the fundamental level is that of *unconscious* structures that
> organize the social production of differences. (Baudrillard 1981, p. 74
> emphasis in original)

This appears to be ambiguous between a view that sign value arises from
the individual unconscious, in which case Baudrillard appears simply to
be adopting a psychoanalytical explanation for consumption, and a view
that sign value depends upon some kind of unconscious social process, in
which case it appears hard to see how such a process could ever be subject to analysis from outside.

Whatever the status of Baudrillard's arguments against institutionalist
and psychological explanations of consumption, they do not seem to
apply to previous Marxist writings on the subject. An obvious argument
against his criticism of Marxism here would be to point to such work,
especially that of the Frankfurt School. More generally, a Marxist might
respond to Baudrillard that Marx's concept of commodity fetishism
deals with many of the same issues as his theory of sign value.

Baudrillard deals with this issue in his article 'Fetishism and Ideology:
The Semiological Reduction'. Here he puts forward two main criticisms
of Marx's theory of commodity fetishism. The first is that it is based
on a dichotomy between material production on the one hand and the
ideological effects resulting from this on the other. Consequently, it

ignores the conditions governing the actual production of ideologies themselves: 'by referring all the problems of "fetishism" back to super-structural mechanisms of false consciousness, Marxism eliminates any real chance it has of analysing the *actual process of ideological labour*' (Baudrillard 1981, p. 89 emphasis in original). Ironically, this is extremely reminiscent of Althusser's account of ideology and thus is potentially sub-ject to exactly those criticisms which Baudrillard went on to make of struc-tural Marxism; that it is forced to view everything through the prism of labour and production. Baudrillard's second criticism is that Marx's con-cept of fetishism deals with the fetishistic character of objects, whereas what is needed is an explanation of the fetishism of the system itself:

> in this sense, fetishism is not the sanctification of a certain object, or value (in which case one might hope to see it disappear in our age, when the liberalization of values and the abundance of objects would 'normally' tend to desanctify them). It is the sanctification of the sys-tem as such, of the commodity as system: it is thus contemporaneous with the generalization of exchange value and is propagated with it. (Baudrillard 1981, p. 92)

What is not clear from this is how one can analyse the fetishism of a system, nor precisely what this means. What Baudrillard appears to mean is that what is fetishised is the sign value of an object, not its material value, and that this is inherently systematic since it is founded on the difference of the object from other objects, not on its inherent character: 'thus, fetishism is actually attached to the sign object, the object eviscerated of its substance and history, and reduced to the state of marking a difference, epitomizing a whole system of differences' (Baudrillard 1981, p. 93). Yet surely Marx's concept of commodity fetishism is also fundamentally about the relationship between objects, rather than the individual objects themselves.

The second problem with Baudrillard's account is that of the link between the critique of classical political economy and the critique of the political economy of the sign. If the latter is to provide the basis for theorising contemporary society, where the conditions for successfully applying Marxist concepts no longer obtain, then it presumably would replace the former. Commodities would have a sign value but not an exchange value. At times Baudrillard appears to be saying this, particu-larly in his discussion of wages and of money in *Symbolic Exchange and Death*. Financial speculation is presented as having broken any ties between flows of money and an underlying concept of exchange value in the Marxist sense:

> today, however, money sanctions a further step: *it also escapes exchange value.* Freed from the market itself, it becomes an autonomous simulacrum, relieved of every message and every signification of exchange, becoming a message itself and exchanging amongst itself. Money is then no longer a commodity since it no longer contains any use-value or exchange-value, nor is it any longer a general equivalent, that is, it is no longer a mediating abstraction of the market. Money circulates at a greater rate than everything else, and has no common measure with anything else. (Baudrillard 1993, p. 22 emphasis in original)

Similarly, now that labour has lost its ties to production and has simply become a means for inscribing workers within the system, there is no determinate exchange value for labour power:

> labour, which in its completed form has no relation to any determinate production, is also without any equivalent in wages. Wages are equivalent to labour power only from the perspective of the quantitative reproduction of labour power. When they become the sanction of the status of labour power, the sign of obedience to the rule of the game of capital, wages no longer possess any such meaning. They are no longer in any proportional or equivalence relation at all. (Baudrillard 1993, p. 19)

Most of the time, however, Baudrillard does not argue that an analysis of sign value should replace one of exchange value. Rather the two are complementary and are presented together as completing the analysis of the commodity, possibly in conjunction with a further analysis of use value. Yet this raises the question both of how they are to be linked, and also that of what the connection is between the rise of sign value and the transition which has led to contemporary society. In other words, Baudrillard tends to oscillate between three positions. Either commodities have always had both a sign value and an exchange value, in which case Marxism only ever told half the story; or they used to have just an exchange value and now have a sign value as well, in which case Marxism was valid but now needs supplementing by a parallel critique; or sign value has replaced exchange value, in which case Marxism has become outmoded.

The third problem for Baudrillard is that of the basis on which the critique of the political economy of the sign is to be carried out. Marx's critique of classical political economy was an immanent critique, based on the dialectical analysis of the internal contradictions in the mode of thought being criticised. Yet Baudrillard is hostile to any notion of dialectical thought: 'the deployment of third-order simulacra sweeps all this away, and to attempt to reinstate dialectics, "objective" contradictions, and so on, against them would be a futile political regression' (Baudrillard 1993, p. 3).

Further, it is precisely the development of consumer society based on sign value, the object of critique in this case, which has led to the impotence of dialectical thought. Consequently, the critique of the political economy of the sign cannot be a dialectical critique. Yet this simply raises the question of what the standpoint of this critique can be, especially given Baudrillard's view that the development of contemporary society is systematically closing off the possibility of critical thought.

The concept which Baudrillard introduces to solve this problem is that of symbolic exchange, which he sees as radically distinct from both commodity exchange and sign exchange. To assess the use to which Baudrillard puts this concept, however, requires examining the second historical transition which he presents, that between societies based on symbolic exchange and other societies.

Baudrillard is rather unclear about when this transition took place. The hunter-gatherer societies analysed by Sahlins are clearly seen as based on symbolic exchange. In *The Mirror of Production*, however, it is also implied strongly that archaic societies, based on slavery, and feudal societies, based on the work of artisans, are also societies founded on symbolic exchange: the artisan, similarly to Sahlins' hunter-gatherers recognises no distinction between himself as labourer and the product of his labour and does not see the work he carries out as an 'investment'. Rather, for Baudrillard the artisan experiences a kind of reciprocity between himself and the material with which he works, in which that material continuously responds to him, so that he is himself as much shaped by the process as shaping it.

Not only is the date of this transition unclear, it is also apparent that symbolic exchange itself resists easy definition. Baudrillard is in many ways clearer about what it is not than about what it is. In *The Mirror of Production* his account of symbolic exchange starts by distinguishing the symbolic from the psychological and then goes on to list a number of relationships which in a situation of symbolic exchange become fluid, so that fixed positions cannot be assigned to individuals or to objects. Among these relationships are those between producers and what is produced, between producers and users, between users and needs, between producers and their labour and between products and their utility.

Baudrillard's point appears to be that in symbolic exchange positions such as 'producer', 'user' and 'product' are not ones which can be assigned unambiguously to one partner in the process of exchange. For example, in the case outlined above, it is not clear whether the artisan is a producer or a product of the interaction with his material. In the case of hunter-gatherers who deliberately restrict the surplus they produce in order to maintain a certain structure of social relationships the relationship between 'use' and 'need' becomes radically disconnected.

In the essay 'The Ideological Genesis of Needs' Baudrillard attempts to give a more positive explanation of just what symbolic exchange consists of, using the example of gifts:

> in symbolic exchange, of which the gift is our most proximate illustration, the object is not an object: it is inseparable from the concrete relation in which it is exchanged, the transferential pact that it seals between two persons: it is thus not independent as such. It has, properly speaking, neither use value nor (economic) exchange value. The object given has symbolic exchange value. This is the paradox of the gift: it is on the one hand (relatively) arbitrary: it matters little what object is involved. Provided it is given, it can fully signify the relation. On the other hand, once it has been given – and *because* of this – it is *this* object and not another. The gift is unique, specified by the people exchanging and the unique moment of the exchange. It is arbitrary, and yet absolutely singular. (Baudrillard 1981, p. 64 emphasis in original)

Gift-giving is always ambivalent, both constituting a relationship between the giver and the receiver and also underlining their difference, since the giver is separating a part of themselves in order to make the gift; 'the gift is a medium of relation *and* distance; it is always love and aggression' (Baudrillard 1981, p. 65 emphasis in original). Consequently, for Baudrillard 'the structure of exchange (cf. Levi-Strauss) is never that of simple reciprocity. It is not two simple terms, but two *ambivalent* terms that exchange, and the exchange establishes their relationship as ambivalent' (Baudrillard 1981, p. 65 emphasis in original). As a result,

> what we perceive in the symbolic object (the gift, and also the traditional, ritual and artisanal object) is not only the concrete manifestation of a total relationship (ambivalent, and total because it is ambivalent) of desire; but also, through the singularity of an object, the transparency of social relations in a dual or integrated group relationship.

In the commodity, on the other hand, we perceive the opacity of social relations of production and the reality of the division of labour. (Baudrillard 1981, p. 65)

Symbolic exchange is thus characterised by the following features. It is not based on equivalence, each exchange is uni-directional and cannot be matched by an equivalent exchange in return. It is not carried out according to the motives of political economy, such as 'rational' investment of time in order to achieve a particular return. The exchange of goods cannot be separated from the constitution of relationships between those exchanging, and these relationships are both transparent and ambivalent, in that exchange both relates and separates those exchanging. It is not based on a conception of 'need'; the purpose of the exchange is not the consumption of the good but the constitution of the relationship.

The detailed historical accuracy of this account, which rests heavily on a particular reading of Mauss, Bataille and Vernant, is not the main question here. What is more important is the role which it plays in Baudrillard's conception of history and his critique of Marx. Symbolic exchange offers a vantage point for the critique of the political economy of the sign which is non-dialectical. Sign value is to be criticised not through its own immanent contradictions but by comparison with a fundamentally different form of exchange, symbolic exchange. Symbolic exchange also offers the possibility of an account of history which differs radically from Marxism. Baudrillard's negative critique of Marxist views of pre-capitalist societies, that they illegitimately extend the concepts of labour and production to areas where they have no place, is now complemented by a positive critique. What these societies are based on is not relations of production but symbolic exchange relations. It is the failure of Marxism to grasp the specificity of symbolic exchange which is at the root of its incapacity to understand pre-capitalist societies, and thus to understand capitalism itself and the transformations taking place within it.

In order to assess the validity of this argument it is necessary to analyse Baudrillard's epistemological standpoint and this is the topic of the next section. However, before doing this it is important to note an important tension in Baudrillard's argument here, between the two accounts of transition which he develops. The central problem with Baudrillard's account of historical transition is that the two ruptures he identifies are not easily commensurate. If the fundamental divide between societies is that between those based on symbolic exchange and those which are not, and if this divide happened around the time of the establishment of capitalist society, as Baudrillard seems to argue, then the transformations taking place in contemporary society appear to lose much of their significance. What is currently occurring is simply a mutation within a social order from which symbolic exchange has already been expelled. If, on the other hand, it is the transformations in contemporary capitalism that are really at issue, then it is not clear what the significance of symbolic exchange is. How can these transformations, and the rise of sign value within capitalism, be understood from the standpoint of a form of exchange based in pre-capitalist societies?

This problem relates back directly to the unresolved question about whether Marxism is obsolete as a result of contemporary developments, or whether it was always misleading. Baudrillard's first transition is closely connected to the former standpoint, since it concentrates on the changes in contemporary society which appear to make the Marxist account of production now problematic. His second transition stems from the latter standpoint, since if the significance of symbolic exchange is accepted then it follows that Marxism never understood the fundamental change at the base of capitalism itself, and that it viewed this mistakenly as a change in the conditions of production and labour rather than as the disappearance of symbolic exchange. Baudrillard's account of history is thus undermined by the ambiguity in his thought about the status of his critique of Marxism. This is hardly surprising, since this account was in large measure developed to provide a basis for that critique.

6.4 Baudrillard and the epistemology of critique

Any examination of Baudrillard's epistemological standpoint immediately faces a striking paradox. The most well-known feature of Baudrillard's philosophy is his denial of objective reality and insistence on the autonomy of discourse. Yet large stretches of his writing, at least in the decade under consideration here, consist of what appear to be straightforward empirical claims either about past societies or about contemporary developments. These claims are presented without any explicit discussion of the methodological approach adopted by Baudrillard in arriving at them or of their epistemological status.

In fact, Baudrillard does have an implicit epistemological position, which can be ascertained by investigating whether it is possible to resolve the above paradox. This position is in large part motivated by his critique of dialectical thought, and Marxism in particular. However, it also contains internal tensions, which relate back to the ambiguities in Baudrillard's characterisation of why Marxism is to be criticised.

A central feature of the code-governed phase which has replaced the era of production for Baudrillard is the detachment of the concepts through which people understand the world from any basis in objective reality. This is presented as a continuing process of separation, which has now been completed:

> today everyday, political, social, historical, economic, etc., reality has already incorporated the hyperrealist dimension of simulation so that we are now living within the 'aesthetic' hallucination of reality. The old slogan 'reality is stranger than fiction', which still corresponded to the surrealist stage in the aestheticisation of life, has been outrun, since there is no longer any fiction that life can possibly confront, even as its conqueror. Reality has passed completely into the game of reality. (Baudrillard 1993, p. 74)

The central concept which Baudrillard uses to describe this process is that of 'hyperrealism'. By this he means the way in which all perception is now mediated through a set of structures of representation which are controlled by the dominant order within the system, such as advertising or photography. The 'real' is never perceived directly but always 'reduplicated' through such reproductive media.

Baudrillard argues that 'at the end of this process of reproducibility, the real is not only that which can be reproduced, but *that which is always already reproduced*: the hyperreal' (Baudrillard 1993, p. 73 emphasis in original). This is a crucial mechanism in closing off any possibility of radical critique within society: 'hyperrealism is only the play of censorship and the perpetuation of the dream, becoming an integral part of a coded reality that it perpetuates and leaves unaltered' (Baudrillard 1993, p. 74).

Baudrillard presents numerous examples of the way in which particular aspects of contemporary communication bring about this process. For example, one mechanism he highlights is the way in which large swathes of the messages presented to people by institutions now take the form of questions requiring a yes/no answer. This applies both to advertising and to the mass media, and has a number of effects. An illusion of choice is created, hiding the way in which the terms of this choice have been tightly structured long before. Communication is moved away from a direct representation of the real towards a statement which conveys no information, but simply demands assent or dissent. The consumer can only enter into the discussion by responding to the message according to the structure of the question and has no opportunity to participate in framing the boundaries within which communication can take place.

In all these ways, such discourse moves away from any connection with an objective external reference and reinforces the code:

> tastes, preferences, needs, decisions: where both objects and relationships are concerned, the consumer is perpetually appealed to, 'questioned' and required to respond. Making a purchase is, in this context, akin to a radio quiz. It is today not so much an original act on the part of the individual aimed at concretely satisfying a need, as, primarily *the response to a question* – a response which engages the individual in the collective ritual of consumption. (Baudrillard 1998, p. 105 emphasis in original)

Consequently, the consumer lives in a world in which the questions asked by the code are precisely those designed to elicit a particular answer. Faced with this continual testing the possibility for escaping the terms laid down by the system becomes narrowed to the point where no independent standpoint outside the framework laid down by the system exists and 'we live in a *referendum* mode precisely because there is no longer any *referential*' (Baudrillard 1993, p. 62 emphases in original).

Marxism is obsolete because it is inescapably tied to a conception of reference back to external reality, and cannot comprehend this new world of simulation:

> following the same basic schema as the central oppositions of rationalist thought (truth and falsity, appearance and reality, nature and culture), all the oppositions according to which Marxism operates (use value/exchange value, forces of production, relations of production) are also neutralised, and in the same way. (Baudrillard 1993, p. 16)

The result of this is that

> all the determinations of 'bourgeois' thought were neutralised and abolished by the materialist thought of production, which has brought everything down to a single great historical determination. In its turn, however, this too is neutralised and absorbed by a revolution of the terms of the system. Just as other generations were able to dream of pre-capitalist society, we have begun to dream of political economy as a lost object. Now, even its discourse carries some referential force only because it is a lost object. (Baudrillard 1993, p. 16)

Baudrillard's account of the rise of hyperrealism and simulation presents a powerful picture of the workings of ideological domination. However, it leaves open the question of the epistemological standpoint from which any critique of these mechanisms in general, and Baudrillard's critique in particular, can be carried out. The more that Baudrillard demonstrates the ability of the code to close off any possibility of contradiction, which might generate a dialectical movement, the more unclear is the basis from which he can analyse this process himself. He appears to be forced into adopting the position that all critical thought in contemporary society has been absorbed into the workings of the system except his own.

Baudrillard's answer to this problem again rests on the concept of symbolic exchange. His argument is that the central mechanism through which the code operates is the assignation of a fixed determinate meaning to each sign. Here his analysis appears to parallel Adorno's critique of identity-based thinking, although Adorno is not mentioned explicitly. The root of all the other means by which systems of communication close off alternative possibilities of thought is through such assignation, a process which is inherently arbitrary: 'the rationality of the sign is rooted in its exclusion and annihilation of all symbolic ambivalence on behalf of a fixed and equational structure. The sign is a discriminant: it structures itself through exclusion' (Baudrillard 1981, p. 149). Consequently, 'only ambivalence (as a *rupture* of value, of another side or beyond of sign value, and as the *emergence of the symbolic*) sustains a challenge to the legibility, the false transparency of the sign' (Baudrillard 1981, p. 150 emphases in original). Such ambivalence is provided by adopting the standpoint of symbolic exchange, which thus becomes the only basis for escaping the hegemony of the sign system and mounting a radical critique.

An immediate question here is that of how the process of a fixed equivalence between sign and meaning precisely relates to the contemporary developments outlined earlier. It appears plausible to argue that the breakdown of such an equivalence would be sufficient to disrupt the mechanisms of control which Baudrillard has described, but it is not clear that it would be necessary. This relates back to the ambiguities inherent in Baudrillard's critique of Marxism. If the domination of the code is taken to rest on the denial of ambivalence and fluidity of meaning as expressed in symbolic exchange, then this would apply not just to the present, but also to the era of production preceding. If that is so, then Marxism was never epistemologically justified. If, on the other hand, the closure of dialectical thought is a more recent development, then it cannot rest on the denial of symbolic exchange, since that is common both to Baudrillard's second simulacra, the era of production, and to the third simulacra in which we are now living. However, if that is the case, it remains unclear exactly what is the basis for Baudrillard's view that he has a privileged standpoint for critique, since symbolic exchange can no longer fulfil that role.

Perhaps even more significant, though, are the epistemological conclusions which Baudrillard draws from his argument that the dominance of the code can only be overcome through the denial of fixed meanings to signs. He takes from Saussure the premise that the relationship between signifier and signified must be an arbitrary one. Yet in order to argue that the denial of ambivalence in this relationship is inherently oppressive he has to go further than this. He assimilates the referent to the signified, and claims that both are constructed by the signifier. Baudrillard's justification for this move is not entirely clear, but appears to depend upon the view that if each signified denotes a distinct objective referent then it can no longer be argued that it is the signifier, which is part of the system of signs governed by the code, which is enforcing a prohibition on ambivalence. Rather that prohibition will spring from the nature of objective reality. Thus, to save his argument that the denial of symbolic exchange is based on the role of the signifier, and that this lies at the basis of the domination of the code, he has to argue not just that the relation between signifier and signified is arbitrary but that the relation between signifier and referent is as well. It follows from this that perceptions of reality become determined by discourse:

> the referent does not constitute an autonomous concrete reality at all; it is only the extrapolation of the excision established by the logic of the sign onto the world of things (onto the phenomenological universe of perception). It is the world such as it is seen and interpreted through the sign – that is *virtually excised and excisable* at pleasure. The 'real' table does not exist. If it can be registered in its identity (if it exists), this is because it has already been *designated*, abstracted and rationalized by the separation which establishes it in this equivalence to itself. (Baudrillard 1981, p. 155 emphases in original)

It is now possible to resolve the paradox which began this section. Baudrillard's account of contemporary society is framed in terms of a progressive detachment from objective reality. However, this raises the question of the standpoint from which he can analyse such a process. This leads him to an analysis of linguistic meaning based on the concept of symbolic exchange. Yet the outcome of this analysis is a denial of any objective reality outside discourse. This position, then, is not the fundamental basis of Baudrillard's thought, as it is often taken to be. It is a consequence of his account of contemporary society, and in particular of his attempt to explain the closing off of the possibility of dialectical critique. Further, it is problematic for this account, since if all reality is constructed by discourse it becomes harder to ascertain what is specific about the mechanisms of domination which are currently operating, and about the nature of the current period.

6.5 Conclusion

Baudrillard's thought during this period is centrally structured by his engagement with the key problems arising out of the crisis of Marxist thought; the nature of epistemological justification, the ontology of historical development and the links between social change and individual subjectivity. His main aim was to provide an alternative account of these to both that of humanist and structural Marxism, which did not depend upon allotting an ethical or ontological privilege to labour. However, his attempt to do this encountered a crucial problem which affected his analyses of each of these areas of debate. This problem was that of whether Marxism was a mode of thought which had been the basis of a viable critique of society in a previous period, but was now obsolete, or whether it had always been misconceived. If the former is the case, Baudrillard had to explain what had changed in contemporary society to make Marxism outmoded. However, his attempts to do this led him into further problems which led to the concept of symbolic exchange becoming ever more central to his account. This concept provided a more radical standpoint from which to criticise Marxism, but it also implied, not just that Marxism was no longer an adequate standpoint for critique, but that it never had been. Hence Baudrillard appears to have salvaged his critique of Marxism at the price of removing the possibility of explaining what is specific about contemporary society.

The key question which this raises is that of whether his failure to link the two aspects of his analysis springs from a particular weakness in his theoretical framework, or whether it reflects a more general difficulty in the kind of account he is trying to give.

There is a difficulty which confronts Baudrillard in mounting his critique which does not spring simply from his own standpoint. This is the difficulty of giving a dialectical account of the end of dialectical thought. Central to Baudrillard's view of the obsolescence of Marxism is his belief that the operation of the code has closed off the possibility of dialectical critique. His account of contemporary society thus has to explain why dialectics is no longer possible. Yet the conception of history which

Baudrillard brings to this task, in Chapters 1 and 2 of *Symbolic Exchange and Death*, is in many ways a Hegelian one. It rests centrally on the view that the concepts which have a valid critical role in one historical period become socially dominant in the following period, precisely when their critical function is exhausted. Not only that, but their critical function becomes exhausted because of their universality. In the case of labour, for example, the spread of capitalist exploitation in the era of production, which gave the Marxist account of labour its validity as a critical concept, also undercut that validity, since when everything has become an example of labour then the concept of labour is no longer a possible basis for social critique.

Baudrillard's conception of historical development, then, remains deeply marked by a dialectical viewpoint. Yet he also wishes to reject the idea that social criticism can be based on dialectical thought. The concept of symbolic exchange is in large part a way of resolving this dilemma. It allows for a conception of history which is not based on dialectical development, but on a single rupture between two kinds of society with nothing in common. By taking this step, however, Baudrillard makes it almost impossible to link his general theory of history with his concrete analysis of contemporary society.

It appears then, that Baudrillard's conception of the obsolescence of Marxism as resting on the impossibility of dialectics leads him inevitably to a view of history in which Marxism was always misconceived, and which undercuts the specific nature of the current period.

Baudrillard's criticism of dialectical thought is rooted in his horror at the kind of communication into which individuals are forced by the operation of the code. Such communication, for him, has no progressive component, nor any possibility of being developed in a positive direction through a dialectical critique; it can only be rejected utterly through the restoration of a completely different kind of interaction. Thus Baudrillard's ethical commitments lead him to the dilemma of trying to explain why dialectical thought is no longer possible while maintaining a theory of historical change which is in large measure Hegelian and dialectical. Baudrillard's solution to this dilemma, the adoption of the theory of symbolic exchange, maintains his ethical standpoint, but at the cost of negating his historical account. His work thus embodies a constant movement between two incompatible viewpoints. His understanding of history leads him to present an account of social change in which recent developments, dialectically understood, have led to the growing obsolescence of Marxism as a critical theory of society. His ethical critique of these developments leads him to a perspective in which Marxism was always misconceived.

A critical assessment of Baudrillard's work thus leads to the question of whether the specific features of contemporary capitalism which he identifies do, in fact, mean that a dialectical approach to political economy is no longer possible, or whether, on the other hand, such an approach can be maintained. This issue is considered in more detail in the conclusion to this book.

References

Baudrillard, J. (1975) *The Mirror of Production*, translated by M. Poster. St Louis: Telos Press.

Baudrillard, J. (1981) *For A Critique of the Political Economy of the Sign*, translated by C. Levin. St Louis: Telos Press.

Baudrillard, J. (1993) *Symbolic Exchange and Death*, translated by I. Hamilton Grant. London: Sage.

Baudrillard, J. (1996) *The System of Objects*, translated by J. Benedict. London: Verso.

Baudrillard, J. (1998) *The Consumer Society*, translated by C. Turner. London: Sage.

Gane, M. (1991) *Baudrillard: Critical and Fatal Theory.* London: Routledge.

Gutting, G. (2001) *French Philosophy in the Twentieth Century.* Cambridge: Cambridge University Press.

Sahlins, M. (1974) 'The Original Affluent Society' in M. Sahlins, *Stone Age Economics.* London: Tavistock.

7
Lyotard: Postmodernism, Capital and Critique

Lyotard began his career as a Marxist and throughout his varied intellectual career his thought retains a Marxist imprint. The impact of Marxism on his thought is expressed at least partially negatively. His espousal of postmodernism, for instance, expresses his turn against general theories such as Marxism that purport to explain or to prescribe what is to be done. On the other hand, throughout his career Lyotard registers continued resistance against the power of capital and against the dominance of the economic sphere. He perceives a postmodern appreciation of difference and creativity as being overshadowed by a global development of performativity that reduces all questions to the instrumental (see Lyotard 1993b).

At the outset of his career Lyotard appears as an unorthodox Marxist, whose thought exhibits tensions by incorporating a variety of elements, disturbing traditional Marxist commitments. Lyotard's early writings are ambiguous in aiming self-consciously to extend the scope of Marxism without undermining its foundations. Subsequently, Lyotard stretches and breaks with Marxist theory in assuming theoretical standpoints invoking the inventiveness and disruptive difference that he takes to be blocked by capitalist society, Marxist critique and all grand narratives.

Lyotard's essays relating to the events of May 1968 reflect a movement away from Marxism, and a valorisation of revolutionary disruptive creativity at the expense of what he diagnoses to be the normalising pressures of both capital and orthodox Marxist politics. The publication of *Libidinal Economy* in 1974 marks Lyotard's increasing distance from Marxism and his most ambiguous estimate of capital. It is a radical working through of scepticism over the power of theory to capture the discordant movements of desire within its representational logic. This scepticism applies to the critique of capital as much as to capitalist apologetics.

130

Lyotard maintains that political economy is not susceptible to a critique purporting to encapsulate and transcend it. Instead of Marxist critique, Lyotard aims to subvert the systemic character of capital by dissimulation from within so as to intensify discordant affects.

Lyotard's *The Postmodern Condition: A Report on Knowledge* opposes all general theories that purport to explain society. It suggests rather than demonstrates resistance to prevailing normalising pressures and countervailing expressions of critique. Grand narratives of modernity, such as Hegelianism and Marxism, are dismissed in the name of a postmodern exploration of creativity, difference and plurality. Lyotard offers a considered philosophical analysis of the unbridgeable character of difference in his later notion of the *differend*. A *differend* expresses the absolute incommunicability of divergent standpoints in a common discourse. Lyotard's hostility to the unificatory language of Keynesian political economy and critical political economy in the form of Marxism, however, is mitigated by his sense of how Marxism operates as a *differend* vis-à-vis the language of the capitalist. He recognises how the economic genre of discourse in the guise of capital and standard political economy, operates imperialistically by dominating other discursive genres. Lyotard's writings subsequent to *The Differend*, such as *The Inhuman* and *Postmodern Fables*, are pessimistic about the prospects for social and political change. Despite retreating from his former revolutionary credo, however, Lyotard continues to valorise divergent creativity, but he now takes the ubiquitous instrumentalism of contemporary liberal capitalism to admit of only an aesthetic, fugitive resistance.

Lyotard's career evinces an ambiguous relationship to both Marx and political economy. He questions Marxism consistently but ambiguously in renouncing its generalising critique of capital and in turning to disruptive anti-systemic forms of creativity and difference. Lyotard's critical engagements with Marx are not to be read as a straightforward shift from orthodoxy to unremitting apostasy. Lechte, for instance, in suggesting that Lyotard breaks decisively from Marxism fails to recognise how aspects of Lyotard's postmodernism, notably his unease at he prevailing imperialist logic of instrumentality, connect to Marx's critique of political economy. Lechte asserts, 'Although a political activist of Marxist persuasion in the 1950s and 1960s, Lyotard became the non-Marxist philosopher of postmodernity in the 1980s' (Lechte 1994, p. 246). In contrast to this unilear reading of his career, Lyotard actually explored tensions and lacunae in Marxism throughout his career. His continuing affiliation to aspects of Marx's critique of capital underlies *The Postmodern Condition*'s unease at the prevalence of the logic of performativity. It also informs his recognition of the exclusionary force of the economic genre of discourse in *The Differend* and his late melancholy testimony to the remorseless instrumentalism of contemporary liberal capitalism.

Subsequent sections of this chapter trace the changing treatments of political economy, capital and Marx that are to be found in Lyotard's writings. Lyotard develops a form of post-Marxism, in which it is postdated because of its alleged resemblance to Hegelianism in its projection of an unsustainable general theory, thwarting creativity and divergency. Lyotard's post-Marxism, however, draws on aspects of Marxist theory in its continuous commitment to disturb the force of capital. Williams suggests Lyotard's *Libidinal Economy* is both after and with Marx and within and against capital. He maintains that this ambiguous formulation can be applied to all of Lyotard's work (Williams 2000, pp. 35–8). The ambiguities of Lyotard's standpoint are compounded by his failure to address them. The upshot is that Lyotard's reading of political economy and Marxism is suggestive but undersupported. His conception of the force of global performativity is a suggestive reading of contemporary political economy but it is undeveloped and relates uneasily to his advertised disavowal of grand narratives. His critique of Marx is likewise problematic because it is insufficiently supported by textual analysis.

7.1   From critique to the end of critique

a. Early writings

In his early philosophical and political career Lyotard was a committed Marxist, a member of the Marxist group, *Socialisme ou barbarie* from 1954 until 1964 and another Marxist group *Pouvoir ouvrier* until 1966. The *Phenomenology* (1954) culminates in a resolute affirmation of Marx and materialism at the expense of a phenomenological approach. If Lyotard's *Phenomenology* is Marxist it is revisionary in responding to cultural and philosophical developments within twentieth-century capitalism. Its closing sections epitomise the tension within Lyotard's bifurcated conception of Marxism. On the one hand, he advocates a form of Marxism that is neither rigidly deterministic nor narrowly economistic. On the other hand, he presents an uncompromising and relatively unsupported defence of materialism and the class struggle.

Lyotard's *Phenomenology* engages with Husserlian phenomenology so as to open Marxism to dialogue with other styles of thought. It signals an opposition to what he takes to be the closure of Hegel's phenomenological style. Lyotard takes the priority of the economic infrastructure to be compatible with superstructural elements retaining significance. He allows for an influence of phenomenology upon Marxism. Gane (1998) interprets Lyotard to be against phenomenology. Lyotard, in fact, adopts a subtler position. He admits a role for phenomenology. He observes,

> There is thus room at the heart of Marxist analyses for phenomenological analyses bearing on consciousness, and allowing us precisely to interpret the dialectical relation of this consciousness, taken as source of the superstructures, to the economic infrastructure where it finds itself engaged in the final analysis (but *only* in the final analysis. (Lyotard 1991, p. 49)

Allied to the relative autonomy, which he allows to the superstructure, Lyotard also recognises that Marxism should admit freedom and contingency in history, observing, 'we must therefore escape this impasse of equally total freedom and necessity' (Lyotard 1991, p. 49).

The meaning of Lyotard's non-deterministic, non-reductionist Marxism and his reading of the relations between Marxism and phenomenology are ambiguous. He concludes by asserting the absolute, objective truth of Marxist materialism and the class struggle, noting 'the insurmountable oppositions that separate phenomenology and Marxism' (Lyotard 1991, p. 49). For Lyotard, Marxism reveals the 'meaning of history' in identifying its determination by class struggle (Lyotard 1991, 49). Lyotard repudiates the phenomenological originary constitution of the world, because it renders reality neither objective nor subjective. The phenomenologically real appears ambiguously neutral. In contrast, Lyotard reads Marxism as affirming the materiality of reality. He notes, 'Marxism is materialism: it holds that matter constitutes all of reality and that consciousness is a particular material mode. This materialism is dialectical' (Lyotard 1991, p. 50).

In *Phenomenology* Lyotard's Marxism is an uneasy discordant theory. Lyotard allows for freedom and superstructural independence and yet asserts an uncompromising materialism that is insulated from the quasi-idealism of phenomenology. Lyotard's condensed defence of Marxist materialism is questionable in itself. It is also highly problematic as a reading of Marx. Marx's hyperbolic materialist rhetoric in *The German Ideology* is generated by a polemical concern to overplay his break from *other* Young Hegelians (Browning 1993). Marx's most considered methodological *credo* is in the introductory section of the *Grundrisse*, where he relates his approach to Hegel's. Marx maintains the relational character of social reality. He observes that these social relations, 'can be grasped, of course, only in ideas' (Marx 1974, p. 164). Marx's materialism, then, is more nuanced than its portrayal in Lyotard's *Phenomenology*. Lyotard underplays the complexity of Marx's thought and the possibilities for an open pluralistic reading of Marx's texts. The complexity and openness of Marx's thought are glossed over in Lyotard's closed reading of his texts. Lyotard's reading of the grand narratives of both Hegel and Marx suffers from being closed. He does not allow for the possibility that either could be read as maintaining the openness and pluralism canvassed by Lyotard's own theoretical standpoint.

The ambiguities evident the *Phenomenology*'s defence of Marxism inform Lyotard's political essays on Algeria, which he wrote during the 1950s for the Marxist journal, *Socialisme ou barbarie*. Lyotard's preoccupation with Algeria and his exile from philosophy testify to his dedication to Marxism, and to his opposition to exploitation, imperialism and alienation (see Lyotard 1993b, p. 17). At the same time, Lyotard's essays identify features of the political situation in Algeria and in France that do not fit easily with Marxism.

Rather than seeing nationalism as a smokescreen masking class interests, Lyotard sees nationalism as an affective lived reality that exerts an impact across class lines of allegiance. The events in North Africa also inspire Lyotard to reflect back on France and to interrogate developed forms of political economy in ways that stretch and challenge traditional Marxist categories. He recognises discordance between the actual attitudes and behaviour of the French working class and the theory of proletarian internationalism. In a retrospective essay 'The Name of Algeria', Lyotard observes, with a clarity heightened by the perspective provided by intervening events, how he sensed an unresolvable *differend* in a commitment to Algeria and its independence that could not be translated into theoretical terms (Lyotard 1993b, 17).

Lyotard's break with Marxist orthodoxies is intensified by his involvement in the build-up to and the events of May 1968. His essays relating to those events, *Derive a partir de Marx et Freud* mark a decisive turn against the rigidities of a dogmatic framework. He dispenses with formulaic Marxist notions of class and class consciousness, and disciplined class- or party-based notions of revolution. He supports imaginative unplanned rebellion and the *élan* of revolutionary extemporisation. Lyotard adheres to a form of revolutionary Marxism, while acknowledging how historical developments have forestalled the classic Marxist route to revolution. In 'On Theory' he maintains allegiance to Marx's general formula for capital, and against Althusser he retains the concept of alienation so as to make continued sense of social experience. He notes, however, his own drift from Marxism by remarking, 'in the situation we know today, and have known for at least a decade, in fact, traditional Marxism isn't wholly satisfactory from a theoretical point of view' (Lyotard 1984, p. 19). He questions the projected revolutionary development of the proletariat, denying that there is an identifiable group or class that can enact revolutionary change. Instead, he looks to the deconstructive activities of modern art to serve as exemplary revolutionary acts. He repudiates the idea that the revolution and revolutionary acts will produce predictable outcomes. He identifies seemingly pointless disruptive actions as being exemplary revolutionary ones.

In 'March 23', another essay included in *Derive à Partir de Marx et Freud*, Lyotard reviews the movement of March 22 with which he was involved. He supports a politics of dissonance and rejects the aspiration to exert control that he imputes to the parties of order and to the parties of counter-order (like Marxist ones). He declares, 'The explicit question of the March 22 movement is the critique of bureaucracy, not only of the state apparatus set against society, not only of the (revolutionary) party that confronts the masses, not only of the organisation of productive labour against free creativity, but also of alienated life as a whole against – what?' (Lyotard 1993b, p. 14).

Lyotard's introductory essay to *Dérive à Partir de Marx et Freud*, 'Adrift', written shortly after 1968, reflects on those events and highlights his movement away from Marx and Freud. In 'Adrift' Lyotard observes, 'Everyone knows that socialism is identical with capitalism. Any critique far from transcending the latter reinforces it' (Lyotard 1984, p. 15). In a partial anticipation of *Libidinal Economy* Lyotard valorises libidinal energy at the expense of carefully formulated critique of the capitalist system. He supports disruptive, creative revolutionary energy unleashed in the events of May 68, and the turn against organised Marxism. Lyotard, in praising nihilistic destructive revolutionary energy, notes, 'In its practice, the young generation occasionally anticipates this destruction, acts and thinks without consideration for equivalence, takes as its sole guide, instead of a potential return, affective intensity, the possibility of decoupling libidinal force' (Lyotard 1993a, pp. 14–15).

b. Political and libidinal economies

Ricke, Tholen and Voulliehe, in the foreword to their German translation of *Libidinal Economy*, highlight how it subverts standard perceptions, notably in regard to theory and political economy. They observe, 'Lyotard wants to show that in capital, in language and in knowledge just as in art and sex, intensities of desire are at work' (Ricke, Tholen and Voulliehe p. xx). *Libidinal Economy* Lyotard In aims to show that Hegel and Marx purport to frame overall critiques of political economy, and thereby presume independence for theory and a settled, stable world to explain. In contrast, Lyotard wants to disturb things by asserting the interfusion of the libidinal, the economic and the theoretical.

The unsettling character of *Libidinal Economy* is evident in its unremitting subversion of theory as the arbiter of truth. The independence and security of Marx's critical constructions are deconstructed in *Libidinal Economy*. Lyotard's rhetoric is directed against the absolutizing structuralism of the Althusserians whose claims to theoretical truth and completion presume the great zero that *Libidinal Economy* aims to efface. The great zero is Lyotard's metaphor for what representational theories take to divide the signifier from the signified, the theoretician from the object of her theory (Lyotard 1993a).

Libidinal Economy is post-Marxist. It is a work of post-critical political economy in that the object and practice of Marx's critical political economy are disturbed and recast. The possibility of rational critique, insulated from the unpredictable flows of libidinal energy, is denied. The susceptibility of the capitalist system to cool rational analysis is denied by observing that its circuits of exchange and the theoretician's study of their inner logic are infused with unpredictable libidinal energy. Rather than signposting a new alternative system to political economy, Lyotard exploits possibilities for intensifying desires within capital. In *Libidinal Economy*, Lyotard is decidedly after Marx in renouncing Marx's project of theoretical critique. He retains a revolutionary sense of disturbing the self-reproducing systemic character of capital, however, in assuming openness to intensifying creative and discordant possibilities amidst its transits.

In criticising erstwhile Marxist colleagues of *Socialisme ou barbarie*, Lyotard, in *Libidinal Economy*, deconstructs their language of critique. He exposes what he construes as the fantasies of an unalienated communism and an unalienated pre-capitalist society. He observes,

> To restart the revolution is not to rebegin it, it is to cease to see the world as alienated, men to be saved or helped, or even to be *served*, it is to abandon the masculine position, to listen to femininity, stupidity and madness without regarding them as evils. (Lyotard 1993a, p. 121)

Lyotard repudiates Marx's Feuerbachian yearning for a social world of transparent immediacy, just as he insists, against Baudrillard, that there is no primitive society in which desire can operate without intersecting with a mediating, systemic form of political economy (Lyotard 1993a, pp. 128–9).

Libidinal Economy opposes critique and the process of critique. For Lyotard libidinal energy and its unpredictable transmissions cannot be mastered by systemic theorising or counter-theorising. In removing authorial access to a critical truth external to libidinal affects, Lyotard accordingly disparages his own capacity to provide foundational rational criteria for his standpoint. Lyotard sees *Libidinal Economy* as a libidinal investment, rather than as a critique. He declares, 'Let's repeat it over and over again, we are not going to do a critique of Marx, we are not, that is to say, going to produce the theory of his theory, which is just to remain within the theoretical' (Lyotard 1993a, p. 106). For Lyotard, reality and theory dissimulate ungovernable desires, which can be intensified by releasing their capacity to produce new previously unexplored affects. He sees his own text as libidinal, just as he takes Marx's theory and proletarian labour to harbour unpredictable forms of libidinal energy.

In *Libidinal Economy* Lyotard's method is appropriately inappropriate to standard notions of conducting theoretical analysis and critique. He makes a series of seemingly disconnected and provocative moves that are designed to release new ways of relating to phenomena. Marx's endless stalling on completing his critique of political economy is a sign of his endless pleasure in dedicating his life to capital's movements and ruses. Rather than providing detailed textual support for this reading or intricate Althusserian theoretical analysis, Lyotard sets up a provocative rhetorical figure to insinuate the libidinal energy lurking within Marx's critique. He imagines Marx's critique as the libidinal interplay between two sides of Marx, a young girl and an old man Marx. It turns upon the old man Marx providing a critical, theoretical alternative for the prostituted, mediated commodified world of capital from which the young girl recoils in horror.

The prostituted world of capital horrifies Marx because it approximates Bataille's image of *Madame Edwarda*, God figured as a public whore gone crazy (Lyotard 1993a, p. 111). On this reading, it is not capital's presumed denaturing of relations between man and woman and man and man that disturbs Marx but capital's motion and its insane pulsions of sexuality. Provocatively, Lyotard muses on the fascinating libidinal possibilities offered by capital.

> Now we must completely abandon critique . . . we must take note of, examine, exalt the incredible, unspeakable pulsional possibilities that it

sets rolling, and so understand that *there has never been an* organic body, an immediate relation, nor a nature in the sense of an *established site of affects*, and that the (in)organic body is a representation on the age of capital itself. Let's replace the term critique by an attitude closer to what we effectively experience in our current relations with capital, in the office, in the street, in the cinema, on the rods, on holiday, in the museums, hospitals and libraries, that is to say a horrified fascination for the entire range of the *dispositifs* of *jouissance*. (Lyotard 1993a, p. 36)

Libidinal Economy forecloses on ethical and critical judgement. It provides a disturbing re-reading of the process of industrialisation and the development of capital. Lyotard sees the proletariat as experiencing rushes of libidinal energy amidst its exploitation and suffering during the industrial revolution. In reviewing the operations of capital, Lyotard imagines an interlocutor objecting,

> But you will say it gives rise to power, domination, to exploitation and even extermination. Quite true, but also to masochism; . . . And perhaps you believe that 'that or die' is an *alternative*?! And that if they choose that, if they become the slave of the machine, the machine of the machine, fucker fucked by it, eight hours, twelve hours, a day, year after year, it is because they are forced into it, constrained, because they cling to life? Death is not an alternative to it, it is a part of it, attests to the fact that there is a *jouissance* in it, the English unemployed did not become workers to survive, they – hang on tight and spit on me – *enjoyed (ils ont joui de)* the hysterical, masochistic, whatever exhaustion it was of *hanging on* in the mines, in the foundries, in the factories, in hell, they enjoyed it, enjoyed the mad destruction of their organic body. . . (Lyotard 1993a, 36)

In his subsequent writings Lyotard maintains his refusal of the very idea of a generalised alternative to capital. He is however, critical subsequently of what he admits to be the reductionism of *Libidinal Economy*, whereby all phenomena are conceived as discharges of libidinal energy. Within *Libidinal Economy*, distinctions, notably between reason and desire and ethics and power, are overridden in the valorisation of the libidinal. Subsequently, Lyotard highlights radical disjunction between distinct spheres of activity, noting, for instance, the incommensurability between normative and denotative discourses. He continues to oppose grand theory and overarching critique, but the focus of his opposition rests on the impossibility of theory capturing differences in one single overarching scheme.

c. Modernity and postmodernism

In *The Postmodern Condition* Lyotard's declaration of postmodernity is a post-dating of Hegel, Marx and critical theory. Grand narratives of modernity, for Lyotard, purport to explain reality by way of general theories. Lyotard's rejection of modernity and his concomitant embrace of postmodernity are announced by way of an obituary for Marxism as an absolutist paradigm of critical theory. The essence of Lyotard's critique of grand narratives is that their closed, self-referential circle of concepts cannot capture a contingent world, expressive of many divergent perspectives. This critique is forceful and plausible. The human world is a world of socially situated discursive agents who understand themselves in relation to divergent contexts that resist encapsulation in a single perspective of historical development.

The Postmodern Condition announces the redundancy of grand narratives. It signals the advent of postmodernity, a token of which is the ubiquity of the logic of performativity. In the contemporary, postmodern world pragmatic efficiency is supreme. The optimisation of performance supersedes normative and theoretical forms of justification for activities. The pliability of performativity harmonises with a postmodern reluctance to frame general normative theories. The ubiquity of performativity, however, also testifies to the ongoing power of capital, which extends and intensifies the reach of instrumental criteria in appraising activities such as higher education that operated traditionally outside the sphere of the market. Postmodernity, then, is a condition postdating a general critique of political economy, but Lyotard's critical reading of the pervasiveness of instrumentalism reflects a continued, if unacknowledged critical perspective on the development of political economy.

In *The Postmodern Condition* Lyotard distinguishes between styles of grand narrative, assuming that classic modernist grand narratives tend to be configured either philosophically or politically. On this view, Hegelianism is a philosophical form of grand narrative that comprehends the pathways of modernity as contributing to its own supervening philosophical perspective. Marxism is a grand narrative that is justified either as a 'scientific' Marxism or politically. The scientific form sees the end of history to be documented by a Muscovite Communist Party that has a monopoly of truth. The countervailing political form sees history as dialectic of consciousness that will be consummated by the proletariat becoming for itself (Lyotard 1984, p. 12). For Lyotard, these formulations suffer from their grand presumption of a single co-ordinating truth that is to be realised in history. Hegelianism and Marxism are condemned as being paradigmatic grand narratives that purport to provide a universal theory, overriding the contingency of history and the diversity of language games. Lyotard maintains that the social bond is not to be reduced to an essentialised unity. Society is envisaged as a diversity of incommensurable language games. This notion of incommensurability is epitomised in the gap separating prescriptive from denotative language games. Marxism, in mingling these registers, is confused. In criticising a political grand narrative Lyotard avers, 'There is nothing to prove that if a statement describing a real situation is true, it follows that a prescription based upon it (the effect of which will be necessarily a modification of that reality) will be just' (Lyotard 1984, p. 40).

Lyotard diagnoses the problems besetting the Hegelian grand narrative as entailing that it can operate by merely cataloguing differing aspects of reality. Marxism's problems are seen to be evident in the realities of contemporary history. Lyotard takes the totalitarian practice of Eastern European communist regimes and the emasculation of critique in western societies as indicating the redundancy of Marxism. Critique is nullified by its incorporation into the programming of capitalist 'open' systems. The refined, sensitive critiques of the Frankfurt School and *Socialisme ou barbarie* testify to the emasculation of Marxism, the blurring of class analysis and the end of effective opposition (Lyotard 1984, p. 13). The inexorable ubiquity of performativity leaves no space for the effective and independent operation of critique.

Lyotard's recognition of different versions of Marxism and his appreciation of how Hegelianism may be read as a mere cataloguing of experience intimates that his image of grand narratives is questionable. Lyotard fails to consider the implications for his own standpoint of the multiple forms of Hegelianism and Marxist theory and practice that he identifies, The general redundancy notice, which he serves on Hegelianism and Marxism, derives from the absolutism that he ascribes to them, but the susceptibility of Marx and Hegel to multiple interpretations raises questions over this ascription. Moreover, Lyotard's own analysis of history and society is highly general and under-theorised. He designates modernity to involve the operation of grand but overly general narratives, but his notion of postmodernity turns upon a highly schematic sketch of the operation of performativity. Paradoxically, Lyotard's conception of postmodernity presupposes a general formulation of performativity, which lacks the theoretical and empirical particularity and richness of both Hegel's and Marx's critical political economy.

d. *The Differend* and after

The linguistic perspective of *The Differend*, which takes discourses to be multiple and divergent, rules out the generalising perspective that Lyotard attributes to standard critiques of political economy such as Marxism. In so doing, however, Lyotard unmasks the perspectival imperialism of the economic genre of discourse, whereby economic imperatives of efficiency and profit override other discourses. Lyotard's sense of the discursive domination of capital is clearly drawn from the continuing impact of Marxism on his thought. *The Differend* diverges from Marxism due to its focus upon incommensurable difference, but it bears an affinity to Marx due to its antagonism to the discursive imperialism of capital. Lyotard's concern over the perspectival imperialism of economic discourse also evokes Hegel's determination to limit the scope of political economy. Lyotard, however, neither addresses the provenance of his reading of the economic genre of discourse, nor explains how it avoids the problems that he identifies as bedevilling the totalising explanations of grand narratives (Lyotard 1988, pp. 181–2). Lyotard fails to specify the boundaries of an intellectual tradition, and hence he is disinclined to discuss how his own theory trades with or participating in a repudiated grand narrative.

In *The Differend* Lyotard develops a conception of language as expressing incommensurable modes of discourse, which determine the linking together of contingent phrases. Phrase regimens and genres of discourse regulate the linking of phrases. Disparities between them entail that particular ways in which phrases might be taken are excluded by the operation of exclusionary discourses. The consequent suppression of a phrase is a *differend* that can be felt but not communicated, because there is no general discourse into which phrases from differing, incommensurable discourses can be translated. For Lyotard grand narratives operate as imperial discourses. They are oppressive in their determination to encompass contingent and differentiated events within a single synoptic discursive perspective.

For instance, Lyotard counterposes the contingency and incommensurability of phrases to the alleged necessity and essentialism of Marxism. The Marxist notion of the proletariat, for Lyotard, operates as a Kantian idea of reason, in its transcendence of actual experience. It incarnates attributes and duties that supersede actual instantiations. Lyotard lists a series of names that evoke historic events that disrupt the totalising claims of Marxism. Berlin 1953, Budapest 1956 and Prague 1968 are seen as self-evident postmodern counters to Marxist myth (Lyotard 1988, p. 179).

Notwithstanding his rejection of Marxist universalism, Lyotard draws upon and transposes Marxism. He understands Marxism as itself testifying to a *differend*. He remarks, 'Marx tries to find the idiom in which the suffering due to capital clamours for' (Lyotard 1988, p. 171). Lyotard, though, takes Marxism to represent an illicit resolution of this *differend*. He sees Marxism as tracing a counterfeit resolution via the universal role, which it assigns to the proletariat. According to Lyotard, a *differend* can only be registered and in some manner negotiated by evincing a sense of the suffering that it occasions (Lyotard 1988, p. 171). In *The Differend*, though, Lyotard implicitly resumes and continues a Marxist critique of political economy by recognising the linguistic imperialism of the economic genre. Lyotard understands capital to be a hegemonic discursive force. All phrases under capital are instrumental responses to the logic of saving or accumulating time so as to maximise efficiency in the pursuit of profit. For instance, work can be conceived in a variety of idioms; as a therapy, as a diversion, as an aesthetic act or as the enhancement of human powers. For Lyotard, though, work under capitalism is reduced to a means of gaining time. Lyotard remarks, 'Working conditions in a capitalist system all result from the hegemony of the economic genre, in which the issue is to gain time' (Lyotard 1988, p. 176).

In *The Differend* the political economy of capital, the economic genre of discourse, is diagnosed to be unjust insofar as it silences alternative possibilities of phrasing. Lyotard signals this commodification of phrases by remarking,

> Under this condition, phrases can be commodities. The heterogeneity of their regimens as well as the heterogeneity of genres of discourses (stakes) finds a universal idiom in the economic genre, with a universal criterion, success, in having gained time: and a universal judge in the strongest money, in other words the most creditable one, the one most susceptible of giving and therefore reviving time. (Lyotard 1988, p. 174)

Lyotard invokes the dominance of capital and its exclusionary discourse in a related essay, 'A Svelte Appendix to the Postmodern' that was published in *Tombeau d'intellectual et autres papiers* in 1984. Here capital is likened to an infinite aggrandisement that restlessly resists its fixing in any determinate state. Lyotard cites *The Communist Manifesto* as registering a sense of this infinity of capital, though the *Grundrisse* actually invokes this very notion of capitalism's infinity to which Lyotard alludes (Lyotard 1993b, p. 26). In the *Grundrisse* Marx observes, 'The immortality which money strove to achieve by setting itself negatively against circulation, by withdrawing from it, is achieved by capital which preserves itself precisely by abandoning itself to circulation' (Marx 1974, p. 261). Lyotard, in 'A Svelte Appendix to the Postmodern Question', identifies what he terms the 'big deal of the past twenty years' as being 'the transformation of language into a productive commodity' (Lyotard 1993b, p. 27). Lyotard avoids opposing this commodification of language by what he terms an essentialised discourse of alienation drawn from a theological or metaphysical discourse (Lyotard 1993b, p. 28). He aims to resist the prospective domination of discourse and the accompanying instrumentality of performance optimisation by a svelte, postmodern sensitivity to paradox and difference. Postmodern resistance is seen to be distinct from Marxist critique despite Lyotard's identification of Adorno as a precursor of this standpoint.

Lyotard's work subsequent to *The Differend*, such as the essays in *The Inhuman* and *Postmodern Fables*, present an aestheticised pessimistic reading of the present and future. They mark a decisive severance from revolutionary critique, for they suggest a systemic incorporation of all forms of social intercourse into a global pattern of development driven by performance optimisation. This incorporation precludes identification of and protest against contradictions actively undermining capitalism. Lyotard's later writings, however, resume Marx's notion of the voracious power of capital in determining the conditions of its self-reproduction. Lyotard's recognition of a neo-totalitarian form of unimaginative instrumentalism also reflects Marx's critical reading of the endemic thwarting of human creativity under capital (see Marx 1975). Lyotard's late work remains opposed to the political economy of capital, but its pessimism defers to its presumed sustainability. Lyotard accepts resignedly the indefeasibility of the open system of liberal capitalism (Lyotard 1995).

Lyotard's repudiation of large-scale emancipatory change, and, in particular, his recognition of the redundancy of critique as a redemptive philosophy inform his late essays, presented as 'The Wall, the Gulf and the System' and 'A Postmodern Fable' in his *Postmodern Fables* (1996), which are developed out of his 'The Wall, the Gulf and the Sun', in Lyotard's *Political Writings* (1993b). In the latter Lyotard remarks,

What was ultimately at stake for Marxism was the transformation of the local working classes into the emancipated proletariat . . . capable of emancipating all humanity from the disastrous effects of the injury it had suffered . . . society was viewed as being possessed by the *mania*, haunted by a ghost, doomed to a tremendous *catharsis*. . . The rights of the workers were the rights of mankind to self-government, and they were to be fought for through class struggle. I mean class against class, with no reference to nation, sex, race or religion. . . The mere recall of these guidelines of Marxist criticism has something obsolete, even tedious about it. This is not entirely my fault. It is also because the ghost has now vanished dragging the last critical grand narrative with it off the historical stage. (Lyotard 1993b, p. 115)

Lyotard's reading of Marxism, in 'The Wall, the Gulf and the Sun: A Fable', is elegiac for but decisively against the very possibility of social emancipation. Lyotard derides the recently overturned Marxist regimes of Eastern Europe and sees the West as inviolable to radical critique. Western liberal democracies operate as effective open systems that assimilate critique in their inexorable instrumentalist development. Lyotard's postmodern fable sees development as a supra-human phenomenon, whereby the universe is complexified. It is only to be threatened by a future explosion of the sun. But Lyotard imagines that this contingency will, in turn, promote a further complexification, whereby thinking will go on without a body. This scenario is sketched without comment, but it points to the inexorable complexification of technological development as depriving human beings of their corporeal links with imaginative creative thought. Inventiveness, creativity and difference are to be sacrificed to the instrumental goal of maintaining development (Lyotard 1995, pp. 99–100).

In his essays of the later 1980s and 1990s Lyotard forecloses on emancipatory and revolutionary rhetoric. Resistance to systemic instrumentalism is to be effected, if at all, by openness to the sublime sense of the limits of experience. This sense of the conditionality of existence is only to be glimpsed in the creative suffering of writing and the corporeal, sexual nature of thinking. This identification of resistance with a non-demonstrable, aesthetic awareness of the *inhuman* limits of experience rules out the very idea of collective action to achieve fundamental change. This corollary is made explicit in Lyotard's critique of Arendt's politicised notion of anti-totalitarianism in an essay of the late 1980s, 'The Survivor', where Lyotard stresses how contemporary neo-totalitarianism operates by suppressing the powers of judgement, imagination and anxious, inspirational thinking. What prevails is the one-dimensionality of performativity. He renounces his former Marxist and revolutionary activism as well as Arendt's nostalgia for public, political action in derogating the capacity for inspirational renewal of the revolutionary workers' councils' set up in Hungary in 1956 (Lyotard 1993c).

7.2 Conclusion

Throughout his career Lyotard is critical of political economy while repudiating the possibility of large-scale critique. Recognising how Lyotard's standpoint on capital and critique receive changing but persistently ambiguous formulations, whose ambiguities are unacknowledged heightens the ambiguities of Lyotard's thought. From the outset Lyotard's thought expressed tensions arising out of his concern to probe the conditions of the political economy of capitalism in ways that did not square with Marxist orthodoxy. Lyotard is a revisionist, who postdates Marx insofar as he re-reads capitalist society by recognising features, traditionally misrecognised in Marxist literature. On the one hand Lyotard highlights the force of the cultural politics of nationalism and appreciates the assimilation of the French proletariat to the conditions of mid-twentieth-century capital. On the other hand, Lyotard remains decidedly against capital in his subscription to the cause of a Marxist group. He also dogmatically affirms Marxist materialism in *Phenomenology*, notwithstanding his empathy for the phenomenological standpoint.

Lyotard subsequently renounces classic Marxist formulae such as the notion of the proletarian revolution, opting to look for the disruptive potential of unprogrammed revolutionary acts. *Libidinal Economy* is emphatically post-Marxist in its break from Marxist critique and in its promotion of a strategy of amplifying discordant libidinal possibilities in the theory and practice of political economy. Lyotard's commitment to disrupting capital by exploiting its possibilities for discordance maintains a link with a Marxist revolutionary *credo*. Lyotard's continued resistance to capital, though, expresses a trademark non-Marxist valorisation of disorder and difference.

Lyotard's turn towards postmodernism is an emphatic postdating of grand narratives such as Hegelianism and Marxism. It is a rejection of a modern wholesale critique of political economy. Lyotard's repudiates grand critiques, and self-consciously adopts a contrary style of theorising, namely postmodernism. Lyotard emphatically rejects the claims of grand narratives such as Marxism to provide a summative reading of the directionality of history. Lyotard identifies currents within capitalism running counter to the essentialising critique of Marxism, observing the assimilation of the working class to capital and exploring how the range of language games, operating within capitalism, allow for a postmodern pluralistic and inventive subversion of essentialising critique. Lyotard's postmodernism, however, should not be read as neo-conservative and simply against critique, for Lyotard's creative and pluralistic postmodernism is set against the one-dimensionality of the logic of performativity operating in modern capitalism. Lyotard's notion of performativity is akin to Marx's conception of the increasing homogeneity in the modern world due to the inexorable intensive and extensive commodification of activities and sites previously outside the orbit of capital. Lyotard's opposition to performativity signals a continuing affinity between his standpoint and that of Marx and the tradition of critical political economy.

Lyotard's subsequent concentration on language, as reflected in his analysis of a *differend*, attends to particular forms of difference and incommensurability rather than grand critique. *The Differend* explores discourse within capitalism, rather than prescribing an alternative form of political economy. The intimation of incommensurable differences between genres of discourse runs counter to the unificatory assumptions of generalised critique. Nonetheless, Lyotard's recognition of the discursive imperialism of the economic genre of discourse is affiliated to Marx's critical reading of the self-reproducing dynamics of capital. *The Differend* maintains an allegiance to Marx and an antagonism to the political economy of capital. In Lyotard's late work, the negative stifling character of contemporary capitalism is an object of mourning but not for combative revolutionary or reformist political action. Their aesthetic resistance to prevailing neo-totalitarianism is a fugitive reminder of Lyotard's hostility to the alienation of capital that thwarts human creativity.

An irony of Lyotard's critical engagement with Marxism and Hegelianism, the paradigmatic grand narrators of modernity, is his reluctance to re-read Marx or Hegel in a postmodern, creative way so as to evoke the possibilities for divergent interpretations of their work. In contrast to Lyotard, Carver, in *The Postmodern Marx* (1998), urges that the development of postmodernism allows for a perspective on Marx that can discard previous certainties, so as to appreciate the indeterminate, plural and fragmented character of Marx's writings. Lyotard's postmodernism contributes to a critical atmosphere, in which an absolutist, deterministic Marxism, maintaining a schematic, necessary reading of historical development, dictated by and reduced to a self-contained economic formula, is no longer credible. Lyotard himself, however, does not allow for the possibility that Marx is an open theorist, who is neither a determinist nor a reductionist. Likewise Lyotard's rejection of Hegelianism assumes it to operate via an absolutist external logic, and hence he ignores, still less engages with, alternative non-metaphysical readings of Hegel.

Lyotard's lack of reflexive engagement with his own constrained reading of Marx, Hegel and political economy is unfortunate. It allows him to ignore how his own conception of social development, his intimation of an inexorable global process of complexification, resembles the modernist grand narratives that he renounces. Marx, for instance, provides a rich account of the internal dynamics driving the constant expansion of capital. Capital, for Marx, describes an ever-widening circle of intensive and extensive commodification, which absorbs traditionally unmarketised activities and reaches across the globe. Lyotard, throughout his career, valorises the inventive and the disruptive at the expense of the unity and connectedness of thought and unificatory practical action. His theoretical talents are turned against general systems of thought, so that he deconstructs the constructions of critical political economy and the constructive political theories of Rawls and Habermas. Lyotard is alert to the dangers of sublimating dissonance and difference within an essentialising unity, but by focusing on the singular and intractable at the expense of unifying norms and shared social practices Lyotard undertheorises the persisting problems of modernity to which Hegel and Marx attended. While Hegel examined closely and aimed to reconcile the particular and the universal, Lyotard's identification of the incommensurability of distinct standpoints is shadowed by an undifferentiated and relatively unexamined notion of development. In criticising Lyotard from an Hegelian perspective, O'Neill observes, 'One does not "post" modernity by dissolving the dialectical transformation of contradiction in the grand narrative into the mini-narrative of unlimited individuation versus total conformity' (O'Neill 1998, p. 131).

Lyotard's rejection of critical political economy and his espousal of a postmodernism are direct challenges to modern grand narratives and, in particular, to the Heglian–Marxist tradition of dialectical political economy. Lyotard's recognition of the intractability and incommensurability of constituents of the social world undermines the presumption that theory is able to frame a general framework to explain society. Likewise, Lyotard's identification of refactory, dissonant features of social reality intimates that the social world is insusceptible to the generalisations about it that are contained in the grand narratives of Hegel and Marx. What emerges, though, from an encounter with Lyotard is an appreciation of how he cannot avoid the large-scale theorising, which is the hallmark of Hegel and Marx. A resort to large-scale generalising theory is unsurprising in that the significance of differing forces in the social world is only to be evaluated by viewing them in relation to the wider web of relations within which they exist. If a dialectical perspective can avoid the pitfalls of absolutism and undue abstraction, then its holistic, critical perspective can analyse and evaluate the role of political economy in the social world in a way that is precluded to a postmodern celebration of the merely singular.

148   *Critical and Post-Critical Political Economy*

References

Browning, G.K. (1993) *The German Ideology*: The Theory of History and the History of Theory, *History of Political Thought*, 14(3).

Carver, T. (1998) *The Postmodern Marx*. Manchester: Manchester University Press.

Gane, M. (1998) Lyotard's Early writings 1954–1963; in C. Rojek and B. Turner (eds), *The Politics of Jean-Francois Lyotard: Justice and Political Theory*. London: Routledge.

Lechte, J. (1994) *Fifty Key Contemporary Thinkers – from Structuralism to Postmodernity*. London and New York: Routledge.

Lyotard, J.-F. (1993) 'A Svelte Appendix to the Postmodern Question', in Lyotard, *Political Writings*. London: UCL Press.

Lyotard, J.-F. (1984) 'Adrift', in Lyotard, *Driftworks*. New York: Columbia University Press. This piece was originally published in Lyotard, *Derive à partir de Marx et Freud*.

Lyotard, J.-F. (1993a) *Libidinal Economy* trans. by I.H. Grant. London: Athlone Press.

Lyotard, J.-F. (1993b) 'March 23: Unpublished Introduction to an Unfinished Book on the Movement of March 22', in Lyotard, *Political Writings*. London: UCL Press. This is included in French in Lyotard, *Derive à partir de Marx et Freud*.

Lyotard, J.-F. (1984) 'On Theory: An Interview', in J.-F. Lyotard, *Driftworks*, ed. R. Mckeon, trans. R. McKeon, S. Hanson, A. Knab, R. Lockwood and J. Maier. New York: Columbia University Press. This piece was published in French in J.-F. Lyotard, *Derive à partir de Marx et Freud*. Paris, Union Generale d'Editions, 1973.

Lyotard, J.-F. (1991) *Phenomenology*. Albany, NY: State University of New York Press.

Lyotard, J.-F. (1993b) 'The Name of Algeria', in J.-F. Lyotard, *Political Writings*, trans. B. Readings and K. Geiman. London: UCL Press.

Lyotard, J.-F. (1988) *Peregrinations: Law, Form and Event*. New York: Columbia University Press.

Lyotard, J.-F. (1984) *The Postmodern Condition: A Report on Knowledge* trans. G. Bennington and B. Massumi. Manchester: Manchester University Press.

Lyotard, J.-F. (1995) *Postmodern Fables* trans. G. Van Den Abeele. Minneapolis: University of Minnesota Press.

Lyotard, J.-F. (1988) *The Differend: Phrases in Dispute*, trans. G. Van Den Abbeele. Manchester: Manchester University Press.

Lyotard, J.-F. (1993c) 'The Survivor', in J.-F. Lyotard, *Towards the Postmodern* ed. R. Harvey and M. Roberts. New Jersey, Humanities Press. This piece is published in French as 'Survivant: Arendt' in J.-F. Lyotard, *Lectures d'enfance*. Paris, Galilee, 1991.

Lyotard, J.-F. (1993b) 'The Wall, the Gulf and the Sun: A Fable', in J.-F.Lyotard, *Political Writings*, trans. B. Readings and K. Geiman. London: UCL Press.

Marx, K. (1975) *Early Writings*. London: Penguin Books.

Marx, K. (1974) *Grundrisse*. Harmondsworth: Penguin.

O'Neill, J. (1998) 'Lost in the Post: (Post)Modernity Explained to Youth', in C. Rojek and B. Turner (eds), *The Politics of Jean-Francois Lyotard*. London and New York: Routledge.

Williams, J. (2000) *Lyotard and the Political*. London and New York: Routledge.

8
Fraser, Recognition and Redistribution

8.1 Introduction

Nancy Fraser is sensitive to the practical and theoretical issues that define the contemporary context for social theory. She consistently engages with a variety of theoretical perspectives so as to be inclusive in integrating divergent empirical phenomena and normative demands in her critical theory. She examines and draws upon Foucault, Lyotard, Honneth, Butler and Habermas in framing a normative social theory that is alert to the particularity and elusiveness of discursive orders of power and strategies of emancipation. She aims to synthesise contemporary social and political theories so as to develop an avowedly post-Marxist critical theory of society.

As she emphasises in her recent dialogue with Honneth, *Redistribution or Recognition? A Political Philosophical Exchange*, however, she engages with post-Marxist thought and practice so as to continue the project of critical theory (Fraser and Honneth 2003, p. 4). She understands the task of critical theory in the terms that were framed by Marx, and which have been abandoned by many post-Marxist theorists, namely to provide a critique of capitalist society as a whole; to examine critically the totality of social conditions (Fraser and Honneth 2003, p. 4) Fraser, then, is a contemporary theorist, who resumes the theoretical ambition of Hegel and Marx, while accommodating post-Marxist perspectives.

Fraser's standpoint is encapsulated in the title of her most famous essay, 'From Redistribution to Recognition: Dilemmas of Justice in a "Postsocialist" Age'. The title advertises the distinctiveness of the present, which is seen as an age in which classic critical political economy is postdated; it is a postsocialist age. Fraser couples this identification of the present as postsocialist with a sense that the former priority afforded to the struggle for the redistribution of economic resources has receded before a contemporary struggle for the recognition of identities. What Fraser proposes in this essay, and, indeed, throughout her work, is to recognise the seminal features of the *Zeitgeist*, notably its tendency to prioritise the rectification of misrecognised cultural identities, while at the same time continuing to press the normative case for a fair overall distribution of economic resources. She aims to continue the project of critical political economy in an age where recognition of distinctive and disparate cultural identities threatens to fragment and divide society rather than allowing for unity and fairness.

Fraser observes how the defining contemporary idiomatic discourses of emancipation demand recognition of an undervalued identity and conceive of social identities as being complex and variegated. Fraser is a feminist and she characteristically reviews many analyses of concrete practical social issues by tracing how contemporary feminist agitation arises out of misperceptions over identity rather than simply reflecting a gendered imbalance of resources. Just as new social movements more generally accentuate the complexity and plurality of politics by supporting the political claims of distinct groups, who represent differing races, cultures, nations and attitudes, so Fraser recognises how the women's movement has turned away from attributing an essential identity to women. This anti-essentialism of feminists breaks with an androgynous assimilation of female to male identity and questions presumptions about the homogeneity of the category, woman. Since the 1980s, feminism has attended more closely to the differences between women and the differing situations in which women find themselves. This tendency to disavow the universalism of erstwhile feminism is reinforced by a feminist cultivation of a deconstructive style of postmodern discourse theory. Essential identities are denied and identities are seen, rather, as contingent upon particular discourses of power, with which women are to contend by a continuous process of deconstruction.

Fraser works with the grain of the contemporary feminist turn. She aims to reconcile the universalism of a feminist claim to justice on equal terms with men to a nuanced appreciation of the particular discursive contexts in which feminist identities are framed.

Fraser's engagement with the politics of identity and her sensitivity to the recognitive claims of heterogeneous social identities render her rehearsal of the tradition of critical political economy distinctive and contemporary. Culture is not subordinated to the economy, for she aims to equilibrate culture and the economy. In so doing she expressly devises a new idiom in articulating a critical political economy. She professes an expressly bivalent standpoint, which includes the economic and the cultural. In defining her approach, she tends to contrast her incorporation of cultural recognition with what she styles a Marxist exclusively economic standpoint. While she acknowledges that Marx may and indeed should be read in non-reductive ways, she also characteristically defines her express support for cultural recognition and economic redistribution by contrasting it with Marx's allegedly exclusive focus upon economic exploitation. The upshot is that she tends to deflect from Marx's holistic sense of political economy. Political economy, for Marx, is not a sphere that is neatly detachable from the wider cultural practices of society. Marx, for instance, defines class in cultural as well as economic terms. Class is a dynamic term, and while classes may be identified in terms of their structural position within a mode of production, the complete specification of working-class identity requires cultural inflection. Marx understands the working class to develop its own sense of identity by its members recognising its class character, needs and powers. Moreover Marx conceives of human identities as flourishing and developing in distinct but imbricated ways in the non-class society of communism. While Marx does not spell out all the implications of his cultural reading of class and identity, the *Economic and Philosophical Manuscripts* points to the prospective development of a wide range of powers on the part of members of communist society, who will have emancipated themselves from the shackles of class under capitalism. Marx imagines that relations between men and women will have altered so that there will be a mutual recognition of their respective powers and capacities. Marx takes relations between men and women under capitalism to be restricted by the structural properties of capital, imagining bourgeois men as possessing women so as to deny their subjectivity. This interpretation of sexual relations shows how Marx integrates the economic and the cultural in his conception of political economy.

Marx's developmental reading of the working class reflects his inclusive dialectical theorising, which he derives from the Hegelian tradition. Hegel himself develops a perspective on political economy, which is directed decidedly towards combining the economic with cultural and political structures and practices. Hegel sees the sphere of political economy, civil society, as depending upon the practice of family life, in which individual identities are nurtured in a loving context that is opposed to the egoism of economic life. Likewise Hegel sees the classes and corporations within civil society, and the political institutions overseeing civil society, as reconciling the claims of cultural particularity, economic freedom and the unity of political community. Hegel is an inclusive theorist, the dialectical sweep of whose imagination is attuned to the several dimensions of the social world, and his aspiration to balance specifically economic practices with countervailing nurturing and corrective political institutions. Hegel's particular integrative understanding of social practices, however, is problematic because his support for patriarchal family life and undemocratic political institutions does not recognise sufficiently the subjectivity and freedom of all persons within a community.

Fraser is a contemporary social theorist, who follows a route that had been travelled by Hegel and Marx. She aims to be a critical theorist, who develops a critical perspective on political economy that is inclusive in incorporating complex and intersecting features of social life. She develops a vocabulary in dealing with rival claims in the contemporary world, which is distinctly post-Marxist, and which postdates the classic critical political economies of Hegel and Marx. She frames her social theory in terms of its bivalent inclusion of the claims to recognition of diverse social groups and to the fair redistribution of economic resources within a social community. She operates in a theoretical and practical context, which is shaped in part by postmodernism and the cultural turn, so that she is mindful of how a community will include a number of heterogeneous cultural identities demanding recognition, and that the demand for recognition is not of a piece with the moral aspiration to treat all members of society in a fair but uniform fashion. Fraser's vocabulary is designed to deal systematically and theoretically with distinctive features of a post-critical age. What she draws upon in so doing is the legacy of critical political economy. She is self-consciously a critical theorist, who aims to respond to new unsettling cultural claims while maintaining a critical interest in the structural features of political economy. Her work indicates the continuing relevance of Hegel and Marx as well as showcasing significant new idioms in articulating critical political economy. Fraser is particularly insightful in highlighting how social theorists in the contemporary setting ought to be inclusive in dealing with issues of culture and economy. What her work also signposts, but does not provide, is the need for a systematic exploration of the political economy and such a systemic approach to political economy is what remains of particular value in the work of Hegel and Marx.

8.2 *Unruly Practices*: *Power, Discourse and Gender in Contemporary Social Theory*

Nancy Fraser's trademark style as a critical theorist is her commitment to combine differing sorts of normative demands in regulating society with a sensitivity to the key practical issues of the day. The trajectory of her own negotiation of diverse ways of perceiving political economy and her sense of the imbrication of cultural and economic issues can be tracked through her career. In the Introduction to *Unruly Practices: Power, Discourse and Gender in Contemporary Social Theory* she reflects on the trajectory of her thought, recognising how she engages with a diversity of theories and practical issues. She observes, 'The essays in this book grew out of this specific generational history. Accordingly, they are bifocal in nature, responding simultaneously to political conditions and to intellectual developments' (Fraser 1989, p. 20). Three of the essays in the book reflect upon how her intellectual encounter with Foucault was seminal in shaping her thinking and political commitments. Foucault elicits a bivalent response from Fraser. On the one hand, he is recognised to be an innovative, productive theorist, tracking the diversity of ways in which modern forms of power are articulated in the cultural discourses of the social world. On the other hand, Foucault is condemned for failing to theorise, to acknowledge and to account for the normative perspective informing his work. Fraser's reading of Foucault reflects her wider development as a radical social critic and feminist. Throughout her career, she aims to combine strategies and standpoints, which, on the face of things, appear incompatible or unresolvable. In respect of Foucault, she admires and incorporates Foucault's sociological insight into the ubiquity of modern power, which resists standard forms of dissent, within her own theoretical perspective, but she also aims to develop a constructive normative critique that is lacking in Foucault's work.

Fraser sees Foucault's genealogical study of power/knowledge regimes as providing 'the holistic and historically relative study of the formation and functioning of incommensurable networks of social practices involving the mutual interrelationship of constraint and discourse' (Fraser 1989, p. 20). Foucault, for Fraser, offers a productive insight into modern forms of power by tracing its genealogy to the unco-ordinated development of disciplinary regimes, whose micro-practices of discipline and surveillance enabled the effective operation and dispersal of power throughout the practices of the modern regime of power. Hence modern power is capillary, and continuous. It is everywhere and self-amplifying, enmeshing all components of its discursive regimes within its production. Fraser draws out implications from Foucault's reading of power for a study of political economy, noting that Foucault highlights how power is embedded in actual practices or the body, rather than operating as an ideology to be assessed or rejected. Again she observes, 'The second strategic implication of Foucault's insight into the capillary character of modern power concerns the inadequacy of state-centred and economistic political orientations' (Fraser 1989, p. 22). Fraser's sense of critical theory is informed by Foucault, in that she standardly takes it to be concerned with the interimbrication of power in areas designated cultural and private, and in practices standardly designated economic or political. Her critique of Foucault, however, also informs her critical theory in that she is at once sensitive to particular critical discourses, constraining or allowing for particular styles of cultural expression, while, *pace* Foucault, she expressly favours emancipatory discourses that are inclusive in their democratic and egalitarian aims.

Fraser's distinctive theoretical style can be seen in her critical essay, 'What's Critical about Critical Theory? The Case of Habermas and Gender'. This essay is of a piece with the critical essays on Foucault in *Unruly Practices: Power, Discourse and Gender in Contemporary Social Theory*, in that she draws positively on the work of Habermas while subjecting aspects of A *Theory of Communicative Action* to a critique owing much to Foucault's sense of the ubiquity of power in modernity. She observes how Habermas produces a conceptual map of the modern world that is insightful. She notes, however, that it is vitiated by the rigidity with which its classification system operates, diagnosing how Habermas' treatment of women and feminism is particularly problematic. She observes how Habermas differentiates the modern world from premodern societies by recognising that modern societies function by splitting their overall organisation into system and life-world processes. In the modern world certain functions, dealing with material reproduction systems, are split from the former unified life world, so as to form system interrelated action contexts constituting the (official) economy and the state. In contrast, the modern nuclear family, 'the private sphere' and the space for political debate and opinion formation, 'the public sphere', perform differentiated symbolic reproduction roles. The sphere of the family is distinguished from the public sphere because its actions are normatively or conventionally secured rather than communicatively achieved.

Fraser takes Habermas' modelling of modern society to allow for a complex reading of the sites and struggles of classical capitalist society and its more recent manifestation as a welfare state capitalist system. She recognises it to possess emancipatory potential, consisting in its recognition of the role of communicatively achieved contexts of interaction (Fraser 1989, pp. 135–6). Habermas' recognition of the potential of communicatively achieved interaction to advance normative political goals is seen to contrast positively with the normative deficiencies that she detects in Foucault's work. Fraser, however, is critical of Habermas for failing to explore sufficiently the ways in which the areas that he schematises in his model of modern society act and interact. She highlights how the experience of women does not bear out the schematised way in which Habermas conceives of society, observing the complex and intersecting ways in which women's lives are subject to the power of men. Women's needs tend to be interpreted and channelled by a number of interrelated discourses, which include those of: 'the private sphere' of the family, the official economy and the state. These discourses require to be understood and challenged in ways to which Habermas does not attend. Fraser, for instance, perceives Habermas' schematic model to occlude the fact that 'the private sphere' functions as a mode of material reproduction as well as a sphere of symbolic reproduction, and that women are subject to non-negotiated constraints in its conventional practices (Fraser 1989, pp. 122–9). She also is critical of Habermas's characterisation of the feminist movement as particularistic. Like Habermas, Fraser conceives of the normative ideal to be espoused by critical theory as universalistic at the meta dialogical level, but unlike Habermas, she recognises a need for women to counteract the particularistic judgements on their bodies and needs that define patriarchal society. More generally, she observes, 'Substantive social meanings and norms are always necessarily culturally and historically specific' (Fraser 1989, p. 136).

In *Unruly Practices: Power, Discourse and Gender in Contemporary Social Theory* Fraser applies her syncretic, inclusive style to issues of political economy that affect women, notably in the two essays, 'Women, Welfare, and the Politics of Need Interpretation' and 'Struggle over Needs: Outline of a Socialist-Feminist Critical Theory of Late Capitalist Political Culture'. These essays, dating from the late 1980s, analyse the pressure that was being exerted on welfare institutions in the prevailing context of the global reassertion of economic liberalism. In 'Women, Welfare and the Politics of Need Interpretation', she urges that the contemporary struggles over welfare centre upon women and involve both the actual economic assistance that is offered to women and the discursive context in which women's welfare needs are calculated and articulated. She notes the gendered character of the welfare system, in which women are the principal agents of care within families. She identifies women as assuming the burdens of caring for families without the material support of men, and as being employed in the administrative system of welfare support. Yet in comparison with men, she points to their distinctly second-class welfare support. Men receive insurance-linked schemes of support for unemployment, which are generous and less administratively intrusive than the welfare support that is standardly offered to women. Fraser, then, shows how economic and political issues are imbricated by gender and that the administratively interpreted system of welfare support exerts power over women. She urges that this power be contested by women on normatively justifiable grounds (Fraser 1989, pp. 153–8).

In 'Struggle Over Needs: Outline of a Socialist-Feminist Critical Theory of Late-Capitalist Political Culture' Fraser discusses the notion of needs in late-twentieth-century political economy, taking it to be a discursively contested concept. In doing so she adopts a signature theoretical stance combining divergent elements. She focuses upon how the notion of needs is contested in a 'social' space, where apparently domesticated and corralled terms can be challenged. She notes how feminist forms of action and debate have successfully challenged prevailing views of the family and the private sphere, so that, for instance, the notion of rape in marriage is increasingly accepted. She observes how welfare cutbacks have been undertaken at the behest of neo-liberal, patriarchal orthodoxy. She notes challenges to these cutbacks and to the contemporary style of servicing welfare needs that have been mounted by radical groups, who resist the injustice of welfare provision, and the lack of respect afforded to recipients. She observes how the process of contestation stirs traditionalist supporters of the discursive status quo to agitate so as to retrench the previously dominant discursive interpretation. Fraser supports an interpretation of needs promoting just and egalitarian claims to welfare on the part of women. She recognises that women are currently undervalued in society and urges that women's welfare claims be pressed by invoking the language of social rights, for the discourse of rights possesses interpretative power in liberal societies (Fraser 1989, pp. 181–3).

8.3   *Justice Interruptus*: *Critical Reflections on the 'Postsocialist' Condition*

Fraser's book, *Justice Interruptus: Critical Reflections on the 'Postsocialist' Condition*, contains essays that she wrote during the 1990s in the context of a global resurgence of neo-liberalism and untrammelled capitalism, combining interests in theory and political and economic practice. They also reflect her commitment to unify differing theoretical positions and practical standpoints. Perhaps her most renowned contribution to contemporary political economy and social theory is the lead essay in this book, 'From Redistribution to Recognition? Dilemmas of Justice in a "Postsocialist Age" '. This essay epitomises Nancy Fraser's contribution to political economy and her concern to explain the inter-relations between culture and the economy. Recognising its links with other themes and essays in *Justice Interruptus: Critical Reflections on the 'Postsocialist' Condition*, however, deepens an appreciation of this essay. Collectively, the essays combine universalism, in the form of critique appealing to general criteria and notions of equality and justice, with sensitivity to the contingency and particularity of the constructed identities and concerns of social actors, such as is exhibited in new social movements, notably the feminist movement. Her assessment of a range of theories and theorists in the essays, including Habermas, French discourse theory, Iris Marion Young, Carole Pateman, Judith Butler and Seyla Benhabib, and practical issues such as the welfare state, democracy, the public sphere and the family wage, aims to reconcile contingency and difference and to support inclusive normative claims. Fraser's synoptic theoretical standpoint, and her sensitivity to heterogeneous normative demands, underlie her stylised and differential treatment of the relationship between the achievement of substantive equality, which is to be effected by the rectification of inequalities in the socioeconomic structure, and the remedying of cultural or symbolic injustices by alleviating prevailing cultural oppression, which is to be effected by recognising/affirming the symbolic claims of social groups. This complex set of aims is the focus for her considered and significant intervention into a complex and postsocialist political economy.

In the essay 'Rethinking the Public Sphere: A Contribution to the Critique of Actually Existing Democracy' Fraser reconsiders western-style existing democracies in the light of western celebration of the demise of Soviet-style socialism and via a theoretical review of Habermas's notion of the public sphere. She focuses upon Habermas's *The Structural Transformation of the Pubic Sphere*, and notes how his conception of the public sphere is useful for a contemporary evaluation of democracy, in allowing for a differentiated reading of the public domain, whereby state institutions and administrative arrangements can be distinguished from the formation and expression of public opinion. Habermas recognises how his idealised image of a public sphere, in which a restricted bourgeois public, operates so as to undertake open rational criticism of public matters, is declining in the face of the rise of new publics and new modes of organisation of the public sphere. Against Habermas, Fraser accepts contrary revisionist views of the pubic sphere, highlighting how the bourgeois public sphere operates so as to exclude alternative voices, though she urges that these voices are nonetheless recognised, in being articulated in alternative public foras (Fraser 1997, pp. 72–7).

Fraser develops a revisionist notion of the public sphere in assessing the extent to which the ideal of the bourgeois public sphere, which brackets differences of status amongst its participants in the interests of an open and unrestrictive discourse about public matters, can operate effectively in contemporary democracies. She urges that the ideal of a discourse transcending status differences is problematic, for discourse cannot be separated from the conditions of its production. She prescribes a plurality of public spheres, because she considers that the most effective conduct of diverse public opinion formation and wide-ranging, inclusive discourse about public matters will not spring from simply one public sphere. To contribute to an effective ongoing democracy, these spheres should engage with one another to debate general normative claims. A diversity of spheres also allows for the generation of independent standpoints, which are blocked by oppressive perspectives, such as androcentrism. Fraser's standpoint is characteristically integrative, in its promotion of the claims of the particular and the universal.

In her essay 'False Antitheses: A Response to Seyla Benhabib and Judith Butler', Fraser reviews a debate between Butler and Benhabib, in which critical theory and deconstruction are opposed. Characteristically, Fraser proposes a combinatory non-dogmatic stance as an alternative to the entrenched dichotomies, prolonging and distorting the debate between feminists and between opposing styles of argumentation. She refers to an essay 'Social Criticism without Philosophy: An Encounter between Feminism and Postmodernism', which she co-wrote with Linda J. Nicholson (Fraser 1988). She endorses the drift of that paper's qualified support for generalising perspectives, notably feminist claims to rectify androcentric forms of injustice. The qualification to her support for generalising perspectives stems from her acknowledgement that universalising foundational metanarratives are not to be accepted uncritically. If general perspectives are to be reasonable contributions to theoretical and practical social life, they must be expressly held as only provisionally true, and should be open to critical questioning from alternative standpoints and allow for the possibility of countervailing theories. Her complaint against Benhabib is over the priority she assigns to advancing general argumentative claims, overriding particularity and the contingency of discursive identities. Butler's recursive resort to the deconstruction of identity claims is seen to threaten to undermine any form of normative standpoint that might justify her practice.

In 'False Antitheses: A Response to Seyla Benhabib and Judith Butler' Fraser shows a nuanced attitude to postmodern versions of feminism such as Butler's, admiring their deconstructive techniques of analysing discourse, which disturb androcentric identities, but criticising their tendency to override constructive social theorising. Fraser shows a similarly balanced appreciation of the possibilities of French discourse theory for feminism in the essays she contributed to her co-edited book, *Revaluing French Feminism: Critical Essays on Difference, Agency and Culture* (Fraser 1992). Fraser provides a similar insightful overview of the developments constituting contemporary feminism in a short essay within *Justice Interruptus*, which is entitled 'Multiculturalism, Antiessentialism and Radical Democracy', the manifest concern of which is to explore the meaning of radical democracy in its contemporary context. She takes the contemporary goal of radical democracy to involve the overcoming of two sorts of impediments to inclusive democratic participation. On the one hand, radical democracy requires the elimination of social inequality, and on the other hand it requires the recognition of difference. Fraser at once acknowledges that recognition of difference is problematic in that it raises questions over which differences are to be recognised. She urges that discussion of difference should not be separated from discussion over social equality and questions of redistribution, observing how treating the politics of recognition as a cultural phenomenon unrelated to questions of political economy is unfortunate, because it undermines the character and agenda of radical democracy. To interrogate the politics of recognition and their relationship to the achievement of radical democracy, Fraser reviews the recent history of feminist engagement with the notion of difference.

Fraser retails how feminist debates in the 1970s concentrated on two positions. Some feminists saw differences between men and women as having been constructed along androcentric lines and hence should be eliminated in favour of equality. Difference feminists, conversely, saw important singularities in the female identity that were unrelated to androcentrism and hence constituted differences to be supported and recognised. Subsequently Fraser sees the terms of the difference debate as changing, because feminists appreciated the interweaving of identities perceiving how issues of sexuality, race, class and nation intersect with gender and acknowledged significant differences between women. Fraser sees the consequential complication of notions of difference as potentially linking identity to social equality, in that multiple identities might be related to overall patterns of distribution in society. However, this potential for linking identity and equality has not been realised. Instead Fraser notes how feminism and identity politics have been internally riven and disconnected from more general social and economic questions. She takes ongoing feminist debate over identity and recognition to be internally divided between anti-essentialist discourse theorists like Butler, and feminist supporters of multiculturalism, who support the cultural recognition of identities espoused by new social movements. She sees both sides of this debate as deficient, in their one-sidedness. Anti-essentialist theorists perceive the constructed nature of identities without possessing the means to discriminate between them, while multicultural feminists proclaim allegiance to a notion of identity that is insufficiently theorised. Both sides of the debate are problematic because they fail to relate questions of recognition and difference to the world of political economy and social inequality. Fraser urges that commitment to radical democracy must link questions of recognition and social justice to provide a basis for discriminating between competing claims for recognition, and to appreciate how identities are shaped in unequal circumstances.

Fraser ends the essay 'Multiculturalism, Antiessentialism and Radical Democracy' with the programmatic slogan, ' "No Recognition without Redistribution" ' (Fraser 1997, p. 188), which resonates throughout her work and is the express focus for the lead essay of her book *Justice Interruptus: Critical Reflections on the 'Postsocialist' Condition*, 'From Redistribution to Recognition?' For Fraser, the question of the ways in which the distinct claims of recognition and redistribution are to be taken is central to developing a critical form of contemporary political economy. She takes her conception of this question to be distinct from preceding exponents of critical political economy, and she highlights its distinctiveness by the subtitle of the latter essay – 'Dilemmas of Justice in a Postsocialist Age'. Indeed its post-Marxist flavour is emphasised by her elucidation of the conceptual distinctness of redistribution and recognition claims in the essay. While she acknowledges that there can be no water-tight division between economic injustice, arising out of an unequal distribution of resources that is to be remedied by redistributive measures, and cultural injustices that invoke cultural remedies, her schematised model of pure economic injustice is drawn expressly from Marxism (Fraser 1997, p. 17).

She imagines a Marxist representation of a capitalist collectivity as being differentiated purely by means of its economic structure. Cultural hardships of the proletariat are assimilated to the proletariat's place in an economic order that can be defined in non-cultural terms. She conceives of the injustice suffered by the proletariat as being quintessentially a matter of distribution, assuming secondary cultural injustices follow automatically from an unjust distribution of resources (Fraser 1997, p. 17). While acknowledging that this is an overly schematised account of Marxism, and signalling in a footnote that it is not representative of her own reading of Marx, her stylisation of Marxism is presented nonetheless as an orthodox and credible standpoint, serving to make intelligible her notion of the paradigmatic possibility of separating economic injustice from cultural injustice (Fraser 1997, pp. 34–5). Moreover it echoes her observation in a related essay, 'Culture, Political Economy and Difference', where a Marxist view of proletarian struggle is seen as depending purely on the issue of redistribution (Fraser 1997, p. 201). The upshot of Fraser's stylised use of Marxist political economy to demonstrate a purely economic rather than cultural sense of injustice, is to divorce Marx and preceding critical political economy from contemporary discourse on social justice (see also Fraser 1999, p. 28).

Fraser herself, in this essay, imagines a heuristic schematised model of injustices and remedies for injustices in which economic injustice, as exemplified by her Marxist paradigm, is distinguished from cultural injustice, which she takes to be exemplified by the cultural oppression of a cultural minority such as the gay community. Fraser's schematism is designed to highlight how redistribution claims are distinct from recognition claims. The respective claims for redistribution and recognition are characteristically held to be in tension, as claims for recognition, such as those pressed by the gay community, tend to value and promote group specificity, whereas claims for socioeconomic redistribution, such as those pressed by the schematised proletariat of her model, tend to be geared to eliminating differences between groups in the interests of realising an overall standard of justice. Her simplified model of collectivities suffering either from economic injustice or cultural oppression is complicated when she invokes groups, like women or races that manifestly suffer both cultural and economic forms of injustice.

In reconsidering the relationship between economic and recognitive forms of injustice in the context of groups experiencing both forms simultaneously, Fraser offers a refinement to her designation of remedies to these forms of injustice. Instead of simply observing how remedies can be distinguished in terms of the distinct forms of injustice they are designed to act upon, she also distinguishes between affirmative and transformative styles of remedy for both recognitive and distributionist forms of injustice. Affirmative remedies tackle issues of injustice by affirming the claims of groups to recognition or by asserting the right to redistributive welfare provision, while maintaining existing structures of society. Alternatively, transformative remedies aim to transform the problems that the injustice claims signal by altering underlying structural conditions. Transformative remedies to the misrecognition of group claims are exemplified in queer politics, aiming to destabilise and to alter perceptions of sexual identity rather than simply affirming the identity of the gay community. Likewise transformative redistributive measures involve the restructuring of society to eliminate the conditions whereby poverty and inequality are produced.

Ultimately, Fraser favours a bivalent reading of social justice whereby cultural and economic injustices are to be tackled simultaneously by transformative strategies. Affirmative strategies tend not to tackle the issues in a radical way. Non-transformative redistributive welfare measures for instance presume rather than overcome the social divisions arising out of inequality. The consequent discordance between egalitarian measures of redistribution and underlying structures of inequality can lead to a backlash against the recipients of welfare, who tend to be groups whose identities are misrecognised. Likewise the affirmation of cultural identities fails to tackle underlying structural causes of the oppression of groups, which are connected to society's social and economic structure and the totality of patterns of cultural identification so that its reformist strategy can generate a backlash of resentment amongst privileged groups.

8.4   *Redistribution or recognition? Justice in a global age*

Fraser's concern to link questions of redistribution with questions of recognition so as to produce an encompassing theoretical overview of justice is developed further in her work subsequent to *Justice Interruptus: Critical Reflections on the 'Postsocialist' Condition*. In her essay 'Social Justice in the Age of Identity Politics: Redistribution, Recognition and Participation' (1999), she revisits the argument of 'From Redistribution to Recognition', reaffirming her commitment to a bivalent approach by insisting upon a perspectival dualism in social theory that accommodates both redistribution and recognition (Fraser 1999). Together with perspectival dualism she proposes a two-dimensional concept of justice on the plane of moral theory, invoking the notion of parity of participation as its moral core. She urges this moral theory can include issues affecting recognition and distribution by stipulating conditions by which individuals are to enjoy parity of participation. She holds that individuals should possess formal equality before the law and sufficient means to enable them to be respected and independent. Additionally, institutionalised cultural patterns of interpretation and evaluation should express equal respect for all participants and ensure equal opportunity for achieving social esteem. This moral theory is a programmatic sketch, and Fraser refrains from theorising in detail over the kind of economic structure that would be consonant with parity of participation. It is a standpoint on social justice, though, that continues her commitment to unite demands for recognition and redistribution in an integrative theory (Fraser 1999).

Fraser reworks this essay, 'Social Justice in The Age of Identity Politics: Redistribution, Recognition and Participation', in a published exchange of views with Honneth, in *Redistribution or Recognition? A Political-Philosophical Exchange* (2003). In revising the essay, Fraser concludes by considering what features of recent history are responsible for the present conjuncture, in which recognition struggles have both superseded claims over redistributing resources and have been decoupled from issues relating to distribution. She maintains that post-Fordism, postcommunism and globalisation have promoted the present conjuncture. The end of Fordism entails that recognition claims could no longer be subordinated to the distributionist concerns of a national Keynesian settlement, while the end of communism in Europe signifies an end to the suppression of cultural difference and cultural dissidence. The ensuing maelstrom of cultural claims for status in Western and Eastern Europe at the same time thereby coincided with the defining postwar projects to ensure just distributive orders. Globalisation and the dominance of a neo-liberal economic ideology exacerbate this change in the social and cultural order. Globalisation promotes awareness of cultural difference and at the same time undermines national projects for securing social justice. Fraser concludes that the present conjuncture demands a dualistic concern for redistributive and recognitive justice along the lines that she recommends and that there should be a heightened sensitivity to the political frame in which these issues are tackled. In the context of globalisation issues need to be tackled at the local, regional, national and global levels. The nation state is no longer to be presumed to the supreme site for remedial political action (Fraser and Honneth 2003, p. 93).

In *Redistribution Or Recognition? A Political-Philosophical Exchange*, which contains Honneth's 'Redistribution as Recognition: A Response to Nancy Fraser' as well as Fraser's 'Social Justice in the Age of Identity Politics: Redistribution, Recognition and Participation', Fraser and Honneth add additional rejoinders to one another's arguments. In her rejoinder, 'Distorted Beyond All Recognition: A Rejoinder to Axel Honneth', Fraser reaffirms her commitment to a bivalent interpretation of contemporary society, observing that Honneth 'overextends the category of recognition to a point that loses its critical force' (Fraser and Honneth 2003, p. 201). In highlighting the imperative for social critique of framing a theory that harmonises with the complexity of contemporary society, Fraser signals the discontinuity of her standpoint with that of the critical political economy of Marx and Hegel as well as its underlying continuity of aspiration. She discusses the empirical reference point of Critical Theory by expressly abrogating what are seen as unacceptable epistemological and metaphysical aspects of Marxism. She maintains, 'At a time when Marxian metanarratives have lost all credibility, there can be no metaphysically designated agent of emancipation and no a prioristically identified addressee of critique' (Fraser and Honneth 2003, p. 200). Likewise she observes that the cultural homogeneity that has been assumed by left Hegelianism can no longer be assumed in the contemporary context of pluralised and cross-cutting value horizons (Fraser and Honneth 2003, p. 198). While Fraser points to the need for critical political economy to respond to the distinctive contemporary discursive and empirical context, her capacity to continue the project of critical political economy by incorporating differentiated empirical and normative aspects of the contemporary social world has been questioned. Honneth in the debate between himself and Fraser questions why Fraser settles for a bivalent approach to analysing society and suggests that she does not account for issues pertaining to the principle of legal equality (Fraser and Honneth 2003, pp. 151–2). More fundamentally Thompson in a review article on the Fraser-Honneth debate questions the adequacy of both Fraser's and Honneth's overall accounts of capitalist society. He suggests, 'it could be argued that neither Fraser nor Honneth really try to theorize capitalist society as a totality' (Thompson, 14). Certainly, Fraser's programmatic critical standpoint, which is designed to include the claims of culture and of the economy, does not possess the sweep and dialectical inclusiveness of Marx's or Hegel's critical political economy.

In her article 'Mapping the Feminist Imagination: From Redistribution to Recognition to Representation' (2005), Fraser reviews the contexts in which second wave feminism developed after the Second World War. She observes how it originated amidst the ferment of ideas and activities of the new social movements in the 1960s, who as part of the New Left questioned the preceding economistic perspective of the traditional left. As the utopian energies of the New Left declined, however, feminism was resignified so as to foreground cultural issues as constituting a new political imaginary. Feminism became preoccupied with identity politics and claims for recognition while social democracy declined in the context of a resurgence of a conservative agenda of neo-liberalism and the dynamic of globalising capital (Fraser 2005, p. 296).

In the light of its recent history and present situation Fraser sees feminism as now needing to reassert redistributive claims and to recognise the importance of supra-national sites of political activity. She identifies European feminism as constituting the vanguard of feminist political actors, who recognise the significance of acting transnationally. Fraser sees European feminists as acting so as to achieve the bivalent claims of recognition and redistribution while also seeking to extend political representation to new sites that can act upon issues that go beyond states. Fraser concludes this article by offering the hope that this style of feminist politics can achieve an equilibrated approach to the question of justice, balancing its economic, political and cultural aspects. She observes, 'Above all such a politics could permit us to pose and hopefully to answer the key political question of our age: how can we integrate the claims for redistribution, recognition and representation so as to challenge the full range of gender injustices in a globalizing world?' (Fraser 2005, p. 306). Fraser's conclusion is a programmatic endorsement of a form of critical political economy in which heterogeneous aspects of the economic and social world are the object of concerted an imaginative political action, but she does not develop a systematic critical political economy of the present conjuncture.

8.5 Conclusion

Nancy Fraser is a social theorist, whose sensitivity to seemingly discordant divergent normative claims, on the one hand for recognition and on the other hand for distributive fairness, motivates her to frame a wide-ranging, inclusive conception of social justice. In do doing she is sensitive to the contemporary context. A significant way in which the contemporary world is different from preceding ones is the pre-eminence attached to the normative claim of difference itself. New social movements exemplify this trend; asserting their identities without reference to an encompassing unitary social world. Ethnic minorities, feminists and adherents to diverse social causes express distinct identities and standpoints, looking for recognition for these identities from fellow members of society, rather than aiming to fit in with prevailing standardising cultural norms. Nancy Fraser's work stands out as a systematic engagement to incorporate differential normative claims to identity within a wider critical theory that articulates a general notion of a just society in political economy. The terms of the identity of the social whole for which justice is sought are destabilised by this development of what may be called 'the cultural turn'. Fraser works with rather than against the grain of this instability.

Fraser deals expressly with contemporary manifestations of cultural complexity, and in so doing she differs from Hegel and Marx, accepting social identity to be fragmentary and to be the product of political negotiation; sexual and cultural differences disbar a univocal sense of social unity. She is alert to the constraining character of received customary social identities; as a feminist she is sensitive to a rigid divide between public and private, which consigns women to a subordinate, private identity. Feminists' deconstruction of standard gender identities, the emergence of divergent discourses of sexuality and the complexity of a multicultural society are seen by Fraser as aspects of a just society with which social theorists must engage. Notwithstanding this contemporary aspect of Fraser's theorising and vocabulary, she is at one with Hegel and Marx in conceiving of social theory as a critical, comprehensive project. Like Hegel and Marx she envisages the project for a critical political economy as incorporating centrifugal claims for recognition and centripetal claims to establish a just distribution of resources. Nancy Fraser's work stands out as a contemporary attempt to renew the project of a critical political economy in a new post-Marxist context. For Fraser, this new context, which is constituted in part by the emergence of divergent identity claims and in part by the global impact of capital, is one in which the prospect of the proletariat achieving a unificatory form of global emancipation is redundant.

Fraser's work, however, remains programmatic and it leaves questions unresolved, notably on the continued viability of contemporary economic structures. Rosemary Hennesy, in a sympathetic but critical review of *Justice Interruptus: Critical Reflections on the Postsocialist Condition*, observes how Fraser does not provide systemic analysis of the economy, class or production, even if she signals the salience of economic issues as well as cultural ones, and points to the persistence of class. Hennessy is critical of Fraser's postdating of socialism, condemning her uncritical perspective on the contemporary turn away from historical materialism. She observes,

> conceptualising political economy in terms of distribution forfeits the opportunity to acknowledge that under capitalism there are and historically have always been uneven, complex material conditions between the unequal relations of production (another way of understanding class) and the production of identities, knowledge and culture (Hennessy 1999, p. 128)

Fraser's work intimates the continuing relevance of Hegel and Marx without highlighting the ways in which they are of contemporary relevance. She calls for the simultaneous resolution of cultural and economic questions without engaging with historic critical dialectical theories, whose relational, inclusive approaches are designed to achieve exactly this critical and systematic resolution of questions. Certainly, the theoretical language of Hegel and Marx does not tally with the rhetoric of contemporary normative claims for cultural identity. For instance, they are relatively insensitive to issues of gender. Hegel's theory is decidedly androcentric, and contemporary feminism points to the contradiction in Hegel's reading of the social world, whereby the freedom of women is sacrificed on the altar of female subservience to men and the family. Marx, while gesturing at the need for women's capacities to be valued in a public recognitive world, tends to ignore issues of gender, underplaying, for instance, the role of women in domestic service. In so far as gender issues are imbricated with other social categories, however, the relational dialectical philosophies of Hegel and Marx offer models of how particular cultural categories such as gender and sexuality might be integrated within synoptic critiques of political economy. They see the world of work and production as offering structural possibilities for and constraints on human development, in restrictive notions of gender and sexuality might be seen arising in a wider context of social oppression and resistance. Moreover, both Hegel and Marx explain the structure of political economy by tracing its historical and social development, and their comprehensive investigations are paradigmatic for the kind of integrated account of social justice that Fraser aims to provide.

Fraser urges a bivalent approach, which combines redistributive and recognitive normative claims in a transformative, integrated review of political economy, but she does not spell out how structural transformation of society is to be achieved. Moreover, she indicates the conjunctural conditions of historical development, and highlights the significance of the current global age, but she does not provide a systematic historical conception of the character of the contemporary world. Marx and Hegel develop systematic ways of reviewing the present in the context of the past and conceive of the structure of political economy in *systematic*, integrated ways. It is because of the relational, constructive and conceptual patterns exhibited in the social world that political economy is to be explained and appraised in terms of the patterns it inscribes in relation to more general criteria of human identity. Fraser's work intimates but does not elaborate upon the continued relevance of Hegel and Marx and the project of critical political economy. For Fraser, recognition and distribution are falsely opposed, but both recognition and distribution imply structures within which judgements are to be made. Hegel is a theorist of social recognition, who takes mutual recognition to be the resolution of the dilemmas of social interaction, but mutual social recognition demands integration within a community in which the economy operates productively and freely but subject to interventions that curb its arbitrariness. Marx, notwithstanding Fraser's schematised model of a Marxist notion of the proletariat, takes the proletariat to become a class for itself in developing a collective consciousness, breaking with the divisiveness of class society, and allowing for the social recognition and acceptance of differences. It was only on the basis of this prospective cultural development that the overthrow of capital and the establishment of emancipatory social structures, allowing for mutual self-recognition amongst the people, could be established. Moreover, both Marx and Hegel predicate their conceptions of political economy on comprehensive readings of the modern world, which, while not furnishing precise maps of current global economic and cultural developments, nonetheless provide paradigms for critiquing political economy in a historical context.

References

Butler, J. (1990) *Gender Trouble*. New York: Routledge.

Fraser, N. (1997) *Justice Interruptus: Critical Reflections on the 'Postsocialist' Condition*. New York and London: Routledge.

Fraser, N. (2005) 'Mapping the Feminist Imagination: From Redistribution to Recognition to Representation', *Constellations* 12(3), 295–307.

Fraser, N. and A. Honneth (2003) *Redistribution or Recognition? A Political-Philosophical Exchange*. London and New York: Verso.

Fraser, N. and Sandra Lee Bartky (1992) *Revaluing French Feminism: Critical Essays on Difference, Agency and Culture*. Bloomington, IN: Indiana University Press.

Fraser, N. (1999) 'Social Justice in the Age of Identity Politics: Redistribution, Recognition and Participation', in L. Ray and A. Sayer (eds), *Culture and Economy After the Cultural Turn*. London: Sage.

Fraser, N. and L. Nicholson (1988) 'Social Criticism Without Philosophy: An Encounter Between Feminism and Postmodernism', *Theory, Culture and Society* 5(2–3) (June), 373–94.

Fraser, N. (1999) *Unruly Practices: Power, Discourse and Gender in Contemporary Social Theory*. Cambridge: Polity Press.

Hennessy, R. (1999) 'Book review, *Justice Interruptus: Critical Reflections on the "Postsocialist" Condition*. By Nancy Fraser', *Hypatia* 14(1).

Marx, K. (1996) *Later Political Writings*. Cambridge: Cambridge University Press.

Okin, S.M. (1979) *Women in Western Political Thought*. Princeton: Princeton University Press.

Thompson, S. 'Is Redistribution a Form of Recognition? Comments on the Fraser-Honneth Debate', *Contemporary Review of International Social and Political Philosophy* 8(1) (March), 85–102.

9

Hardt and Negri: *Empire, Multitude* and Globalisation

9.1 Introduction

In *Empire* and *Multitude: War and Democracy in the Age of Empire* Hardt and Negri offer a radical reading of the contemporary world political economy and an agenda for revolutionary change. Their radicalism is presented as new. They perceive the contemporary world as operating in a novel way. Political power is no longer concentrated in states; state sovereignty has given way to imperial sovereignty. Hardt and Negri are theorists of globalisation, who take the contemporary world to function in a way that is distinct from its modern past. The power that states have harnessed and wielded and which has been criticised by preceding modern critics is no longer to be inspected and denounced from a standpoint that is situated outside the boundaries of the power exercised by states and empire. New imperial power is exercised globally and has no inside or outside. They observe,

> There is a long tradition of modern critique dedicated to denouncing the dualisms of modernity. The standpoint of that critical tradition, however, is situated in the paradigmatic place of modernity itself, both 'inside' and 'outside', at the threshold of the point of crisis. What has changed in the passage to the imperial world, however, is that the border no longer exists, and thus the modern critical strategy tends no longer to be effective. (Hardt and Negri 2000, p. 183)

The corollary of empire, for Hardt and Negri, is a new agent of emancipatory revolution, the multitude. The multitude differs from preceding social subjects that have been designated as agents of liberation. Its identity is neither given nor specifiable; it is to be achieved via heterogeneous

169

activities. In *Multitude* Hardt and Negri observe,

> As a first approach we should distinguish the multitude at a conceptual level from other notions of social subjects, such as the people, the masses and the working class. The *people* has traditionally been a unitary conception. The population, of course, is characterized by all kinds of differences, but the people reduces that diversity to a unity and makes of the population a single identity: 'the people' is one. The multitude, in contrast, is many. The multitude is composed of innumerable internal differences that can never be reduced to a unity or single identity. . . (Hardt and Negri 2004, p. xiv)

Just as Hardt and Negri claim to be dealing with radically new objects of social investigation, so they also announce an innovative theoretical framework. In the preceding quotation from *Empire*, they expressly distance themselves from a critical tradition presuming a metaphorical space between critique and its object. For Hardt and Negri there is no inside and outside, whereby imperial power can be sequestered for external critique, and there is no critical and emancipatory pathway that can be discerned and mapped out on behalf of the multitude. They designate no essentialized core to the character of the multitude; for there are simply multitudinous acts that in their irreducible plurality create a 'common' emancipation. Hardt and Negri align theory and practice by identifying novel social subjects and espouse a new form of radical theory. Empire constitutes a form of global power that demands conceptual elaboration to be recognised, for it is insusceptible of straightforward empirical designation. Imperial power is neither distinct from nor exercised in opposition to state power. The evident influence and power that is exerted by the USA in the contemporary world does not in itself undermine the arguments of Hardt and Negri over the operation of a new globalised form of empire. The level at which imperial power operates is conceptually but not empirically distinct from that of states, so that the power of the USA is co-extensive empirically with the operation of a new form of power, that of global empire. Likewise, the revolutionary impetus of the multitude is exercised in discrete campaigns against particular grievances or forms of repression, for example, campaigns of the landless movement in Brazil or those of the Save the Narmada movement in India are to be taken as enacting a common resistance to imperial power (see Hardt and Negri 2004, pp. 280 and 282).

   Hardt and Negri's recasting of the framework for social and political analysis harmonises with the contemporary revision of populist radicalism. The current anti-capitalist movement rejects the discipline and hierarchy associated with traditional leftist movements and traditional Marxism in particular (see Tormey 2004, p. 172). Anti-capitalism is neither focused upon specific states nor preoccupied with particular issues; it is a movement of movements targeting a diversity of targets rather than acting as a centrally co-ordinated party directed to the achievement of pre-formulated goals. Negri recognises the identity between his standpoint and the contemporary practice of anti-capitalist and anti-globalisation movements. In *Negri on Negri*, he observes, 'And another thing: with Genoa the antiglobalization forces became truly globalized for the first time. The fate of the world destined by the G8 for war rested on the testimony of the *noglobal* protestors alone. These protestors thus became a multitude in every sense of the term . . .' (Negri 2004, p. 76).

If Hardt and Negri's open-ended, pluralistic reading of the multitude is aligned to the contemporary practice of the anti-capitalist movement, then the focus of their de-alignment with the past is their opposition to the critical dialectical style of Hegel and Marx. Marx and Marxism serve as paradigmatic bearers of critical theory from which Hardt and Negri aim to break. In *Multitude* Hardt and Negri define the multitude by opposing it to the notion of the proletariat. They observe, 'the concept of the multitude is meant to repropose Marx's political project of class struggle' (Hardt and Negri 2004, p. 105). They urge that the notion of the proletariat or the working class has tended to operate restrictively, in which particular kinds of work and activity are privileged and prioritised. In contrast, the notion of the multitude embraces all categories of worker that resist the prevailing imperial order. Hardt and Negri note, 'In contrast, to the exclusions that characterize the concept of the working class, then, the multitude is an open and expansive concept' (Hardt and Negri 2004, p. 107). Hardt and Negri self-consciously oppose Marxist theory and practice by highlighting the complete socialization of labour in the contemporary world, which they assume entails the redundancy of a critique of capital purporting to rest on a universal measure of value (Hardt and Negri 2004, pp. 140–53).

As well as contesting key aspects of Marxist theory, Hardt and Negri abrogate Marx's treatment of history in accepting the postmodern disavowal of grand narratives of historical development. They break with dialectical, teleological standpoints, which assimilate the past to what is implied in an imputed end of its development. In repudiating dialectics, they disassociate themselves from Hegel as well as Marx, condemning the content and the form of Hegel's philosophy. They perceive Hegel to provide, 'the self-satisfied and triumphant conception of the sovereignty of the modern state' (Hardt and Negri 2000, p. 90). Hegel is impugned for his vindication of the modern state and capital. Hegel's theory of sovereignty is derogated for celebrating the role of capital in sustaining the state, and for exalting the state as the supreme, sovereign body. Hardt and Negri see state sovereignty as anachronistic, and Hegel's celebration of it as constituting the end of history is presumed to signal the unwarranted closure perpetrated by his philosophical method. Hardt and Negri are postmodern in their opposition to a closed reading of history. For Hardt and Negri, openness is inscribed in the historical process and this openness is distorted by dialectical teleology, which aims to bridge the gaps between historical actors and actions so that the past is seen as leading inexorably to a predetermined end.

In providing a radical theory of globalisation and a new agenda for revolution Hardt and Negri highlight significant aspects of the contemporary world. Sovereignty is undoubtedly complex in a contemporary world, in which agencies operating at differing levels intersect, and forms of transnational interaction proliferate. Contemporary radicalism is resolutely opposed to the discipline and central organisation characterising communist movements in the twentieth century. History is a contingent process, whose conceptual presuppositions of agency and alternative courses of action disturb deterministic teleological readings of progress and regress (see Collingwood 1999). But Hardt and Negri's criticisms of Hegel and Marx and the project of critical political economy are problematic. They ascribe closure to Hegel and Marx's dialectical method, assuming that Hegel and Marx's critical readings of the modern world operate from a closed position *outside* the phenomena with which they deal. They also attribute to Hegel and Marx a clear specifiable ending to the substantive process of history in the shape of the modern state and proletarian revolution. These ascriptions of closure in the form and substance of Hegel and Marx's theories are at the least contestable. Hegel and Marx can be read in a multitude of ways, and their conceptions of the modern state and revolution should not be seen as determinate, fixed endings to historical development. As Carver (1999) observes, the advent of postmodernism can legitimate open readings of Marx.

Hardt and Negri's explanatory map of the contemporary world operates by making comprehensive claims about its development and by connecting diverse diachronic and synchronic phenomena. The area covered by this explanatory map is of a piece with the grand narratives that they and postmodernism more generally stigmatize. Hardt and Negri share with Hegel and Marx a *global* style of theorising. This shared style embraces the content and form of their theorising. Hegel and Marx develop forms of world history. For Hegel, the modern state is sovereign, but the meaning of this form of sovereignty and its affiliated political economy is evidenced in world history. World history operates as a court of judgement in which the general significance of the modern development of freedom is to be judged. For Marx, capital is neither a local nor a limitable phenomenon, for it is of the essence of capital that it develops and that it extends its networks on a global scale. Likewise, Hardt and Negri rehearse Hegel and Marx's theoretical ambition, sharing a common tendency to explain complex phenomena via systemic causes and to minimise qualifying an overarching theory of historical development.

In particular, there is continuity between Hegel and Marx's theories of the world-historical significance of the modern state and the proletariat and Hardt and Negri's identification of empire and multitude as culminating points of the historical process. Hegel begins his *Lectures on the Philosophy of History* by remarking on its global content, observing that his philosophical history is a history of the world, which is universal in orientation (Hegel 1956, p. 12). In developing a systematic dialectical system of thought that connects its concepts, Hegel turns to the history of how human relations have become generalised to become of world significance. The modern European world for Hegel is significant on a global basis, and the modern state constitutes the end of the historical process, in the sense that it consummates the notion of freedom. Likewise Marx interprets capitalism as globalising in its reach. Mankind, for Marx, is social, and individuals are constituted by their social relations and capital develops this sociality by extending patterns of relations across the globe as well as intensifying the social aspects of human activities. The completion of this process of socialisation is to be achieved by the projected world revolution of the proletariat. Hardt and Negri read history as leading to the global power of empire; preceding forms of sovereignty are superseded by the direction of historical development ushering in a new kind of sovereignty. Likewise the emancipation that is to be enacted by the multitude is signposted by contemporary developments, notably the global spatial and temporal power exercised by empire. Hardt and Negri read past, present and future in the light of a theory that discriminates the normative significance of empire and multitude as imparting an overriding directionality to the innumerable events that compose the historical process.

Marx and Hegel reflect upon how they are able to link diachronic and synchronic events and levels of analysis. They provide a critical interpretive and unifying framework for the sets of processes that they identify and offer a justification of their critical perspective. Hardt and Negri, however, reject critical dialectical political economy, and emphasise their postdating of Marxism. In so doing Hardt and Negri exaggerate their originality and thereby underplay significant aspects of their work. In fact, like Hegel and Marx they entertain a grand narrative of historical development, and they frame their reading of historical events within a teleological perspective. Their claim to develop a distinctive postmodern and immanent radicalism masks their debts to dialectical predecessors. Their egalitarian emancipatory and abstract conceptualisation of the multitude rehearses aspects of Marx's reading of the proletariat, for whom he prescribed neither a precise route to, nor a detailed plan for its post-revolutionary activity.

The multitude, like the proletariat, is determined by its historical context in that preceding diachronic conditions have opened up the global possibilities of freedom, and the logic of emancipation for the multitude, as for the proletariat, precludes determination of the course of revolutionary action. In *Multitude* Hardt and Negri acknowledge more directly their debt to Marx's concepts and methods, admitting to a suspicion that their thesis has been anticipated (Hardt and Negri 2004, p. 141). Nonetheless, their distinctive postmodern standpoint purports to break decisively with the dialectical heritage of Marxism. In the succeeding analysis of this chapter, Hardt and Negri's key concepts, empire and multitude will be examined and their affinity in both form and content with the theories of their dialectical predecessors will be highlighted. Hardt and Negri operate with interconnected concepts that draw upon Hegel and Marx in developing a generalised theory of history and the present, which is revealed to be problematic given that its logic and status is largely unjustified.

9.2 Empire, multitude and essentialism

Empire by Hardt and Negri has become what Murphy and Mustapha term 'a lightning rod for criticism from the left and right as well as a fundamental point of reference for many activists in the growing struggle over globalization' (Murphy and Mustapha 2005b, p. 1). *Multitude* continues the controversy generated by the former book in amplifying their notion of the multitude, designated by Hardt and Negri to be the revolutionary agent of the destruction of empire. *Empire* and *Multitude* assume and subvert the language of globalisation, maintaining a postmodern revisionary conceptualisation of the social and political landscape. *Empire* is an elaborated engagement with the theory and practice of what has become the distinguishing concept of the contemporary world, globalisation. It rehearses standard features of globalisation theory, which postdate the narratives of preceding radical forms of political economy, for example the incorporation and eclipse of nation-state sovereignty in wider global power networks, the prevalence of decentred, de-territorialising apparatuses of political economic power such as the World Bank and the identification of a new phase of production characterised by intensive socialisation and mediatisation.

Empire and the succeeding *Multitude* rehearse standard features of accounts of globalisation signposting an alternative emancipatory future. Hardt and Negri reject the entire political economy underlying contemporary dispositions of power, and thereby undercut the celebratory rhetoric of contemporary western politicians and theorists, who either endorse the neo-liberal form of the global economy or call for its mere modification. They provide a radical subversion of contemporary globalism, by their injection into its topography of a new conceptualisation of contemporary global power and an innovative depiction of an agency of global emancipation (see Walker 2002, p. 341). Hardt and Negri maintain the irreversibility of globalisation and acknowledge its wholesale socialisation of production, but they project the prospective supersession of prevailing imperial power.

Hardt and Negri's innovative radicalism, however, is problematic on account of their unconvincing essentialised reading of key terms. The multitude for Hardt and Negri is defined as instantiating singularity and commonality. The radical socialisation of production at a global level is taken to entail that all emancipatory struggles against prevailing forms of globalised power are immediately conjoined. Just as empire is a universal form of global power so the multitude is an immediately universal entity that is composed of innumerable forms of resistance to empire. Negri observes the necessary simultaneous plurality, singularity and universality of the multitude in *Kairos, Alma, Venus, Multitudo*, 'The postmodern multitude is an ensemble of singularities . . . if the singularities that constitute the multitude are plural, the manner in which they enter into relations is co-operative' (Negri 2000, in Negri 2003, pp. 233–4). In *Negri on Negri*, Negri maintains this apparently discordant character of the multitude by asserting its irreducible plurality, while investing it with a cohesive ontological power to incarnate desire and to transform the world' (Negri 2004, pp. 111–12). Hence the multitude exists as a plurality of independent subjects, but it is at the same time reified as an essential entity, assuming powers of cohesive collective agency. Laclau observes incredulously, 'the unity of the multitude results from the spontaneous aggregation of a plurality of actions that do not need to be articulated between themselves' (Laclau 2004, p. 26, in Passavant and Dean 2004). Hardt and Negri's essentialised notion of the multitude in practice abstracts from the divergencies between the material conditions of the poor and oppressed in different parts of the world. As Bull (2003, 89) notes, 'It is difficult to see how this analysis (of the multitude) comprehends the reality of powerlessness.'

The essentialised character of the multitude harmonises with the stipulated universality of the concept of empire. Empire is both plural and unitary, signposting a topography of power, a configuration of sovereignty that is decentred and flexible and yet relentlessly co-ordinated in its exercise of hegemony. Empire is not a form of hegemony exercised by a state, in which the manner of ruling can be seen as a means separate from and instrumental to the ends pursued by a hegemonic state. The hybrid dispersed forms of domination exercised by empire are not forms assumed by a distinct and self-contained political power; empire is the universality of power exhibited and maintained in its diverse forms of domination. These claims about the novel unity of empire are difficult to substantiate because they are shielded from empirical discrimination by imperial rhetoric, which obscures the conceptualisation that in fact determines its alleged character. Hardt and Negri invoke empirical phenomena to support their arguments in *Empire* and affiliated writings, but, given the ubiquity of the power that empire is presumed to maintain, their reference to examples of imperial power are suggestively illustrative rather than offering precise empirical evidence of a clearly specifiable entity (see Barkawi and Laffey 2002, p. 111).

Hardt and Negri make a virtue out of empire's lack of a precise articulated conceptual structure. Like the multitude it is a subject, which is designated to operate as a pure plurality. It is construed as a pure plurality, precluding the dialectical combination of unity and multiplicity in a structured and developmental way (see Deleuze and Guattari 1988). While Hardt and Negri's characterisation of a range of diverse empirical phenomena as being essentially unified in terms of the constitution of empire and the multitude, the phenomena and the concepts necessarily lack clear articulation. Their argument for the sovereignty of empire depends not so much on the specification of new and clear-cut empirical political phenomena but by elaborated rhetorical designation. Empire, for Hardt and Negri, is a paradigm of political power that is both systemic and ubiquitous. 'The systematic totality (of empire) has a dominant position in the global order, breaking resolutely with every previous dialectic and developing an integration of actors that seems linear and spontaneous. At the same time however, the effectiveness of the consensus under a supreme authority of the ordering appears ever more clearly' (Hardt and Negri 2000, p. 14). The identification of empire is not to be read off unproblematically by apprising empirical phenomena, for its specification turns upon recognising phenomena to reflect a level of operation and set of values that supersede the state and localised forms of power. Hence, for Hardt and Negri, the values to which forms of power are directed and to which everything is attuned, are the promotion of imperial order and the cessation of conflict (Hardt and Negri 2000, p. 38). Imperial sovereignty is decentred, operates via deterritorialized apparatuses of rule and yet establishes a common global power.

The advertised globality of empire renders it impervious to external critique and occludes easy identification of its distinguishing empirical features. Its purview includes the smooth operation of hierarchical forms of power and disruptive forms of rule, where rebellion is endemic. Recalcitrant phenomena, such as the emergence of local or regional forces antagonistic to higher forms of control, are taken to be the necessary outlets of energy and dissonance that enable the system to reproduce itself. Hardt and Negri, however, indicate contemporary empirical phenomena that highlight the operations of imperial sovereignty. They point to an increasing reliance on global policing, a developing role for international institutions such as the United Nations and, above all, an acceptance of a right of intervention, whether undertaken by international institutions or powerful states. They remark,

> Now supranational subjects that are legitimated not by right but by consensus intervene in the name of any type of emergency and superior ethical principles. What stands behind this intervention is not just a permanent state of emergency and exception, but a permanent state of emergency and exception justified by *the appeal to essential values of justice.* In other words, the right of the police is legitimated by universal values. (Hardt and Negri 2000, p. 18)

Hardt and Negri's reading of the current empirical situation is suggestive without being compelling. While the ending of the Cold War has ushered in a new historical situation, the postdating of preceding dualities is insufficient in itself to herald the advent of an imperial power that is global in its reach and that is absolutely distinct from what has gone before. The USA under Bush's presidency is prepared to operate on is own initiative in offensive operations, such as the war against Iraq, and is relaxed about resisting pressure from other nations to support international environmental initiatives. Hardt and Negri, though, are not disturbed by the relative autonomy of the USA, for their conceptual reading of empire stretches so as to include unilateral operations by the USA. The USA is held to play a privileged role in the operations of empire. In *Multitude* they diagnose the contemporary global condition as being one of a permanent state of war, echoing Hobbes's diagnosis of the conditions predisposing the absolute sovereignty of the nation-state. They imagine that in this contemporary state of war the USA simultaneously prosecutes its own interests and works for the co-ordination of global, ideological concerns such as the promotion of human rights. In pressing their case, they urge, 'We should not get caught up here in the tired debates about globalization and nation-states as if the two were necessarily incompatible' (Hardt and Negri 2004, p. 60). Their recognition of the complexity of contemporary sovereignty is plausible, but they do not provide a convincing account of how contemporary international political actions might be deconstructed so as to show how the national and global aspects of political action are to be distinguished as well as combined. A convincing analysis of the contemporary operations of power requires pertinent distinctions to be made about how power is being exercised in specific situations and why and how it makes sense to identify national or trans-national aspects of its exercise.

Hardt and Negri develop the notion of empire by invoking suggestive yet indeterminate features. For instance, they intimate the illimitable aspect of empire by associating it with the sense of the inexorably expanding American frontier (Hardt and Negri 2000, pp. 160–82). It is a metaphor that harmonises with the key role of the USA in contemporary global transactions and also suggests without constraining the elasticity of their sense of empire. It trades upon the mythic quality of the frontier in the American imagination. Hardt and Negri's essentialised account of the contemporary condition of empire provides an evocative sense of the power that is exercised in the name of international causes. Their analysis of global imperial sovereignty provide a rationale for the way in which the exercise and defence of global power is currently trans-national. They point to the character of modern warfare as demanding its prosecution on a networked, non-hierarchical basis so as to counteract the networked, global character of contemporary resistance to empire (Hardt and Negri 2004, p. 62). They do not, however, specify how the networked opposition to empire actually operates. International terrorist and resistance groups are not examined in detail and the actual conduct of recent wars is not investigated. The foreign policy of the USA and its wartime mode of operations are likewise under-researched.

9.3 The end of critique or revisiting dialectic

Hardt and Negri claim to be offering a new and distinctive perspective. Central to their claim to originality is their sense of breaking with the past, and more specifically of dishing critique and critical political economy. In his account of Negri's theory and political practice between 1968 and 1973, 'Into the Factory: Negri's Lenin and the Subjective Caesura (1968–1973)' Hardt emphasises how Negri rightly distances himself from the standpoint of a critical political economy that assumes an external perspective from which to criticise capital. He remarks,

> The critical approach never adequately deals with the subjectivity of the actual working class; the critique of capital never succeeds in unifying itself with the standpoint of the working class so as to recognise the proletariat as the effective agent of social transformation. (Hardt 2005, p. 14)

Hardt and Negri in *Empire* and *Multitude* are suspicious of a critical theoretical approach that purports to dictate how history will develop and how social realities are to be articulated according to an external dialectical logic. They contrast the immanence of their standpoint to what they take to be the external teleological dialectic of Hegel and Marx. Where Hegel and Marx are stigmatised for operating by means of logical or scientific doctrines, purporting to be independent from the phenomena to which they are applied, Hardt and Negri aim to limit themselves to the immanent conditions of historical development.

Hardt and Negri's claims to originality and their repudiation of dialectical critique can be criticised, however, on at least two counts. On the one hand, their disavowal of Marx and Hegel and their practice of critical political economy is problematic. They repudiate what they take to be the closure and externality of Hegel and Marx, without examining in detail the actual operations of Hegel and Marx's dialectical perspectives. Hegel and Marx can be interpreted in differing ways. Chapters 2 and 3 of this book have urged the openness and immanence of Hegel and Marx's dialectical theorising. On the other hand, the immanence of Hardt and Negri's own advertised postmodern perspective depends crucially on a reading of history and the present in terms of a framework of thought that is highly schematic and implicitly dialectical. They proclaim a pure immanentism, dispensing with dialectic and teleology, but their radical theory of globalisation intertwines its key concepts of empire and multitude, and recognises these notions to operate within a wider web of concepts encompassing past, present and future. This web of concepts revisits the dialectical paradigms of Hegel and Marx. Fitzpatrick in, 'The Immanence of *Empire*', notes how this interdependence of empire and multitude establishes a conceptual frame for supposedly purely immanent events, redolent of those theorists and power regimes that Hardt and Negri purport to subvert. He observes, 'With some wariness, then, the objection to Hardt's and Negri's *Empire* pursued here is that its founding ontology of liberation is ultimately at one with the very *imperium* it is so resolutely directed against' (Fitzpatrick 2004, p. 31 in Passavant and Dean 2004).

In *Multitude*, their successor to *Empire*, Hardt and Negri consider possible criticisms of their methodological standpoint. In doing so, they expressly consider a possible Hegelian critique of their standpoint. They conjecture,

> One criticism, the Hegelian criticism, sees the multitude as merely another version of the traditional dialectic relation between the One and the Many, especially when we pose the primary dynamic of contemporary global politics as a struggle between Empire and the multitude. (Hardt and Negri 2004, p. 225)

In refuting this indictment, they argue unconvincingly that their reading of concepts allows for a relational dynamic and the possibility of the multitude operating autonomously (Hardt and Negri 2004, p. 225). In disavowing the symmetrical dichotomy between the One and the Many, however, Hardt and Negri are not effectively distancing themselves from Hegel and Marx. Hegel allows for multiple reading of identity and difference, with the concrete development of identity incorporating increasingly determinate modes of negation that allow for a non-dichotomous relationship between identity and non-identity. Hegel's sensitive reading of Plato's *Parmenides* is devoted to showing how Plato reads the One and the Many in differing but related ways, so that in some sense their relationship is symmetrical and dichotomous but in other senses they are distinct and other (see Hegel 1892, pp. 1–10). Similarly Marx envisages the proletariat as emerging from the structures of capital to which it is related, but he also maintains that proletarians are capable of constructing their own post-capitalist identities.

Hardt and Negri's sensitivity to dialectical critique is warranted because the conceptual character of empire emerges most clearly out of reflection upon its dialectical interdependence with the multitude and with the ubiquitous, global force of capital. Just as Marx perceives the dynamic of state forms to reflecting the functional requirements of economic interests, so the novel forms of power exercised by the operations of empire are related to the exigencies of capital. The motive force behind the dynamic of empire's hegemony is the momentum of global capital. Global capital orders the completely socialised world of production, which incorporates industrial, transactional, co-operative and affective labour. Hardt and Negri's conceptualisation of the unrelenting dynamic of imperial power harmonises with their conception of the illimitable force of global capital. They assert, 'The absoluteness of imperial power is the complementary term to its complete immanence to the ontological machine of production and reproduction, and thus to the biopolitical context' (Hardt and Negri 2000, p. 41). For Hardt and Negri contemporary global capital no longer operates within a sequestered sphere of production, but rather directs universal biopower.

For Hardt and Negri capital and empire are mutually reinforcing agencies that preclude an external critical perspective. They deny the possibility of a critical standpoint by which history can be ordered and the future projected by reference to a supposedly underlying force that is insulated from the open creative possibilities of the multitude and that is external to the hierarchical system of prevailing power. They deny an essential agency of radical change to a preformulated entity that is detached from prevailing hegemonic forces. Negri, in *Kairos, Alma, Venus, Multitudo*, derides critiques of constitutive power, because they become involved in complex relational patterns of thought that link the possibilities for future initiative action to an opposition to past forms. Negri looks to a postmodern openness in the creative decision of the multitude. He remarks, 'Dialectics, in so far as it is the capitalist (bourgeois and/or socialist) form of transcendental thinking of Power, is incapable of grasping the power of the relation of poverty and love in the decision' (Negri 2000, in Negri 2003, p. 251). Hardt and Negri's disavowal of dialectics and critique assumes that a dialectical critical political economy operates by framing an external logical basis for the critique of existing society. Their own theoretical practice, however, can be said to be dialectical and critical in so far as they connect concepts and forms of practice with one another. For instance, they gloss resistance to global capital and imperial power as integral to the maintenance and development of empire. They observe,

> These struggles, however, have their own weight, their own specific intensity, and moreover they are immanent to the procedures and developments of imperial power. They invest and sustain the processes of globalization themselves. Imperial power whispers the names of the struggles in order to charm them into passivity, to construct a mystified image of them, but most important to discover which processes of globalization are possible and which are not. (Hardt and Negri 2000, p. 59)

Hardt and Negri read the disunities of space and time as being superseded by the unifying economic operations of production and consumption, which have now become thoroughly socialised so that mediation is part of the operation of universal biopower that precludes a division of the economic from the social and cultural. Hardt and Negri point to the mediating role of trans-national corporations and communications networks in promoting progressive global unification. Their understanding of the role of capital in the development of globalism is closely affiliated to Marx's sense of the infinite dynamic of capital in reproducing and increasing itself (see Marx 1974, p. 102; Browning 1998; and Arthur 1998). Hardt and Negri, however, take their reading of the economic sphere to be distinct from that of Marx. Crucial to their designation of *Empire* as a postmodern and post-Marxist text is its highlighting of the comprehensive socialization of production. They invoke the universality of biopower in the operations of the global economy rather than what they take to be Marx's restrictive notion of materialist production. They urge that a sphere of material production can no longer be separated from an immaterial social and cultural world. They deny the separation of production from life. In *Empire* they observe,

> In the bipolitical sphere, life is made to work for production and production is made to work for life. It is a great hive in which the queen bee continuously oversees production and reproduction. The deeper the analysis goes, the more it finds at increasing levels of intensity the interlinking assemblages of interactive relationships. (Hardt and Negri 2000, p. 32)

Hardt and Negri's criticism of Marx's conception of production harmonises with their inclusive notion of the multitude. Resistance to empire is not to be restricted to those who produce in traditional forms. Hardt and Negri maintain an expressly post-Marxist notion of immaterial production, according to which what contributes to production cannot be isolated and catalogued as pertaining to a distinct sphere of activity. In *Multitude* they observe that production is no longer susceptible of being analysed a staking place in a definite time span. Post-Fordist production blurs time divisions (see Hardt and Negri 2004, p. 146). If production is no longer a material occupation, then the activity of production is not to be encapsulated by specific designated periods of production time. Creative ideas, for instance, to be creative cannot be produced on demand; they are generated during and outside working hours. Likewise contemporary products may not be self-contained commodities serving the needs of self-contained independently identifiable social consumers. Rather, they might constitute the means and expression of communication and affective life, and hence be inherently social rather than individualised. The fun of texting and the reflective iterations involved in manipulating a powerful search engine are signature expressions of emotive and communicative life of the twenty-first century.

In a variety of works Negri has registered his sense of the redundancy of key aspects of Marxist analysis. In *Marx Beyond Marx: Lessons On The Grundrisse*, he critiques Marx's conception of labour, commenting, 'In fact, the Marxist definition of productive labour is a reductive definition, which is linked to the socialist axiology of manual labour' (Negri 1991, p. 183). Surin, in 'Now Everything must be Reinvented: Negri and Revolution', refers to what he takes to be the defining feature of Negri's works.

> . . . the notion which perhaps provides all Negri's other principles and themes with their *modus operandi* is the one of 'real subsumption', that is the process whereby labour power and capitalist command are extended throughout the social field, a development which in turn makes production inseparable from communication, with the outcome that (all) production is now, unavoidably social production. (Sorin 2005, p. 206)

Negri maintains that the contemporary conditions of production disallow the formulation of a critique of capital, resting upon a generalisable logic of the labour process, independent of the specific modalities of the capitalist economic formation. Negri rejects the counterposing of use value to exchange value, because the use value of labour power only has meaning in the sphere of the capitalist determination of exchange value. Negri attributes to Marx the project of establishing a transcendental critique of political economy and he denies the possibility of a non-immanent reading of contradiction, maintaining instead that contemporary capital subsumes all production under its network of relations. In *The Constitution of Time* he argues,

> If social labour covers all the time of life, and invests all of its regions, how can time measure the substantive totality in which it is implicit? In this way we are brought back to the earlier conclusions. We find ourselves before a tautology that after presenting itself *intensively* as the impossibility of distinguishing the measure of the differentiation of the substance of value, reproposes itself extensively as the impossibility

of distinguishing the totality of life (of the social relations of production and reproduction) from the totality of time from which this life is woven. (Negri 1997, in Negri 2003, p. 29)

For Negri and Hardt contemporary empire and capitalism do not allow for critical perspectives that transcend the actual operations of global capital and imperial sovereignty.

Hardt and Negri's postdating of Marxism and their specification of the originality of their own perspective are problematic, for Marx's writings, as Negri himself acknowledges, are ambiguous, and Marx's alleged materialism and productivism are controversial. On a materialist reading of Marx, production is emphatically material and distinct from cultural relations, but to divorce material production from social relations is to deny how particular modes of production are implicated in specific social forms, such as capitalist relations of production, which constitute forces of production. Marx's identification of labour power as the key force production, does not signify a reading of production whereby social relations do not shape the meaning and reality of labour power; notwithstanding Cohen's celebrated interpretation of Marx's theory of history relations and forces of production are conceptually interrelated (see Cohen 1978). The generality of the *Grundrisse*'s conceptualisation of production is an express process of abstraction that presumes the mutual implication of concepts in historical and social processes (see Chapter 3 of this book; Carver 1998 ch. 3; Marx 1974; and Marx and Engels 1976).

Notwithstanding their criticisms of Marx's political economy, Hardt and Negri's conceptual map of a global economy of empire draws upon a Marxist framework of explanation. Empire follows the immanent logic of capitalist development, the circuits of capital constituting a globalised infinity of transactions whereby an endless supersession of barriers to the operation of expanding circuits ensures that its processes of mediation supersede material and cultural obstacles impeding an inherently globalising process. This process ensures that the merely local, in terms of capital and resistance, is an abstraction from a globalised world of economic and political operations. Marx, like Hegel before him, had conceived of world history as being the consummation of mankind's inherent sociality, and yet this resonance between Marx's social theory and the perspective of *Empire* and *Multitude* does not deter Hardt and Negri from advertising a radical break from the preceding dialectical theories of Hegel and Marx.

Hardt and Negri emphasise that their break from a dialectical perspective is motivated by their concern both to deconstruct the imperial order and to allow for the affirmative, positive construction of a new ethico-political alternative society. They take the dialectical form of Hegelian and Marxist critique to restrict the possibilities of both construction and deconstruction. They expressly deny that they are operating with a philosophy of history and they decry the Hegelian image of philosophy as the Owl of Minerva, theorising the order of historical development in the wake of events (Hardt and Negri 2000, p. 49). They insist, 'This approach breaks methodologically with every philosophy of history insofar as it refuses any deterministic conception of historical development and any rational celebration of the result' (Hardt and Negri 2000, p. 49). Despite their protestations against undertaking a philosophy of history, Hardt and Negri do identify the future possibilities of the multitude by relating them to the current order of imperial rule, which in turn is seen as emerging historically. In *Empire* they remark,

> It is a question of transforming a necessity imposed on the multitude – a necessity that was to a certain extent solicited by the multitude itself throughout modernity as a line of flight from localized misery and exploitation – into a condition of possibility of liberation, a new possibility on this new terrain of humanity. (Hardt and Negri 2000, p. 47)

Hardt and Negri's claim to originality and theoretical innovation is itself susceptible to dialectical critique. Their repudiation of dialectics is predicated upon their insistence on framing a purely immanent undermining of empire. They repudiate merely external critique, and instead point to 'the real alternatives and potentials for liberation that exist *within* Empire' (Hardt and Negri 2000, p. 47). Their normative understanding of empire, however, is shaped by their overlapping recognition of the prospective revolutionary liberation to be enacted by the multitude. If the character of empire and the multitude is reciprocally determined by the relations of resistance to the historical hegemony of empire, then Hardt and Negri are assuming a normative perspective on history implying a general interpretation of its development and directionality. The upshot is that they assume the very style of a teleological, dialectical reading of history, which rhetorically they are at pains to reject.

Hardt and Negri's reading of empire is sustained by a highly generalised interpretation of the logic of historical development. They take postmodernity to supersede modernity, and in doing so they are implicitly appraising the value and directionality of the modern and the postmodern. Likewise they understand the immateriality of biopower under conditions of new informational and communicative technologies to supersede preceding modern productive practices and a materialist view of labour.

Likewise just as Marx imagines capitalism to supersede feudalism, so they imagine imperial sovereignty to outstrip modern sovereignty in the form of the nation-state. The latter, in circumscribing the operation of hegemony, is as superseded as Old Europe. For Hardt and Negri, if modernity is European, postmodernity is American. Hardt and Negri's sensitivity to their apparent dialectical manipulation of concepts and their resort to a teleological reading of history inspire their concern to rebut the criticism that they are reworking rather than repudiating a dialectical style of theorising in their discussion of dialectic in *Multitude*. Here they recognise how their purely immanent unmasking of empire might be construed to be an unacknowledged reworking of dialectical thinking, but urge that their recognition of the interrelations between concepts defining past and present, allows for the emergence of what is distinct and different (Hardt and Negri 2004, p. 225).

Hardt and Negri's disavowal of a dialectical teleological reading of history implies that Hegel and Marx did not allow for the emergence of new forms in the historical process. This is a puzzling and defeasible claim. Civil society, the sphere of political economy, for Hegel, is identified precisely to be a new and significant form of modernity. While civil society can be recognised retrospectively to harmonise with the inherent freedom of the ego, Hegel is adamant that it is pointless to condemn a slave-owning society for failing to instantiate the freedoms of civil society. Civil society is a novel construction of modernity. Likewise capital, for Marx, is not an eternal category but a modern form. In identifying what is irreducibly new in modernity Hegel and Marx simultaneously connect new forms with one another and with past phenomena. In this respect Hardt and Negri follow the dialectical path of Hegel and Marx rather than pursuing a new course. Hardt and Negri present history as dialectical in their actual theoretical practice, even if they repudiate dialectics in their theoretical commentary on their practice. The meaning of new events and concepts, for them as it is for Hegel and Marx, is to be revealed by their interrelations and by preceding developments.

Hardt and Negri assume that the modern is superseded neatly by the postmodern, an assumption which lends itself to a reading of history in which progress is unilear and in which politics involves alignment with the directionality of history. The later Lyotard's reservations over his use of the term postmodernity reflect his own belated recognition of the susceptibility of his own discourse to the grand theorising that he sought to repudiate (Lyotard 1992). Hardt and Negri's reliance on a dialectical, relational reading of events and concepts is evidenced by the logical and practical dependence of empire upon the emancipatory potential of the multitude.

Their notion of the multitude performs a multitude of roles. It is the object of historical imperial development, and the deterritorialising mass of creative sociality subject to the power of empire. Its post-national, post-industrial character distinguishes its variegated resistance to empire from Marx's characterisation of the industrial proletariat's prospective revolution. At the same time, the emancipatory guise of the multitude implies a normative framework for their characterisation of imperial dominion and their reading of globalisation. The telos of global emancipation in Hardt and Negri's work provides a dramatic structure, whereby the figures of empire, the multitude, capital, and the postmodern form intersecting pieces of a grand narrative of historical development. Hardt and Negri's dialectical, teleological style rehearses Marxism and the tradition of critical political economy that they disavow, for they see the limitations of past and present to be exhibited and redeemed in a complete prospective emancipation from the fetters imposed upon social enactment in the imperial conditions of time and space.

Hardt and Negri sporadically address the question of the extent to which their claims to radical originality are compromised by the immanence of the multitude within the sphere of empire. They recognise how this immanence might be construed as of a piece with the perspectives of Marx and Machiavelli (Hardt and Negri 2000, p. 65). They are even prepared to concede that their standpoint might amount to a kind of teleology, but they insist it would only constitute a retrospective teleological reading of historical events (Hardt and Negri 2000, p. 44). To identify their teleological standpoint in this way, however, is not to distinguish their position decisively from that of Hegel and Marx. Hegel and Marx were themselves circumspect in their readings of history. Hegel took the essence of history to reside in the inherent freedom of historical agents, individuals located in political cultures that supersede the merely naturalistic ties of family and tribe. This free activity itself inspires the practice of historical writing that records and celebrates freedom in narrative form. Freedom is therefore central to the rise and practice of the study of history and Hegel recognises that a philosophical teleological reading of history must respect its fundamental presupposition, the freedom of historical actors. Philosophical history is a retrospective teleological interpretation of how freedom, a conceptual precondition of history, has been recognised and developed in history, rather than serving within a causal theory to predict the future (Hegel 1956). Likewise, Marx and Engels in *The German Ideology* are highly critical of fellow young Hegelians, such as Max Stirner, who distort the process of history by imposing upon it a preformulated teleological explanation of its development. Their materialistic reading

of history is a retrospective review of historical development that is expressly designed so as not to foreclose on the openness of historical events (Marx and Engels 1976). Hardt and Negri's *post festum* teleology does not differ profoundly from Hegel and Marx's treatment of history. Rustin is right to maintain, 'Hardt and Negri share – indeed take from – Hegel and Marx a teleological theory of historical development, in which each new evolution creates the potential for a fuller expression of human potential' (Rustin 2003, p. 2).

9.4 Conclusion

Hardt and Negri develop a comprehensive theory of the present, in which the contemporary postmodern globalised world is situated historically and at the same time subject to a transformative critique. They theorise significant and novel aspects of the contemporary situation, notably the current complexity of sovereignty in a global world, and the intensity and extensiveness of social connections. Their concern to capture the present conjuncture supports their presentation of their theory as being post-Marxist. They maintain what can be termed a form of post-critical political economy, because they highlight the supposed nondialectical, immaterial and supra-statist character. In an interview conducted for *Theory and Event* in 2000, Hardt disavows the label of Marxism for the standpoint developed by Negri and himself and prefers that they are seen as communist rather than Marxist because of the substantive criticisms that they have of Marx (see Hardt 2000). Hardt and Negri dispute what they take to be Marx's transcendental critique of capital, the externality of the dialectical method and they claim to develop new post-Marxist levels and objects of analysis, namely the notions of empire and multitude.

The elasticity and interrelations of the concepts of empire and multitude, though, are redolent of classic Marxist notions of class and proletarian universality. What makes the identification of empire complex is the conceptual level at which it is to be taken. Just as the Hegelian notion of the state does not replace civil society but transforms its meaning, so empire includes but does not replace states, IGOs and corporations. It evokes obedient clients and provokes absolute opposition. Empire accommodates a plurality of empirical practices, just as capital accommodates a range of forms of state. To explain a complex world requires a theoretical complexity that accommodates diverse entities, whose conceptual modes of operation differ profoundly. Empire is a superordinate entity, exercising a highly general form of power, and its appropriate conceptualisation demands it to be recognised as a highly generic concept,

overlapping with less generic ones. To reflexively conceptualise the patterns traced by the relations between more specific and more general concepts, however, is to revisit the dialectical conceptual world of Marx's *Grundrisse* and Hegel's *Logic*. Analysis of the conceptual behaviour of generic concepts such as empire and multitude demands elaboration of the logic of dialectical conceptual patterns that is conducted in those seminal texts. Marx's methodological *credo* in the introduction to the *Grundrisse* interestingly specifies a method, which is decidedly immaterial. Marx (1974) conceives of the world as thoroughly social, constituted by social relations that can only be captured by concepts, which trace their dialectical interrelations. Hardt and Negri's insistence on the post-Marxist status of their theory is at odds with the decided continuity between their notion of postmodern immateriality and the connectedness of concepts and Marx's reading of the social, relational character of production. Moreover, Hardt and Negri's reading of the generation and prospective transformation of the universality of contemporary biopower reflects the grand narratives of Hegel and Marx. The identification of the universality of biopower and the supersession of empire as progressive presupposes a dialectical reading of historical concepts, whereby they are appraised on a common gradational scale.

Hardt and Negri offer a singular yet hard-hitting thesis on globalisation. Globalisation is a contested concept, subject to ideological inflection, but proponents of globalisation standardly maintain that the contemporary world is distinguished from preceding eras by the intensity of its global interconnectedness. Neo-liberals endorse the simplifying logic of global capital, while Held is the most notable advocate of the renewal of the tenets of social democracy in the context of globalisation by enacting a cosmopolitan regime of rights (see Ohmae 1990; Held 1995, 2004; and Held *et al.* 1999). Hardt and Negri urge the revolutionary supersession of prevailing norms, and embrace the prospect of global revolution. In 'The Great Globalization Debate', Held and McGrew suggest, 'the very idea of globalization appears to disrupt established paradigms and political orthodoxies' (Held and McGrew 2000, p. 2). The standpoint of Hardt and Negri, however, while innovative in its inclusion of novel aspects of the contemporary situation such as the complexification of sovereignty continues rather than disrupts the dialectical developmental paradigm of Hegel and Marx. Marx and Hegel presumed that the impetus of world history was for it to become progressively more global and Marx's critical political economy was focused upon the revolutionary supersession of the global order of capital, just as Hardt and Negri imagine the multitude will overturn the imperial global order.

Generally, theories of globalisation have tended to accentuate their novelty and to underplay the conceptual connections between themselves and preceding large-scale theories of society. Hardt and Negri are not alone amongst contemporary theorists of globalisation in minimising the extent to which Hegel and Marx recognise the globality of historical development. This relative neglect of Hegel and Marx is unfortunate in that it thereby ignores the dialectical expertise with which Hegel and Marx deal with interlocking concepts. The burgeoning literature on globalisation displays an increasing conceptual refinement, and a readiness to admit that globalisation has a history as well as the propensity to generate ideological debate, and empirical disputes about the character of international trade (see Held 2004; Held *et al.* 1999; and Hirst and Thompson 1996). There remains a tendency, however, notwithstanding acknowledgement of the complexities of global developments and the idiosyncratic tempos of change in differing aspects of society and in different areas of the world, to assume that globalization constitutes a single phenomenon (see Held *et al.*, 1999).

The standard identification of an essential underlying process of globalisation, however, lends itself to reification as globalisation often assumes the guise of a thing that causes manifold events across the globe. Hegel and Marx can help us to guard against conceptual error, as they develop subtle paradigms of how a global world is to be conceived. Hegel sees philosophical world history as providing a conceptual frame within which empirical developments in history can be assessed, and Marx sees the logic of capital as providing a conceptual framework in which the development of global patterns of political economy can be understood and criticised. Hegel and Marx are sensitive to the divergent levels at which concepts operate and they avoid the reification of essentialised concepts. Hardt and Negri, in developing a radical theory of globalisation, accommodate new developments but like other theorists of globalisation exaggerate their claims to be theoretical innovators. They see themselves as breaking from the tradition of Hegel and Marx, but this break is more apparent than real. The form and substance of their theory reflect key aspects of Hegel and Marx's theories. Their criticisms of Hegel and Marx, though, should serve as reminders of how Hegel and Marx can be interpreted in many ways and that they are best seen as open theorists, who do not foreclose on historical development. Hardt and Negri's conceptualisation of empire and multitude reflects their tendency to perceive the world through interlocking concepts. Indeed, their conceptualisation of the multitude assumes a consistency of underlying class composition, which ignores the pluralism that they profess and corroborating empirical data. This disjunction is to be explained, according to Dyer-Witheford, as being motivated by a Marxist concern to establish a smooth conceptual opposition between empire and the multitude (Dyer-Witheford 2005, p. 154). While Dyer-Witheford's implicit characterisation of Marx may be doubted, he is right to identify conceptual links between Hardt and Negri and Marx's dialectical practice.

References

Arthur, C.J. (1998) 'The Infinity of Capital', *Studies in Marxism* no. 5, 17–36.

Balakrishnan, G. (ed.) (2003) *Debating Empire*. London: Verso.

Barkawi, T. and Laffey, M. (2002) 'Retrieving the Imperial: *Empire* and International Relations', *Millenium* 31(1), 109–27.

Browning, G.K. (1998) 'Infinity in Hegel and Marx', *Studies in Marxism* no. 5, 1–16.

Bull, M. (2003) 'You Can't Build a New Society with a Stanley Knife', in G. Balakrishnan (2003) *Debating Empire*. London: Verso.

Carver, T. (1998) *The Postmodern Marx*. Manchester: Manchester University Press.

Cohen, G.A. (1978) *Karl Marx's Theory of History: A Defence*. Oxford: Oxford University Press.

Collingwood, R.G. (1999) *The Idea of History*. Oxford: Oxford University Press.

Deleuze, G. and Guattari, F. (1988) *A Thousand Plateaus*. London: Athlone Press.

Dyer-Witheford, N. (2005) 'Cyber-Negri: General Intellect and Immaterial Labour', in T. Murphy and A.-K. Mustapha (eds), *The Philosophy of Antonio Negri*. London: Pluto Press.

Hardt, M. (2000) Interview with Thomas Dumm, 'Sovereignty, Multitudes, Absolute Democracy', *Theory and Event* 4(3).

Hardt, M. (2005) 'Into the Factory: Negri's Lenin and the Subjective Caesura (1968–73)', in T. Murphy and A.-K. Mustapha (eds), *The Philosophy of Antonio Negri*. London: Pluto Press.

Hardt, M. and A. Negri (2000) *Empire*. Cambridge, MA: Harvard University Press.

Hardt, M. and A. Negri (2004) *Multitude: War and Democracy in the Age of Empire*. London and New York: Penguin.

Hegel, G.W.F. (1976) *Hegel's Science of Logic*. London: George Allen and Unwin.

Hegel, G.W.F. (1892) *Lectures on the History of Philosophy*. London: Paul, Trench and Trubner.

Hegel, G.W.F. (1956) *The Philosophy of History*. London: Dover Books.

Held, D. (1995) *Democracy and the Global Order: From the Modern State to Cosmopolitan Governance*. Stanford: Stanford University Press.

Held, D. (2004) *Global Covenant: The Social Democratic Alternative to the Washington Consensus*. Cambridge: Polity.

Held, D. and A. McGrew (2000) 'The Great Globalization Debate', in Held and McGrew (eds), *Global Transformations Reader*. Cambridge: Polity Press.

Held, D. and A. McGrew, D. Goldblatt and J. Perraton (1999) *Global Transformations*. Cambridge: Polity Press.

Hirst, P. and Thompson, G. (1996) *Globalization in Question*. Cambridge: Polity Press.

Laclau, E. (2004) 'Can Immanence Explain Social Struggles?' in P. A. Passavant and J. Dean, *Empire's New Clothes: Reading Hardt and Negri*. London and New York: Routledge.

Lyotard, J.-F. (1992) *The Postmodern Explained to Children: Correspondence 1982–1985*. London: Turnaround.

Mandarini, M. (2003) 'Translator's Introduction' in A. Negri *Time for Revolution*. New York and London: Continuum.

Marx, K. (1974) *Grundrisse*. Harmondsworth: Penguin.

Marx, K. and F. Engels (1976) *The German Ideology*. Moscow: Progress Publishers.

Murphy, T. and A.-K. Mustapha (eds) (2005a) *The Philosophy of Antonio Negri*. London: Pluto Press.

Murphy, T. and A.K. Mustapha (2005b) 'Introduction', in T. Murphy and A.-K. Mustapha (eds) (2005a) *The Philosophy of Antonio Negri*. London: Pluto Press.

Negri, A. (2000) *Kairos, Alma Venus, Multitudo* in A. Negri (2003) *Time for Revolution*. New York and London: Continuum.

Negri, A. (2004) *Negri on Negri* (with Anne Dufourmantelle and translated by M.B. DeBevoise). London and New York: Routledge.

Negri, A. (1997) *The Constition of Time* in A. Negri (2003) *Time for Revolution*. New York and London: Continuum.

Negri, A. (2003) *Time for Revolution*. New York and London: Continuum.

Ohmae, K. (1990) *The Borderless World*. London: Collins.

Passavant, P.A. (2004) 'Introduction: Postmodern Republicanism', in P. A. Passavant and J. Dean, *Empire's New Clothes: Reading Hardt and Negri*. London and New York: Routledge.

Passavant, P.A. and Dean, J. (2004) *Empire's New Clothes: Reading Hardt and Negri*. London and New York: Routledge.

Plamenatz, J. (1954) *German Marxism and Russian Communism*. London: Longmans.

Smith, T. (2003) 'Globalisation and Capitalist Property Relations: A Critical Assessment of David Held's Cosmopolitan Theory', *Historical Materialism* 11(2), 3–35.

Surin, K. ' "Now Everything Must be Reinvented": Negri and the Revolution', in T. Murphy and A.-K. Mustapha (eds), *The Philosophy of Antonio Negri*. London: Pluto Press.

Tormey, S. (2004) *Anticapitalism*. Oxford: One World.

Walker, R.B.J. (2002) 'On the Immanence/Imminence of Empire', *Millenium* 31(2), 337–49.

10
Conclusion

10.1 Introduction

This book has attempted to delineate the differences between what we have termed the tradition of critical political economy, inaugurated by Hegel and Marx, and a post-critical approach exemplified by a number of more recent figures. Three main issues are raised by this analysis, which will be examined in this concluding chapter. First, there is the question of the defining features of post-critical political economy and of the key differentiating factors between the critical and post-critical frameworks. Secondly, there is the question of the extent to which the rebuttal of critical political economy by the post-critical theorists is valid and of whether they present a preferable alternative to Hegel, Marx and their followers. Thirdly, it is necessary to examine what is left of the critical tradition in the wake of the post-critical account of it, and what, if anything, can be incorporated from post-critical political economy into a rejuvenation of that tradition. These three questions are discussed in the following three sections of this chapter and the chapter concludes with an outline of some possible areas for future development of a critical approach.

10.2 The nature of post-critical political economy

In our view there is no set list of characteristics or positions which can be used to define a writer as a post-critical theorist. Rather, the writers discussed in this book, and others who might be assimilated to a post-critical framework, are linked by a set of 'family resemblances' in the Wittgensteinian sense. No one thinker satisfies all of the following criteria and none of the criteria is met by all the thinkers; however, taken together they provide an interlocking set of standpoints which are closely enough related, we feel, to constitute a distinctive strand within social theory. The following six elements of this strand appear particularly important.

First, post-critical writing is typified by a scepticism about, or rejection of, a dialectical approach to political economy. This is explicit in the case of Baudrillard, Lyotard and Hardt and Negri and implicit in the other writers considered here, especially sharply in the case of Foucault. Hegel and Marx both stress the contradictory nature of the concepts of political economy, which leads either to the necessary opening out of those concepts into a wider framework of analysis or to the supersession of the reality defined by the concepts through a practice of transformation. In contrast, post-critical theorists present two alternatives to dialectical thought. The first is a constantly shifting set of perspectives which relate to each other through an intricate network of changing connections, rather than through structured binary contrasts, as in the work of Lyotard. The second is the notion of an all-encompassing and internally consistent conceptual grid through which the world must be perceived, which is subject to no inherent contradictory dynamic, as in Foucault.

The second key element of a post-critical approach is an emphasis on discontinuities and particularities within the social and scepticism about overarching 'grand narratives'. This has both a synchronic and a diachronic aspect. Post-critical theorists strongly reject anything which implies a historical teleology and stress strongly the contingent and open-ended nature of historical development. They also stress the independence of the political, cultural and other levels of society from the economic. Even the relative autonomy granted to these spheres by Althusser and his followers, with the concomitant formula of determination by the economic 'in the last instance' is regarded as too reductionist. Both particular historical periods and institutional or social structures must be analysed in their own terms and not by reference to some larger framework which determines them. Again, there are differences here between the writers considered, with Lyotard mounting the most explicit, if self-defeating attack on the notion of large-scale explanatory frameworks, while at the other extreme Hardt and Negri can be seen as using just such a framework themselves even if they reject the large-scale paradigms of Hegel and Marx.

Allied to this viewpoint within post-critical writing is a rejection of the notion that history can be seen to be progressive, even if such progression is not tied to a teleological end point. This is one of the reasons why post-critical writers often express an affinity with the work of Walter Benjamin, although Benjamin is in some ways some ways relatively 'orthodox' in the links he draws between economic and cultural factors (and was criticised for this by his friend Theodor Adorno, another thinker whose scepticism about historical development and emphasis on the inability of fixed concepts to grasp the flux of human thought and practice have drawn the approval of post-critical writers). In his 'Theses on the Philosophy of History' Benjamin provides a famous description of Klee's angel of history who faces a storm from paradise which 'irresistibly propels him into the future to which his back is turned, while the pile of debris before him grows skyward. This storm is what we call progress' (Benjamin 1973, p. 260). This can in some ways be seen as a founding text of post-critical theory.

Thirdly, post-critical writers tend to reject what they see as the Marxist attempt to define exploitation and liberation exclusively in economic terms. They emphasise the independence of sexual, racial and other forms of oppression from economic determination and stress that gendered, ethnic and other identities have equal validity and importance to class identity. Some, like Foucault in particular, go further than this and argue that economic factors are less important than other considerations, notably power relationships, as mechanisms of domination, and that consequently liberation cannot be achieved even partially through struggles based on class interests. Others, like Fraser, or Gorz in his ecological writings, stress the equal importance of gender or the environment to economic exploitation and the need for parallel and interlinked struggles which connect these diverse areas.

The fourth key aspect of post-critical writing is a critique of the priority accorded to labour and to production in the critical political economy tradition. This is most notably in Baudrillard's writing, and, from different perspectives, in Gorz's, Fraser's and Hardt and Negri's work. The priority given by critical political economists to labour is rejected both with regard to epistemological and ethical questions. The notion that the experience of labour provides a special insight into the world which can form the basis of radical theory and a practice of transformation is opposed, as is also the view that a key aspect of human liberation can be conceptualised in terms of the creation of the self through labour. The critique of the role of labour is related to an attack on critical political economy for being too centred on production. At a conceptual level this is exemplified in Hardt and Negri's critique of production as a distinct category in postmodern society, and at the empirical level it involves stressing the significance of other aspects of economic life, notably consumption. At a deeper level it is expressed in a rejection of the way in which critical theory itself is framed as a kind of textual production.

Fifthly, post-critical theorists argue that the tradition of critical political economy did not itself interrogate the notion of the economy as a distinct sphere within society and was insufficiently radical in its own relationship to political economy in general. This is exemplified in different ways in accounts of Marx by Baudrillard, Lyotard and Foucault. The claim is that critical political economy did not adequately examine the constitution of political economy as a distinct discourse and the special conditions which gave rise to the possibility of such a discourse. Among other things, it is argued, this encouraged the projection back of the concepts of political economy on to radically distinct societies in which they had no applicability. In addition, the claim is that, rather than challenging the notion of the economic itself, and its influence within social thought and reality, Marx and his followers simply mounted a localised critique within the domain of political economy, which by this token could not be truly revolutionary.

Finally, post-critical writing is typified by a strong epistemological scepticism shading into relativism and perspectivism. The theoretical mediations standing between observers and the 'real' are stressed, as are the multitude of perspectives arising from such mediations. The influence of such considerations is especially strong, in different ways, in the work of Foucault, Lyotard and Baudrillard. Critical political economy is seen as resting on an unsophisticated and erroneous presumption of direct access to the truth which in turn can provide a basis for practical activity. At their most extreme post-critical theorists have claimed that such a presumption can at least in part explain the crimes of Stalinism and Maoism in the USSR, Eastern Europe and China. Less dramatically, it is argued that it has led to theoretical and practical dogmatism which has stood in the way of constructing movements which can lead to social change.

As outlined above, there is no clear logical relationship between these various positions, and so the degree to which they are held differs between particular post-critical analysts. It is, for example, quite possible to hold to an overarching theory of historical development in which the economic plays a key role but on the other hand to reject dialectical method and emphasise other sources of oppression and identity than economic exploitation and class. Such a viewpoint appears to correspond in large measure to the aims of Hardt and Negri for example. Again, one can construct a large-scale theory of changes in patterns of thought while maintaining a strong emphasis on the role of theoretical mediation and the difficulty of direct access to the real, as does Foucault. The examples could be multiplied. However, we believe that the affinities between these different positions are sufficiently strong to outweigh the divergences among them, so that they can be grouped together, with qualifications, as a distinct post-critical mode of thought. There are clear links between an attack on teleology, a rejection of dialectics (at least as commonly conceived) and a stress on the multiplicity of identities and the complexity of social formations. A stress on theoretical mediation and the autonomy of theory from the real leads relatively naturally to an emphasis on the constructed nature of the economic as a realm and a critique of the privileged access to knowledge through labour. Again, various examples could be given. What is more important, however, is to move to an assessment of the validity of the challenge mounted on these lines by post-critical theorists to the tradition stemming from Hegel and Marx. This will be the topic of the next section of the chapter.

10.3 The validity of the post-critical approach

In our view, despite the many illuminating insights of the post-critical theorists, a number of which are of lasting importance for social theory, the post-critical approach is not an adequate substitute for the tradition of critical political economy and cannot be accepted as superseding that tradition. Our reasons for arguing this relate to each of the six defining features of post-critical thought, as outlined above.

We believe that a dialectical approach remains crucial for an emancipatory social theory for a number of reasons. First, as we have tried to demonstrate above, a number of the writers who claim to be rejecting dialectical thought, notably Baudrillard and Hardt and Negri, are actually employing dialectics without due acknowledgement. More importantly, we believe that a dialectical approach is necessary for explaining both theoretical and social change. In our view the oscillation of post-critical theory between the two seemingly opposite conceptions of encompassing frameworks and the interaction of multiple perspectives is no accident. Both the play of concepts without structure and the presentation of structures without movement result from the rejection of a dialectical framework which can explicate both how conceptual thought shapes perceptions of reality and also how such thought must develop both through its internal dynamic and through changes in the world it describes.

Dialectical thought has been rejected by post-critical theorists for two main reasons. It is regarded as inherently teleological and as essentialist, in that the specificity of developments at different social levels is ignored in favour of explanations couched in terms of single foundational contradictions. We would not deny that there are elements of each of these characteristics in the work of Hegel and Marx, particularly as they have been interpreted by some of their followers. However, a dialectical approach is not inevitably marked by teleology or reductionism. It is possible to envisage a more open dialectics in which contradictions are not necessarily finally resolved either by the existence of a perspective which can encompass all competing viewpoints, or by a social transformation which abolishes the mainspring of conflict. In such a framework resolution of competing standpoints would be temporary and provisional and would lay the basis for future dialectical development, which would not be governed by teleological motion or a final end. In a similar way, the existence of dialectical contradictions within the economic, political and cultural spheres of society does not necessarily imply any particular relationship between those spheres, certainly not the reduction of all social tension to one single determining conflict. In fact Fraser's recognition of the multidimensional character of justice points to a dialectical reading of society just as the actual practice of Hardt and Negri recognises internal connections between spheres of society and between past and present.

One important aspect of critical political economy in this context is the notion of differing levels of abstraction and of a movement from the abstract to the concrete in dialectical reasoning. Such a movement allows for an account of contradictions at more abstract levels which provide a set of tendencies embodying the potential for more concrete developments but which may or may not be realised at the level of the concrete, depending on both the interaction between opposing tendencies and more contingent factors. In this way contingency can be incorporated into social explanation without such explanation either collapsing into description or consisting of a mass of influences to each of which no priority or particular weight can be assigned.

It does, however, remain important to examine the relationship between the economy and other levels of society. While recognising the important arguments put forward by post-critical theorists about the autonomy of particular social spheres we believe that they underestimate the role of the connections between such spheres in their opposition to grand narratives. This has two problematic outcomes. First, it leads to analyses of cultural and political developments, which, while they are locally illuminating, are seriously undermined by lack of attention to the economic factors, which are at work. A particular danger here is that of overvaluing the radical nature of such developments, through ignoring the extent to which they can be incorporated within the strategies of economically dominant agents. Fraser has rightly highlighted the way in which the political economy of neo-liberalism was progressing at the same time as radical cultural theorists were championing an identity politics that ignored economic realities. Secondly, such an approach leaves the economic untouched by broader social and cultural considerations to operate according to its own laws and norms. By refusing to analyse the nature of the connecting links between the economy and other spheres, on the basis that such an analysis must lead to economic reductionism, the post-critical theorists in effect legitimise the break up of the holistic tradition of political economy and the constitution of an isolated economic realm within social theory. Set against this, a contrasting strength of critical political economy is its insistence on the irreducibly political and cultural nature of economic concepts.

An emphasis on relating the economic to other aspects of social reality does not imply either a privileging of class identity over other affiliations or an uncritical stress on the centrality of labour and production in social interaction, rather the reverse. A number of points can be made here.

First, a rich tradition of analysis, notably stemming from work in social history, has emphasised the cultural and political aspects of both class position and class consciousness. Just as class inescapably involves economic, political and cultural factors, so too do ethnicity, gender and other identities. Yet post-critical writers have tended to stress the former rather than the latter. The concept of class has been both detached from economic determination and deconstructed, but there has been less attention paid to bringing the economic into the analysis of gender, race and other aspects of oppression. The relative scarcity of writings on feminist economics as compared to other aspects of feminist thought is one example of this. In fact the relationship between, say, class, gender and ethnicity on the one hand and between economics, politics and culture on the other are logically entirely distinct questions. There is no *a priori* reason why the relative primacy of any one of the first triad, in a particular social context, should imply anything about the importance or otherwise of members of the second grouping.

Secondly, any account of lived identities, however subjective, must involve some reference to a wider social framework, which in turn necessitates some kind of account of the relationship between differing social spheres. If there is no such reference point then not only do we have no clear reason for attaching importance to some forms of identity rather than others, but we also have no conceptual basis for forming such identities in the first place. Concretely, an analysis which takes gender or race as a founding concept must start from some kind of criterion for distinguishing different genders or ethnicities, as well as some kind of justification for choosing these as foundational rather than other identities. Such criteria and justifications must involve situating the relevant identities within a broader conceptual mapping and the danger of excluding the economic from such a mapping, as post-critical theorists tend to do is both that other elements are used to constitute it in an uncritical way, for example biological factors, and also that once more the economy is left to go its own way, without being pressurised to acknowledge its own gendered and ethnic nature.

Thirdly, the tradition of Hegel and Marx does not necessitate an uncritical glorification of labour and production. The chapters above on Gorz and Hardt and Negri have shown the ambiguities within Marx's own writing, concerning the status of labour. It is, of course, true that certain strands within critical political economy have tended to value labour and production as absolute goods in a problematic way – though they are scarcely alone in this, as shown by the attitude of the current British government. However, such an attitude is not inevitable. Indeed, as discussed in the chapter above on Baudrillard, for those wanting to analyse the nature of mass consumption in contemporary society and the reasons for its current dominance, a prior analysis of production and the extent to which it has been supplanted by consumption is a necessity. Without analysing labour and production, even if, and in fact especially if, their status has radically changed since Hegel and Marx wrote, it is not possible to understand what is specific about the current period. This is particularly true if, as Baudrillard for example argues, a defining feature of contemporary society is the 'end of production'.

However, it is also the case that there are important reasons for assigning some centrality to labour and production within social theory, without unduly excluding other organising concepts. This is so for both practical and ethical reasons. At a practical level, changes in productive structures and the labour process continue to be central in the lives of many people, especially if we extend the reach of social theory outside Western Europe, North America and Japan. The debate over globalisation is clear evidence of this. In addition, other key concepts of social analysis can only be understood in relation to production. To take one example, feminist writers on political economy have rightly criticised an emphasis on production at the expense of the examination of reproduction, particularly within the family or household structures. However, any detailed analysis of reproduction will inevitably involve specifying the links which it has with production and the interaction between labour outside and within the domestic sphere. Ethically, it is not necessary to assume that human fulfilment only comes through labour to argue that labour continues to be an important aspect of self-expression for many, and, more significantly, that given social transformation this potential could be dramatically extended. If this is accepted then an emancipatory social theory must investigate both the limitations within the current system which stultify and negate the experience of work and the strategies and possibilities for overcoming these limitations.

There is also a third reason for continuing to view labour and production as important. This arises from the epistemological insights which are opened up by participation in work. Again, it is not necessary to assume that the experience of labour is the only privileged source of insight into social and political reality, or even that it is the most important one. The argument here is simply that this experience does convey some key perspectives which are not provided by other forms of activity or contemplation. Such perspectives clearly need to be related to the frameworks which arise from other aspects of social life; however to neglect them entirely would result in an impoverishment within critical thought.

This raises the more general question of the epistemological critique of Hegel, Marx and their followers mounted by post-critical political economy and the implications of this for the conceptualisation of the economic as a realm of analysis. In many ways this is the most difficult of the criticisms made by the post-critical theorists to respond to adequately. However, in our view this is not primarily because of the specific weaknesses of critical political economy, but more because of the inherent difficulty of the issues raised. The questions of the relationship between theory and the real and of the criteria for justifying one theoretical approach over another pre-date Hegel and Marx, since they are traceable in their modern form back to Kant in particular, and while critical political economy has not solved these questions it is by no means alone in this. It should be acknowledged, however, that, contrary to claims of dogmatism and complacency, theorists from this tradition have made a number of attempts to grapple with such difficulties. Some of these have been rather unconvincing, notably attempts to equate truth with a reflection of reality or with success in praxis. Others though have taken the question further. The most notable figure here is surely Althusser, whose attempt to synthesise the French tradition of epistemological analysis represented by figures such as Canguilhem, Bachelard and Cavaillès (which in itself was an important background influence on Foucault and on one element of post-critical thought) with Marxism eventually failed, but could hardly be said to have been neglectful of the importance of the issues discussed. Examples of alternative approaches to the Althusserian one include the critical realism of Bhaskar and his followers (Bhaskar 1975) and Callinicos' attempt to integrate Marxism with the methodology of scientific research programmes developed by Imre Lakatos (Callinicos 1982).

There are serious problems with all of these attempts to provide critical political economy with epistemological criteria of justification. However, the implications of adopting the post-critical standpoint, according to which no such criteria can be found, are at least equally problematic. Three immediate difficulties suggest themselves.

First, at least in practice if not in theory, such an adoption can easily lead to the evaluation of different aspects of social institutions and practices according to their own internal criteria. A general problem here is one of fragmentation of analysis. However, a more particular problem in the case of political economy is that this leads precisely back to the separation of the economic from other aspects of society which the tradition of political economy has tried to break down. This separation is already, to a large degree, hegemonic both in economic analysis (witness the discursive power of neo-classical economics) and public policy. Further reinforcement of it by critical theorists would be unfortunate, to say the least.

Secondly, such a strategy seriously weakens any link between social theory and human liberation, since a theory acknowledged as based only on a partial perspective is in a much weaker position to compel practical assent. Avoiding the problem of dogmatism comes at a high price – that of eschewing any potential for critical thought as the basis for practical interventions. This view has been put forward cogently by Sabina Lovibond in her debate over feminism with Richard Rorty (and to a lesser extent with Lyotard and with Alasdair MacIntyre). Setting out a principle which rejects claims to entitlements that we would not be prepared to recognise universally, she writes that

> It is this egalitarian principle . . . that constitutes the main debt of feminism to the Kantian model of rationality, and hence to 'universalism' and 'realism'. Remove it, and you remove the moral coerciveness of the demand that men give up their sexual prerogative and learn to live like human beings. (Lovibond 1992, p. 69, see also Lovibond 1989)

Thirdly, such an approach leaves social theory unable to adjudicate between competing perspectives. Lovibond, though her interests are primarily in the links between epistemological standpoints and ethical commitments, rather than in epistemology in isolation, provides a useful example here, that of the question of pornography, outlining 'the contest between pornography (considered as a sign system) and the feminist discourse in which pornography is characterized as (symbolic and/or actual) violence against women' (Lovibond 1992, p. 60). Epistemological scepticism as typified by many post-critical theorists would leave no way of investigating which of these two views is correct.

Given the difficulties of adopting a post-critical perspectivist viewpoint, and the epistemological difficulties faced by critical political economy, it seems worth at least investigating the contribution that a dialectical approach might make to this set of problems. The key concept here is that of an immanent critique in which the criteria for assessing a theoretical standpoint are simultaneously internal and external. They are internal in that they are generated by that standpoint itself and by the expectations inherent to it, but they are external in that any limited standpoint cannot fully satisfy its own criteria and as a result dialectical thought is impelled to relate that standpoint to other competing perspectives. Such a notion of critique, interpreted in an open and undogmatic way, appears to us to provide more potential for social theory than the relativism of the post-critical theorists.

This point can be exemplified by looking at the arguments put forward by post-critical writers about the constitution of the economic as a distinct realm. For such writers, as outlined above, the notion of the economic must be criticised from a standpoint entirely outside that sphere. The implications of this for Baudrillard, for example, are detailed in the chapter above. It required the rejection not just of Marxism but of any conception of the economic as a notion based in reality, even viewed in necessary relationship to other concepts and spheres of activity, and the development of a perspective based on the concept of symbolic exchange which attempted to provide an entirely external standpoint for critique of this notion. The problems with this are twofold. Firstly, the concept of symbolic exchange itself necessitates epistemological relativism. Not only does this lead to the problems described above, but it also introduces a dangerous circularity into Baudrillard's argument. The requirement for an external critique is based on epistemological scepticism, but the concepts developed to mount such a critique themselves reinforce such scepticism. Secondly, the concept of symbolic exchange renders all postulated economic relationships subject to an undifferentiated criticism. It thus makes it impossible for Baudrillard to fulfil his original objective of explaining exactly what is special about contemporary capitalism – although it is this project that originally motivated his critique of Marx's notion of the economic. Similar problems arise with a number of the other post-critical theorists.

The immanent critique of the economic offered by Marx and Hegel, while incomplete and problematic in various ways, appears to offer a more promising alternative. Here, as outlined in the introduction, the contradictions latent in economic concepts and practices open up the potential for development both through relating the economic to a wider social reality and through developing new concepts and practices as a result of theoretical and social transformations. The critique is both internal and external.

While acknowledging the validity of a number of the criticisms of Hegel and Marx made by post-critical theorists, we believe that a critical political economy based on a dialectical approach remains a preferable alternative. Such an approach would allot an important place to issues of class, labour and production and would adopt a holistic conception of social reality. However, it would give equal weight to other identities than that of class and to other concepts than those rooted in the productive process, while rejecting the patriarchal readings of sexuality and the family offered by Hegel. It would stress the relationships between concepts and identities within a more general framework, and would also avoid teleology and reductionism.

The above paragraph sets out a summary of the approach we would favour. However, it is also necessary to outline in more detail exactly what the positive contributions of the post-critical theorists to the renewal of political economy have been. That is the topic of the next section of this chapter.

10.4   The contribution of post-critical political economy

Post-critical political economy has made a number of key contributions which are indispensable to the rejuvenation of critical political economy. The following are particularly important.

First, post-critical theorists have created a new degree of sensitivity to the extent to which theorists in the tradition of Hegel and Marx have remained marked by the concepts and arguments of the economics which they are purportedly challenging in a radical way. In particular, the post-critical theorists have encouraged awareness of the ability of the form of arguments to shape their content. They have played an important role in problematising the notion of the critique of political economy and in forcing an evaluation of the notion of critique. Related to this they have developed an innovative analysis of the historical specificity of particular economic concepts and of the illegitimacy of projecting them back to pre-capitalist societies. Post-critical political economy is distinctive (with the possible exception of some forms of anarchist thought) in criticising Marxism for not being radical enough as a theory of capitalist society, rather than for being too radical. In making this point it has opened up an important debate about exactly what constitutes a radical critique of existing theory and practice.

Secondly, post-critical theorists have been amongst the most imaginative analysts of the precise specificity of modern capitalism and the reasons for the failure of critical political economy to lead to transformative political practice in the West. Examples like Baudrillard's account of mass consumption, Gorz's analyses of labour and ecology and Hardt and Negri's discussion of empire and the redundancy of statist sovereignty are crucial attempts to understand contemporary developments at a fundamental level, and can be contrasted favourably with the rather mechanistic nature of much Marxist economic analysis. Previous chapters have argued that the underlying theoretical frameworks adopted by a number of the post-critical theorists have led them away from being able to provide a convincing final answer to the questions that originally motivated them about just what is new about current social realities, and the associated challenges posed for existing radical theories. However, this should not detract from the interest of their initial investigations and the insights provided by these.

Thirdly, post-critical theorists have brought to the fore the implications of epistemological commitments for critical political economy – both in terms of the evaluation of explanations of social reality and in terms of the ethical and political imperatives linking critical thought to practice. To take one example, in the debate quoted above Lovibond is strongly critical of Lyotard, MacIntyre and Rorty with regard to the links between their philosophical positions and the practice of feminism. However, the impetus for her debate with these writers in the first place, and for the relationships which she outlines between epistemology and liberation, came from the challenges laid down by the post-critical writers. Their work has forced a new awareness and sophistication with regard to the links between epistemology and substantive theoretical and practical positions in radical thought. As mentioned above, this sophistication is also due in part to the work of Althusser and his followers; however, the post-critical theorists generalised the debate and took it on to a different level.

Fourthly, post-critical theorists such as Gorz, Fraser, and Hardt and Negri have played an important role in taking the insights provided by social movements, especially in the areas of gender, ethnicity, anti-globalisation and ecology, and relating these to questions of political economy. In so doing they have provided important critiques of the way in which key concepts of critical political economy, notably those of labour and production, have previously been understood. They have introduced new conceptual frameworks into the study of political economy in order to provide a basis for analysing differing forms of oppression, notably power in the case of Foucault.

Fifthly, the post-critical writers have provided important counter-arguments to economic reductionism and teleology. To take just one example, the awareness of economies as cultural formations and of the potential determination of economic changes by cultural factors, so that culture and the economic are seen in terms of reciprocal relationships, is to a large extent due to the post-critical theorists.

All of these contributions mean that, while critical political economy, appropriately conceived, can withstand demands from post-critical writers for its dissolution and rejection, it is also the case that the renewal of critical thought in this area requires imaginative appropriation of the insights which have been provided by those writers, rather than a retreat into orthodoxy. The next section of this chapter attempts to sketch some ways in which this might take place.

10.5 Towards a renewal of critical political economy

In many ways the debate between critical and post-critical theorists can best be seen against the background of the unsolved problems generated by the incorporation of the work of Marx and Hegel into debates around political economy in the 1960s and 1970s. This period saw a wealth of discussion covering areas such as the role of dialectical method in political economy (stimulated both by divergent interpretations of the theory of value and by philosophical arguments, in particular the contrast between the work of Lukács and Althusser), the nature and development of the labour process, the economic basis of the subordination of women and the epistemological basis of economic critique. However, as these debates continued the intractability of the problems raised became apparent. The coupling of increased awareness of the difficulty of constructing a critical political economy adequate to its object with the political defeats suffered by the left from the early 1970s onwards, led to the popularity of the post-critical alternative. Post-critical theory promised an initially attractive explanation of the problems faced by critical thought and a ready response to the political difficulties faced by radical practice. The problems of the tradition of Hegel and Marx were to be traced back to fundamental flaws in the project inaugurated by these thinkers and any more successful practical activity was seen as conditional on rejecting that project, at least in large measure, and substituting a dramatically different perspective. The effect of this, however, was in many ways to short circuit the debate around the problems raised by the initial renewal of dialectical thought in this period in favour of drawing out the implications of one particular position at the expense of others. While this debate was in many ways frustratingly painful and slow, it seems possible to argue that this was the result of the inherent difficulty of the problems being addressed rather than of the shortcomings of a particular tradition or approach. The post-critical promise that a change of perspective would somehow provide a magic key to solving the complexities of social theory was in large measure a chimera. Not only that, but it led to a fragmentation of social thought in which attention turned to philosophical or cultural questions in relative isolation, while the economic was left to go its own way, both in terms of theoretical understanding and practical contestation.

This argument should be distinguished from the position put forward by Callinicos (1989), who sees post-critical thought as largely a frivolous response to a political downturn. We do not see post-critical theorists as frivolous, rather their response to the twin crisis of the inherent problems of the tradition they criticise and the political defeats they respond to, is a deeply serious one, though sometimes couched in aggressively jocular or sarcastic language. It is however, we believe, in the last resort a mistaken one. A more productive approach would be to return to the dialectical approach and try to extend this patiently both to investigate the problems thrown up by the debates of the 1970s and to accommodate the insights of the post-critical writers.

This would involve taking the tradition of critical political economy and developing it in two main directions. The first direction would be conceptual in nature. Dialectical thought would have to be developed to meet the criticisms of teleology, reductionism and epistemological dogmatism. Critical thought would have to be reformulated around concepts of contradiction, development and levels of abstraction which allow for contingency and empirical complexity, and are capable of relating social spheres to each other without trying to reduce one to the other. The post-critical insights about the nature of discourse, the constitution of the economic as a distinct sphere and the problematic nature of the relationship between theory and the real would need to be thought through and incorporated within a renewed dialectical method. The second direction would be more concrete. Critical political economy would have to take up once more the questions raised in the 1970s, and analysed since then in a more localised way, concerning relationships between different identities, the nature of labour and production, their relationship to other concepts such as reproduction, consumption, the role of ecology within political economy, the specificity of contemporary capitalism, the links between the economic and cultural and political spheres and so on. It would embed them within the broader framework that is demanded by Fraser, but which in fact must involve a comprehensive critical and systematic analysis of political economy that is not developed in her work. In developing a broader framework, both the paradigms of Hegel and Marx can be drawn upon, while taking care not to operate with deterministic and absolutist versions of either. Hegel's synoptic, reconciliatory but reformist critique of political economy is distinct from Marx's revolutionary perspective, but both can be seen to operate with complex, holistic perspectives that can provide systematic standpoints to incorporate the more pluralistic and partial insights of more recent theory. Ultimately, the choice between Hegelian and Marxist paradigms might not be susceptible of neat, knock-down answers, but will depend on normative ways of reading global cultural and economic developments. Whatever paradigm might be adopted, the reformist or revolutionary path will need to be questioned and sharpened by relating it to the other as well as to subsequent theoretical and empirical insights.

Such a process cannot, in our view, be carried out either by philosophical thought in isolation from concrete analyses, or simply through empirical studies. Political economy remains crucial as a field of force in which the conceptual and empirical can be brought together to illuminate each other. In this sense, our argument differs from that put forward 30 years ago by Perry Anderson (1974) when he called for a turn away within Marxism from philosophical questions towards concentration on political and economic analysis. Much of Anderson's criticism of the abstraction of Western Marxism was justified. However, his proposed solution overestimated the existing resources of political economy in implying that a ready-made method existed in that area which could simply be adopted as an alternative to methodological controversy, and underestimated the relevance of the philosophical issues raised by the western Marxist tradition to the development of a dialectical political economy. The issue was not so much the need to move from philosophy to political economy but to relate the insights gained from philosophical debate to political economy in order to take both areas forward together. In many ways, a similar situation exists now, in our view, with regard to post-critical political economy, as that analysed by Anderson with regard to western Marxism. A range of insights exist but embedded within a context framed around philosophical and cultural analysis, which both prevents the full development and critical appraisal of those insights, and allows the economic and the political to proceed unhindered as separate realms of theoretical and practical activity. The task is not to decree a straightforward abandonment of such analysis in favour of work in political economy but to bring the insights from it into a relationship with a renewed approach to critical thought. In this way post-critical political economy could function as a stimulus to and agent of the renewal of critical political economy. We would be happy if this book could be seen as an initial contribution to this task.

References

Anderson, P. (1974) *Considerations on Western Marxism*. London: New Left Books.

Benjamin, W. (1973) *Illuminations* translated by H. Zohn. London: Fontana.

Bhaskar, R. (1975) *A Realist Theory of Science*. Leeds: Leeds Books.

Callincos, A. (1982) *Is There a Future for Marxism?* Basingstoke: Macmillan.

Callinicos, A. (1989) *Against Postmodernism*. London: Polity Press.

Lovibond, S. (1989) 'Feminism and Postmodernism', *New Left Review*, (November/December) 178, 5–28.

Lovibond, S. (1992) 'Feminism and Pragmatism: A Reply to Richard Rorty', *New Left Review*, (May/June) 193; 56–74.

Index